ELEMENTS · OF
MUSIC

A Programmed Approach · Third Edition · Michelle Worthing

wcb
Wm. C. Brown Publishers
Dubuque, Iowa

Cover design by Dale Rosenbach

Library of Congress Catalog Card Number: 87-71183

ISBN 0-697-05292-3

Printed in the United States of America by Wm. C. Brown Publishers
2460 Kerper Boulevard, Dubuque, IA 52001

10 9 8 7 6 5 4 3 2 1

Contents

Preface

This text expands upon basic thrusts found useful in previous editions: progressive introduction of a basic intellectual vocabulary in music, avoidance of specific prerequisite musicianship, individual pacing, and exposure to aesthetic concepts influencing practical applications. Assuming no specific course syllabus, the information presented offers a flexible and potentially self-instructed factual basis for diverse classroom applications geared to various curricular instructional objectives. The linear program maintains the sequential relevance of basic elements of musical structure and the analysis/response focus on active participation in the learning process. Apply Your Understanding, Check Your Understanding, and Supplementary activities options, as well as the Song Supplement, again reinforce these information capsules through composite thought processes in more extended musical contexts. A practical, generalized view of basic structural relationships persists in preference to advancing any specific "system" of music theory or stylistic idiom.

The Third Edition offers expanded options for individual users. Exercises for individual or classroom use entitled Developing Performance Skills offer vocal, aural, and physical applications, including the use of piano, recorder, autoharp, or guitar. Individual instructor options are encouraged in identifying drill response modes and languages. The presentation of rhythmic interpretation is extensively revised, as is the Song Supplement which now includes more songs geared to a wider audience and fewer nursery rhyme songs.

In general, instrumental applications will be governed by technical expectations of specific courses. Guitar/autoharp chord symbols are included in appropriate musical examples. Piano reinforcement offers a particularly effective visual reference for harmonic concepts in Chapters 9 and 10. Instrumental fingering charts and a piano keyboard diagram are included as appendices, along with a Glossary of basic musical terms. Free use of additional musical repertoire from any appropriate source is always valuable. Individual frames or sections (such as bass clef notation, more complex scales, and key signatures, etc.) may be omitted as specific syllabi dictate.

The author wishes to acknowledge the interest and assistance extended by William M. Anderson, Virginia Hoge Mead, Susan Kannel Oliver, and Richard Worthing in the completion of this text. A special word of appreciation is extended to the many students and teachers whose use of the previous editions proved invaluable in completing the present publication. Also appreciated were the efforts of the reviewers for this edition: Edward C. McManus, Lane Community College; Lloyd K. Herren, Metropolitan State College; Joaquina Calvo Johnson, Yuba College; Charlotte G. Trautwein, North Dakota State University; La Vaun Beyer, Cypress College; Julianne Vanden Wyngaard, Grand Valley State College; Gayel Gibson, University of Texas, El Paso; and Christine B. Breitanfeld, Adirondack Community College.

To the Student

Music consists of two basic components of sound, pitch and duration. The simplest form of musical expression is a "tune" or melody by itself. In this undecorated state, pitch and duration interact at their most basic levels to create a sense of motion and shape. In a melody, pitch and duration are organized in a horizontal dimension of one event at a time. More complex musical experiences may be created by adding to a melody other simultaneous events (other pitches and durations) of equal or supporting significance. Such simultaneous events produce the harmony, counterpoint, and orchestration with which melody is often adorned. We shall begin with the simple, undecorated horizontal organization of pitch and duration as found in melody.

This presentation of the elements of music is organized into frames that require written responses to test and reinforce your understanding. The correct response appears in the left-hand column opposite each frame. Before beginning each page of the text, cover the answer column of that page with the cardboard provided in the front of this text. As soon as you have written your answer in each frame, reveal the corresponding answer frame to check the accuracy of your response. If you have answered incorrectly, restudy the frame so that you may formulate a correct response. If you do not understand the recommended response, consult your instructor. It is important that you understand the correct solution to each frame before proceeding to the next. In the course of this text you will encounter various terms and expressions that should become a part of your musical vocabulary. The initial appearance of such items is in boldface type.

Most important, music is much more than just the intellectual concepts explaining its structure. It is real sound, sung or played on instruments and heard, by real people just like you. It is entirely appropriate for the study of fundamental facts about music to include experiences in producing these corresponding musical sounds and understanding how they exist and interact through the ear. Opportunities to develop your performance skills through singing, rhythmic activities, playing the recorder, piano, autoharp and guitar, and listening are included at appropriate points in this text. Your instructor will choose those appropriate to course objectives. The degree of challenge presented by these exercises will vary depending upon your previous musical experiences.

Concentrate on those best suited to your skill level in each category. It is important to remember that these are organized to reinforce your understanding of the concepts presented and do not constitute a "complete method of playing technique" for any instrument.

To the Instructor

Elements of Music is designed to present a general core of information regarding basic elements and relationships of musical pitch and duration. The text is appropriate to a broad range of applications and pedagogical preferences requiring basic musical literacy as a foundational step. To the greatest extent possible, general conceptual understanding has been favored over particular "systems" or traditions of music theory. This text does not attempt to address every possible music fundamentals agenda.

GENERAL CHARACTERISTICS

The reading level, deductive reasoning expectations and speed of progression of *Elements of Music* are geared to college-level students. As a text for adult learners, presentations of concepts and applied skills frequently differ from "traditional" approaches familiar in music method books for young children. The programmed format is efficient in presenting facts and is largely self-instructional. It also reinforces patterns of conceptual problem solving applicable to future musical experiences. This focus on self-instruction in developing the basic core of information and concepts is intended to expand class time available for individual emphases, reinforcement activities and the addition of more specific material or musical applications at the discretion of the instructor. Although no prior musical background is expected *Elements of Music* will provide a unifying and fast-paced review for those students with some past experience.

INSTRUCTOR CHOICES ARE IMPORTANT

Opportunities for individual curricular choices occur throughout the text. General possibilities of that nature include de-emphasizing or omitting the study of bass clef (which also implies abbreviated attention to harmonic vocabulary as presented in Chapters 9 and 10,) limiting the number of key signatures and scales studied (emphasis is already on four sharps and four flats,) reducing interval vocabulary covered and restricting harmonic experiences to a few keys.

In Chapter 3 a system of oral counting syllables is presented to demonstrate that process. Students are advised to adopt the particular system favored by their instructor. In Chapter 7 the concept of minor tonality is introduced through the relative-major phenomenon, beginning with the natural minor scale. The harmonic minor scale is developed to the extent necessary to reinforce the use of the dominant triad in minor key harmonization in Chapter 9. The melodic minor scale is also presented. Each of these topics may be expanded or de-emphasized as appropriate. The presentation of intervals in Chapter 8 suggests additional choices. While the concept is valuable in grasping other pitch relationships (triads, etc.,) specific requirements in recognizing, spelling or hearing intervals should be based on individual instructional goals. Chapter 9 presents major and minor triads and dominant seventh chords as used in simple harmonization. Chapter 10 introduces chord inversion and additional harmonization concepts. Either chapter may be abbreviated or omitted. Activities may be limited to selected tonalities. Focusing on autoharp/guitar chord symbols can also deemphasize attention to bass clef notation.

DEVELOPING PERFORMANCE SKILLS

A major new component of this edition is exercises for Developing Performance Skills in singing, rhythmic performance, listening, recorder, piano, autoharp and guitar. These DPS exercises, placed at the end of each chapter, are referenced at appropriate points throughout the text. They are designed to reinforce concepts developed in the programmed material. Instructor choice is an important element in the successful use of these exercises. It is highly unlikely that any single course can accommodate the use of all of the exercises provided. It will be important to decide what performance skills are appropriate to your course and to what level you wish students to develop them. Pace your assignments accordingly. Some skills require greater amounts of material for their introduction (ie. guitar in Chapter 9) and more time to achieve a useful level of proficiency. You will also want to choose those exercises most appropriate for your students; some may be too elementary, others beyond the scope of your course. Omission of various DPS sections will *not* break the intellectual continuity of the programmed material.

GENERAL CHARACTERISTICS

Many DPS exercises begin at a very elementary level but progress quickly to demonstrate the performance level required in practical musical applications. Some are more demanding right at the outset. Several DPS sections include "challenge" sections. These may involve less fundamental applications of concepts presented or explore more advanced performance levels intended to challenge students who readily master basic skills. The overall design of these exercises is cumulative, adding new notes and fingerings while reviewing previously acquired skills. Some combine skill areas such as singing or playing by ear, singing while playing, etc. None of these exercises should be considered a complete or beginning performance method in the medium involved. They are simply practical applications of fundamental concepts presented in terms appropriate for adult students.

The DPS exercises are *not* self-instructional. While they do provide basic physical direction, the text repeatedly encourages students to seek instructor guidance in instrumental technique. In-class demonstration and evaluation of students' skill mastery is expected. Many drills, especially those in aural discrimination involve the use of a partner. Students are also advised to practice together and evaluate each other's performance. Virtually any of these can be converted to class drills with the instructor serving as "partner." Finally, connecting these drills directly to additional musical materials from other sources (including the Song Supplement) is important in helping students to become comfortable with realistic musical situations. The text frequently encourages students (and their instructors) to invent additional similar drills or apply skills to additional musical examples.

The following comments offer more specific suggestions regarding the DPS exercises in each chapter.

CHAPTER 1

The recorder is introduced early as a pitch reference instrument readily available to students during personal study time. The piano offers a sound source capable of producing the bass clef tessitura. Starting pitches are those that correlate best with the text. (Middle C is of no particular advantage, especially for adult students.) Piano exercises progress quickly to two hands to encourage orientation to the pitch spectrum of the great staff. Pianistic virtuosity is not the goal of these exercises. Singing experiences encourage students to internalize pitch relationships in preparation for aural discrimination experiences.

CHAPTER 2

Exercises deal first with rhythm alone. Reviewing recorder, piano and singing exercises in Chapter 1 will provide continuity in developing those skills while beginning Chapter 2. Reciting note names in rhythm is included to reinforce musical reading skills. You may wish to add additional exercises from the Song Supplement or other sources. As recorder and piano skills are combined with rhythmic interpretation, new notes and fingerings are introduced. Aural discrimination is introduced via singing and playing by ear. Students who have difficulty matching or producing pitch relationships vocally might focus greater attention on recorder and piano skills as a step toward developing an aural foundation for singing.

CHAPTER 3

Rhythmic interpretation through counting is combined with singing, recorder and piano. Be sure to insert your own counting system. An emphasis on singing is intended to nuture aural accuity. Isolated rhythmic performance through clapping and tapping is combined with listening skill in "echo" drills with partners. Finally, notation from rhythmic dictation is offered. Instructor evaluation in each performance area is encouraged. Many of these exercises are appropriate for in-class drill. Unnecessary ear training skills may be omitted as appropriate to your course syllabus.

CHAPTER 4

The black keys of the piano and recorder fingerings filling out the chromatic scale are introduced. Singing is combined with recorder and piano as reference points for developing tonal memory of the sound of the whole and half step. Singing with letter names reinforces interval spelling. Ear training drills of a more traditional nature on whole and half steps are available if appropriate. These DPS exercises conclude with practical applications in melodies for recorder, piano and singing emphasizing accidentals.

CHAPTER 5

The octave phenomenon is presented through playing, singing and listening. Playing major scales introduces additional recorder fingerings. Piano exercises introduce traditional major scale fingerings. Playing these scales is more important as aural reinforcement of major scale pitch relationships. While these exercises also provide opportunities for piano technique development, *if desired,* it is not expected that all students will master playing the scales with two hands simultaneously. Singing major scales will reinforce both aural recognition and scale spelling. The exercises conclude with playing and singing major key melodies emphasizing scale-wise motion. It is also important to reinforce rhythmic performance in these exercises as a review of those concepts and skills.

CHAPTER 6

Memory skills and development of tonal memory and intuition are central to the concept and application of key signatures. These exercises reinforce recorder fingerings for accidentals and provide opportunities for additional practice in accurate rhythmic interpretation.

CHAPTER 7

Minor scales are presented in the manner of major scales in Chapter 5. Here again, aural reinforcement is the primary goal, not instrumental virtuosity. The inclusion of harmonic and melodic minor scales *for those who wish to use them* adds a great deal of material. Assign as appropriate to your syllabus. Again, melodies to perform *(and hear)* in all forms of the minor scale review rhythmic skills and emphasize realistic musical context over abstract skill development.

CHAPTER 8

These exercises focus on physical and aural "spatial" relationships of perfect, major and minor intervals while providing additional opportunities to gain technical fluency with the recorder, piano and singing. Listening drills in naming, notating and playing intervals are quite extensive to cover all possibilities. Choose the level of skill development your course requires. Add additional drills as appropriate. Using much of this material in class will provide appropriate levels of instructor input and evaluation. Melodic-rhythmic dictation is introduced at the conclusion of this section. If appropriate to your course, the Song Supplement and other sources can provide additional dictation materials.

CHAPTER 9

These exercises begin with piano and singing drills to reinforce theoretical concepts of major and minor triads and dominant seventh chord construction. Listening skills offer *brief* exploration in basic chord identification. This chapter's focus on harmonization of simple (folk) melodies begins with an introduction to the autoharp for those who wish to use it. Introducing the guitar as an accompanying instrument requires considerable material. The assimilation of related technical skills will also require appropriate time. Courses involving the guitar may wish to move quickly through earlier chapters to allow more time to deal with these skills. More instructor input is also appropriate at this point. Here again, the exercises are not intended as a complete guitar method but merely as application of the theoretical concepts and practical musicianship skills on an appropriate instrument. Pace these materials as appropriate for your students and provide additional resources as desirable.

CHAPTER 10

Piano skills reinforce conceptual understanding of chord inversion principles. Exercises move quickly to practical application of chord inversions in rudimentary keyboard harmonizations. Experiencing the aural impact and musical responsibility of establishing a basic harmonic foundation is the goal, not the development of refined instrumental voicings or piano technique. Guitar exercises emphasize expanded skills for accompanying melodies: new chord fingerings and optional strumming techniques for greater contrapuntal and rhythmic interest if desired. Here again, extended time, additional instructor input and supplemental musical material is appropriate in courses requiring higher development of these skills.

Basic Notation

1

Pitch is indicated by the placement of symbols on a **staff** consisting of five lines and the intervening four spaces.

The following example is a music staff.

Pitch is notated by placement of symbols on a _____.

staff

2

The staff consists of _____ lines and _____ spaces.

five (lines)
four (spaces)

3

The pitches represented by the lines and spaces of the staff are identified alphabetically by the letters A through G.

Circle the letters in the following group that may be used to identify musical pitches.
B J A G I

Ⓑ Ⓐ Ⓖ

4

The lines and spaces of the staff are identified alpha-

betically by the letters_____ through_____.

A (through) G

5

A **clef sign** is placed at the beginning of a staff to deter-mine the specific letter identity of each line and space.

The letter names of the lines and spaces are determined

by a _____ sign.

clef

6

Two types of clef signs will be used in this text. The first is the **treble** clef, also referred to as the G clef.

A treble clef has been placed on the following staff. In this case the staff is referred to as a treble staff.

Which one of the following examples illustrates a treble clef?

a. 𝄢 ═══════   c. 𝄞 ═══════

b. 𝄡 ═══════   d. ═══════

Answer: _____

c.

POINT OF REFERENCE

The treble staff represents the pitch locale in which most women and children sing and in which such instruments as the flute, clarinet, trumpet, and violin sound. The recorder also sounds in this treble register, as do approximately half of the pitches available on the piano.

7

treble

When a treble clef is placed on a staff, that staff is then called a _____ staff.

8

The treble (or G) clef indicates that the *second line* (the line which the center of the clef encircles) is G.

The remaining lines and spaces are named in relation to this second line G.

The pitch of the second line on the treble staff is _____.

G

9

The names of the remaining lines and spaces of the treble staff are as follows:

Name the lines of the treble staff from lowest to highest.

____   G____   ____   ____   ____

E (G) B D F

10

The letter names for the spaces of the treble staff (from lowest to highest) are

____   ____   ____   ____

F A C E

11

The names of the lines and spaces are always recited from lowest to highest.

Name the lines of the treble staff.

____   ____   ____   ____   ____

Name the spaces of the treble staff.

____   ____   ____   ____

E G B D F

F A C E

12

By alternating consecutive lines and spaces, pitches may be indicated in continuous alphabetic sequence.

Identify the pitches of the remaining lines and spaces of this treble staff in consecutive alphabetical order.

---

notes

13

This chapter began with the statement "pitch is indicated by the placement of symbols on a staff." These symbols are called **notes.**

To indicate pitch, _____ are placed on the staff.

No response necesssary

14

A basic note is the whole note: ◗. You will learn more about this and other various note types following some additional drill on pitch involving whole notes.

F B F E A

15

Identify the line or space on which a whole note is placed in each of the following examples.

E A G D C

16

Continue as in Frame 15

G E C E D

17

Continue as in the preceding frame.

	18
	Continue as in preceding frame.
A F B E F	

DEVELOPING PERFORMANCE SKILLS

Recorder, piano, and singing exercises involving the notes of the treble staff begin on page 26.

	19
	The second type of clef sign that we will be using is the **bass** clef or F clef.

	When the bass clef is placed on a staff, the two dots fall on either side of the line F.
	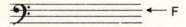 ← F
	All of the remaining lines and spaces of the bass staff are named in relation to the fourth line, F.
F	The fourth line of the bass staff is called _____.

POINT OF REFERENCE

The bass staff represents the pitch locale in which most men sing and in which such instruments as the trombone, bassoon, and cello sound. Approximately half of the pitches available on the piano are also notated on the bass staff.

20

Which of the following is a bass clef?

a. 　　c.

b. 　　d.

Answer: _____

d.

21

The remaining lines and spaces of the bass staff are:

Name the lines of the bass staff from lowest to highest.

____　____　____　F　____

G　B　D　(F)　A

22

Name the spaces of the bass staff.

____　____　____　____

A　C　E　G

23

Consecutive lines and spaces of the bass staff also identify pitches in simple alphabetical sequence.

Identify the pitches of the remaining lines and spaces of the following example in consecutive alphabetical order.

24

Identify the pitch of these notes on the bass staff:

D　G　G　A　E

	25
	Continue as in Frame 24
	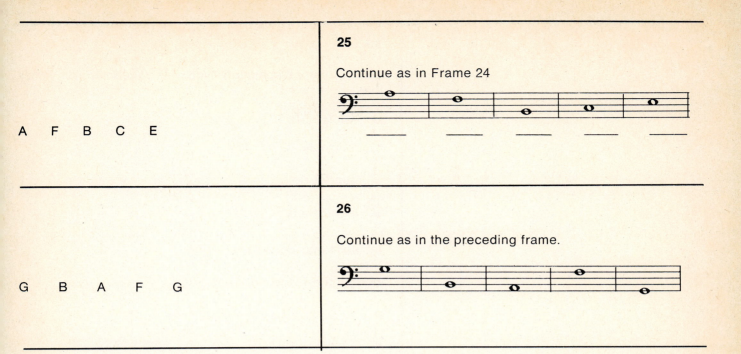
A F B C E	

	26
	Continue as in the preceding frame.
G B A F G	

DEVELOPING PERFORMANCE SKILLS

Piano and singing exercises in bass clef notation begin on page 29.

	27
	Notes are graphic symbols employing as many as three component parts—**note head, stem,** and **flag.** These components are illustrated in the following examples.
	○—— note head
	⌐—— stem ○—— note head
	⌐—— flag │—— stem ●—— note head
	The three possible component parts of a note are the
note head, stem, (and) flag	_____, _____, and _____.

28

Most of the compositions you will encounter will utilize these note types:

𝅝   whole note

𝅗𝅥   half note

♩   quarter note

♪   eighth note

𝅘𝅥𝅯   sixteenth note

Identify the following notes.

𝅗𝅥 _____ note

♪ _____ note

half

eighth

29

Identify the following notes by type.

♩ _____ note

𝅝 _____ note

𝅘𝅥𝅯 _____ note

quarter

whole

sixteenth

30

Write the following notes.

quarter note _____

whole note _____

sixteenth note _____

half note _____

eighth note _____

♩

𝅝

𝅘𝅥𝅯

𝅝

♪

G

half

31

This whole note ♩ indicates the pitch _____.

This _____ note, ♩ , is in the space E.

---

a. quarter   E

b. whole   A

c. half   A

d. eighth   D

32

Identify the following notes by type and pitch.

	type	*pitch*
a.	_____	_____
b.	_____	_____
c.	_____	_____
d.	_____	_____

---

a. sixteenth   C

b. half   G

c. whole   E

d. quarter   F

33

Continue as in the preceding frame.

	note	*pitch*
a.	_____	_____
b.	_____	_____
c.	_____	_____
d.	_____	_____

34

Because common musical usage involves a greater variety of pitches than can be represented on a single five-line staff, additional means of pitch notation are required. One such device is the extension of a staff in either direction by the use of **ledger lines.**

The staff may be extended in either direction through the use of _____ _____.

ledger lines

35

Ledger lines are short horizontal lines, spaced the same distance apart as the lines of the staff. Any number of ledger lines may be used depending upon the specific pitch desired. Place three ledger lines above the staff provided.

36

Letter names of the lines and spaces created by ledger lines continue in ascending or descending alphabetical order from the staff to which they are added.

Identify the following pitches.

37

Identify the following pitches in the bass clef.

38

By using ledger lines, notate the following pitches *above* the staff provided.

B   D   A   C   E

39

By using ledger lines, notate the following pitches *below* the staff provided.

A   C   G   B   F

40

By using ledger lines, notate the following pitches *above* the bass staff provided.

C   E   G   D   F

41

By using ledger lines, notate the following pitches *below* the bass staff provided.

D   E   C   A   B

DEVELOPING PERFORMANCE SKILLS

Performance exercises for the piano dealing with ledger line notation on both the treble and bass staves begin on page 31.

---

great staff

42

Since the use of a great number of ledger lines in association with a single treble or bass staff is quite cumbersome, a simpler solution is employed for instruments of great pitch variety (such as the piano). To serve this need, the treble staff and bass staff may be joined with a brace to form a **great staff.**

This is a great staff.

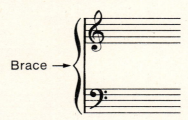

Brace →

When the treble staff and bass staff are joined with a brace, a _____ _____ is created.

C

43

The great staff can accommodate a range of twenty-three pitches without adding ledger lines below the bass staff or above the treble staff.

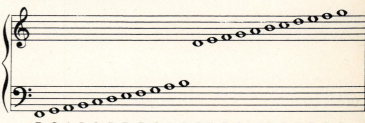

F G A B C D E F G A B D E F G A B C D E F G

At one point, a letter of the alphabet is skipped in the succession of pitches illustrated on the great staff above.

It is _____.

44

The C which completes this sequence requires the use of one ledger line between the bass and treble staves.

The note that occupies a ledger line between the treble

and bass staves is _____.

C

45

Since C is the middle pitch of the great staff, it is commonly called **middle C.** Middle C may be notated in one of two ways.

or   not

Circle each *correctly notated* middle C in the following example.

46

Identify the lines and spaces of the great staff in consecutive alphabetical order beginning with the lowest pitch. Be sure to include middle C.

F G (etc.)

POINT OF REFERENCE

Because of its wide pitch range, piano music is notated on the great staff. Treble staff notes are normally played with the right hand. The left hand usually plays notes on the bass staff.

	47 Identify the following pitches placed on the great staff. _ _ _ _ _ _ _ _
C B D C F E F G	
	48 Continue as in Frame 47. _ _ _ _ _ _ _ _
C E C B A A F E	

DEVELOPING PERFORMANCE SKILLS

Refer to page 32 for piano exercises dealing with the notes of the great staff.

CHECK YOUR UNDERSTANDING

1. The names of the lines of the treble staff are __ __ __ __ __.
2. The names of the spaces of the treble staff are __ __ __ __.
3. The names of the lines of the bass staff are __ __ __ __ __.
4. The names of the spaces of the bass staff are __ __ __ __.
5. Identify the component parts of the following note.

6. Write the following notes.

   a. quarter ___ b. half ___ c. eighth ___ d. whole ___ e. sixteenth ___

7. The staff may be extended in either direction through the use of

   _____ _____.

8. Identify the following pitches.

9. When the treble staff and bass staff are joined with a brace, a _____

   _____ is created.

10. Identify the following pitches on the great staff.

    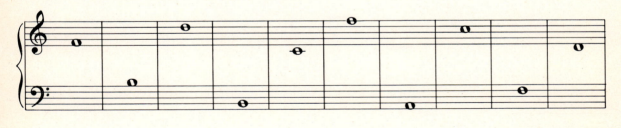

    (Answers may be found on page 353.)

APPLY YOUR UNDERSTANDING

Place the correct letter name below each note in each of the following songs.

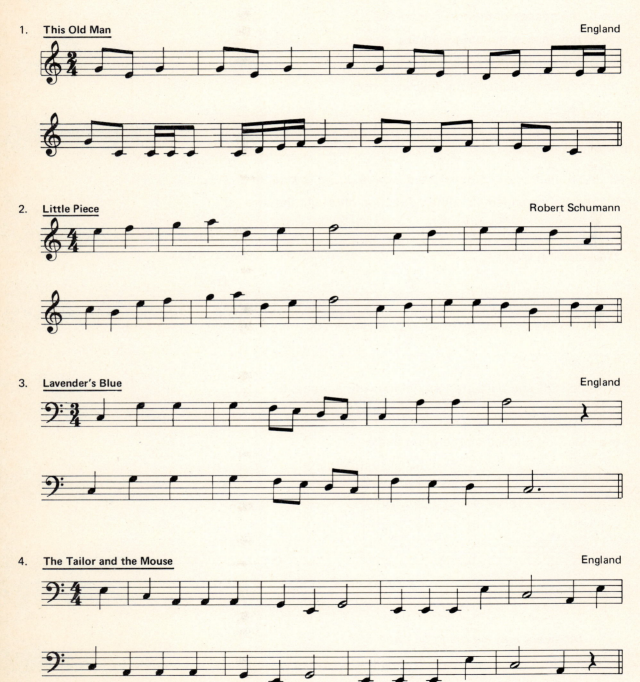

1. **This Old Man**   England

2. **Little Piece**   Robert Schumann

3. **Lavender's Blue**   England

4. **The Tailor and the Mouse**   England

(Answers may be found on page 354.)

49

In addition to pitch, you must also be concerned with the duration of a musical sound. Notes are used to show duration as well as pitch.

Two components of musical sound indicated by notes are

pitch and _____.

duration

50

Notes indicate both relative and absolute duration of musical sounds. The remainder of this chapter will deal with relative durations. These relative durations are evident in the names of the notes, which resemble fractions. A half note is half as long as a whole note, and so on.

The fraction-like names of the various notes indicate their

(relative/absolute) _____ duration.

relative

51

The following chart shows the relative duration of the five common notes you have studied.

For example, two half notes are equal to a whole note.

Two quarter notes are equal to one _____ note.

half

Two eighth notes are equal to one _____ note.

quarter

Four sixteenth notes are equal to one _____ note.

quarter

52

Complete the following equations.

𝅝 = 𝅗𝅥 + ___

𝅝 = ♩ ♩ + ___ ___

𝅝 = 𝅗𝅥 + ___ ___

53

Continue as in Frame 52.

♩ = ♪ + ___

𝅗𝅥 = ♩ + ___

𝅗𝅥 = ♪ ♪ + ___ ___

54

Continue as in the preceding frame.

♩ = 𝅘𝅥𝅯 𝅘𝅥𝅯 + ___ ___

♪ = 𝅘𝅥𝅯 + ___

𝅗𝅥 = ♩ + ___ ___

55

Continue as in the preceding frame.

𝅗𝅥 = ♩ + ___ ___

𝅗𝅥 = 𝅘𝅥𝅯 𝅘𝅥𝅯 𝅘𝅥𝅯 𝅘𝅥𝅯 + ___ ___ ___ ___

𝅗𝅥 = ♪ ♪ + ___ ___ ___ ___

Left column answers:

𝅗𝅥

♩ ♩

♩ ♩

♪

♩

♪ ♪

♪ 𝅘𝅥𝅯

♪

♪ ♪

♪ ♪

𝅘𝅥𝅯 𝅘𝅥𝅯 𝅘𝅥𝅯 𝅘𝅥𝅯

𝅘𝅥𝅯 𝅘𝅥𝅯 𝅘𝅥𝅯 𝅘𝅥𝅯

	56
	Complete the following statements.
whole	Four quarter notes are equal to one _____ note.
half	Eight sixteenth notes are equal to one _____ note.
half	Four eighth notes are equal to one _____ note.

	57
	The eighth and sixteenth notes that you identify by the flag(s) attached to the stem may also be notated in an alternate manner when they occur in groups of two or more. In this manner of notation, the notes are joined by a **beam** or beams that replace the flags.
	♪ ♪ = 𝅘𝅥𝅮𝅘𝅥𝅮 ◄— beam
	♬♬ = 𝅘𝅥𝅯𝅘𝅥𝅯𝅘𝅥𝅯𝅘𝅥𝅯 ◄— beams
	Notice that the number of beams used is equal to the number of flags.
eighth	These four notes 𝅘𝅥𝅮𝅘𝅥𝅮𝅘𝅥𝅮𝅘𝅥𝅮 are _____ notes.

	58
sixteenth	These two notes 𝅘𝅥𝅯𝅘𝅥𝅯 are _____ notes.

	59
	Using beams, notate two eighth notes in the space that follows.
𝅘𝅥𝅮𝅘𝅥𝅮	

60

Using beams, notate four sixteenth notes in the space that follows.

61

Rests are symbols that represent periods of silence. Every note value has a corresponding rest value.

Symbols that represent periods of silence are called

_____.

rests

62

On the staff provided write several whole rests. Note: A whole rest hangs below the fourth line of the staff.

63

On the staff provided write several half rests. Note: A half rest sits upon the third line of the staff.

64

On the staff provided write several quarter rests.

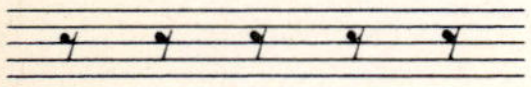

65

Continue as in the preceding frame using eighth rests.

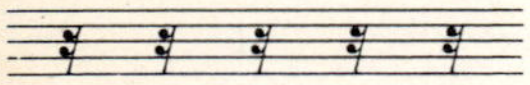

66

Continue as in the preceding frame using sixteenth rests.

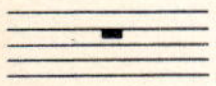

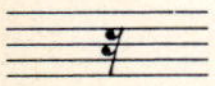

67

Write the corresponding rest for each of the following notes.

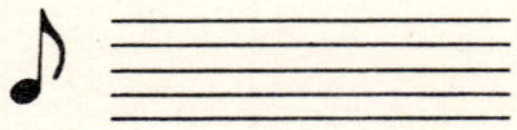

	68 Just as notes are related to one another, so are the rests. For example: A whole rest equals two half rests. four A whole rest equals _____ quarter rests.

four

68

Just as notes are related to one another, so are the rests. For example:

A whole rest equals two half rests.

A whole rest equals _____ quarter rests.

---

two

two

two

four

69

A ▬ rest = _____ ❟ rests.

A ❟ rest = _____ ❞ rests.

A ▬ rest = _____ ▬ rests.

A ▬ rest = _____ ❞ rests.

𝅘𝅥 + 𝅘𝅥𝅮

70

A **dot** may be added to each of the notes or rests. It increases the value of the note or rest by one-half of its original value.

𝅗𝅥. = 𝅗𝅥 + 𝅘𝅥

𝅘𝅥. = __ + __

𝅘𝅥 + 𝅘𝅥𝅮

𝅝 + 𝅗𝅥

71

Continue as in the preceding frame.

𝅘𝅥. = __ + __

𝅝. = __ + __

𝅘𝅥𝅮 + 𝅘𝅥𝅯

𝅗𝅥 + 𝅗𝅥

72

Continue as in the preceding frame.

𝅘𝅥𝅮. = _____ + _____

𝅗𝅥. = _____ + _____

♩. ♩. ♪.	**73** Rewrite the following combinations using dotted notes. ♩ + ♪ = _____ ♩ + ♩ = _____ ♪ + ♪ = _____
𝄽 + 𝄾 ▬ + ▬	**74** Continue as in the preceding frame. 𝄽· = _____ + _____ ▬. = _____ + _____
𝄾· 𝄽·	**75** Rewrite the following combinations using dotted rests. 𝄾 + 𝄾 = _____ 𝄽 + 𝄾 = _____ ▬ + 𝄽 = _____

CHECK YOUR UNDERSTANDING

1. Notes indicate both pitch and _____.

2. Complete the following:

    a. Four quarter notes are equal to one _____ note.

    b. Two eighth notes are equal to one _____ note.

    c. Eight sixteenth notes are equal to one _____ note.

3. Notate the following eighth and sixteenth notes using beams.

    a. =   b.  =

4. Symbols that represent periods of silence are called _____.

5. Notate the following rests.

6. A dot added to a note or rest increases the value of that note by _____.

7. Complete the following equations.

    a. $\mathbf{o}\cdot$ = ___ + 𝅝

    b. ♪. = ♪ + ___

    c. ♩. = ___ + ___

    d. 𝄼. = 𝄼 + ___

8. Complete the following equations using dotted notes and rests.

    a. ♩ + ♪ = ___

    b. 𝅗𝅥 + ♩ = ___

    c. 𝄾 + 𝄿 = ___

    d. 𝄽 + 𝄾 = ___

(Answers may be found on page 355.)

APPLY YOUR UNDERSTANDING

Identify selected notes and rests in the following songs as shown in example a.

1. **Rig-a-jig-jig**

2. **Pony Song**

For additional drill identify each note by letter name below the staff in each of the above songs.

(Answers may be found on pages 355–56.)

DEVELOPING PERFORMANCE SKILLS

Recorder (Frames 13–18)

If you are using the recorder as a class instrument with this text, the following exercises will introduce you to playing and hearing basic treble clef notes. It will be helpful to have your instructor hear you on at least some of these exercises to be sure you are playing the correct pitches. Your instructor will also guide you in proper recorder playing technique.

This illustration shows the placement of your fingers in playing the recorder and the fingering for basic pitches on the treble staff. The exercises that follow present those fingerings in progressive order.

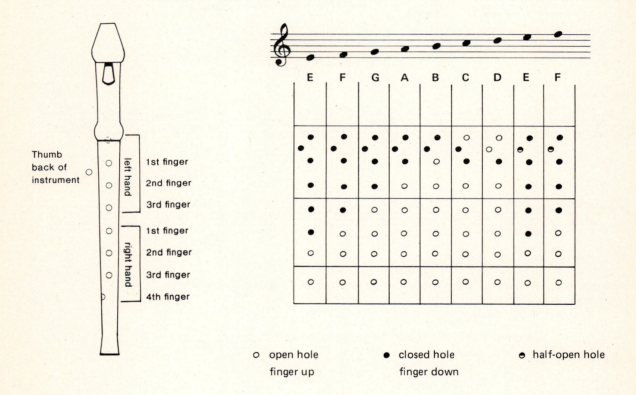

○ open hole
finger up

● closed hole
finger down

◐ half-open hole

Play these exercises at a slow, steady pace. Pause for a breath after each exercise.

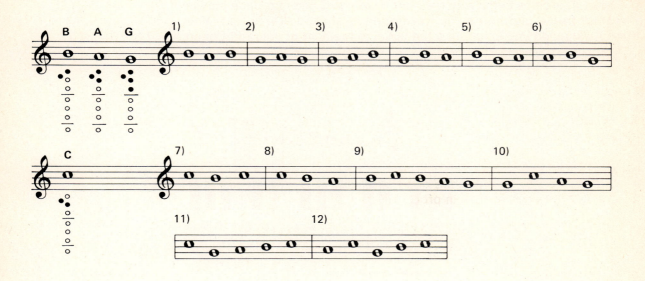

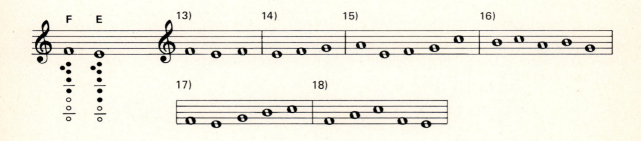

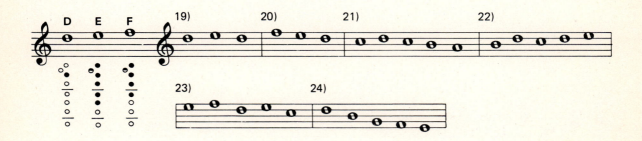

Piano (Frames 13–18)

Beginning piano method books traditionally present "middle C" as the first note. These exercises begin with the right thumb on G and introduce playing and hearing treble clef notes you have already studied in this text. Your instructor will guide you in locating the initial placement of your right hand.

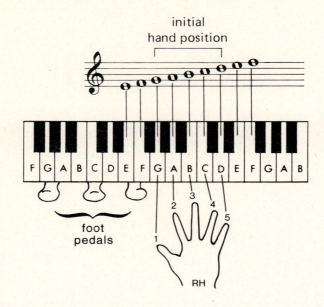

Play at a slow, steady pace, pausing between exercises. Numerals above the notes correspond to the fingering illustration. Begin in the initial hand position shown above.

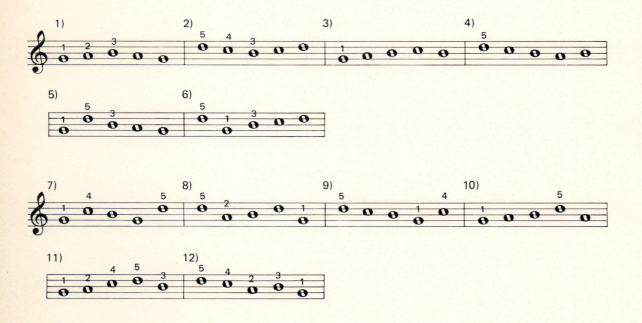

Shift your hand to each new starting position required. Stretch your hand to span the fingering indicated.

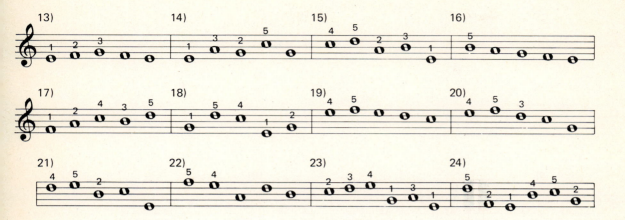

Singing (Frames 13–18)

You can further develop your music reading and recognition of pitch relationships by singing each of the preceding exercises. Sing the letter name of each note on the appropriate pitch in your own vocal range. Use your recorder or the piano to find the starting pitch and to check your accuracy. Most men will sing the corresponding pitches in the octave below the written exercises which is perfectly natural. (The octave concept is explained in Chapter 5.)

Piano (Frames 19–26)

The following exercises introduce playing and hearing bass clef notes you have studied in this text. Ask your instructor if you need assistance in the initial placement of your left hand.

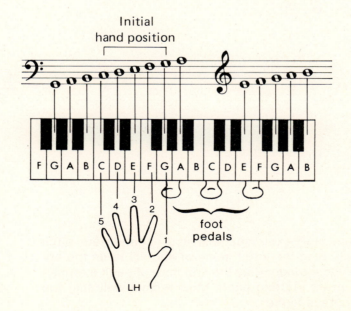

Play at a slow, steady pace pausing between exercises. Begin in the initial hand position shown above.

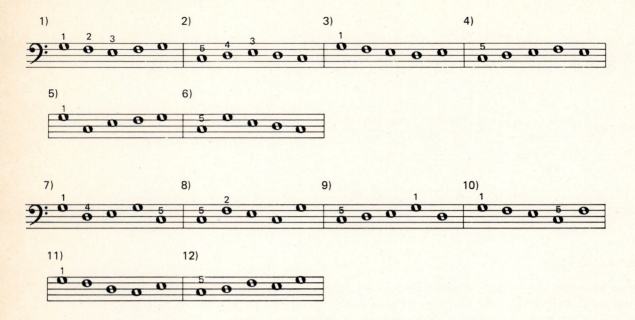

Shift your hand to each new starting position required. Stretch your hand to span the fingering indicated.

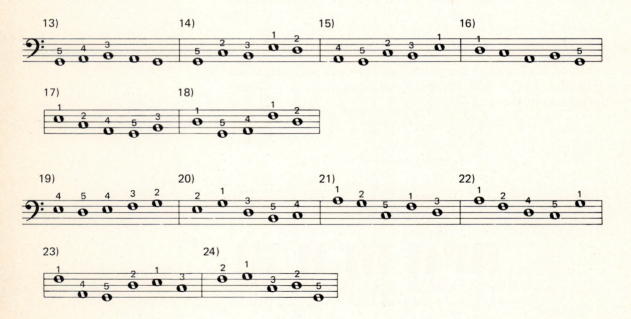

Singing (Frames 19–26)

Singing each of these bass staff exercises will also expand your pitch reading and recognition skill. Sing the letter name of each note on the appropriate pitch in your own vocal range. Play the first note of each exercise on the piano to find the correct starting pitch. Most women will sing the corresponding pitches an octave higher.

Piano (Frames 34–41)

Playing these exercises involving ledger lines will help you become familiar with more of the piano keyboard.

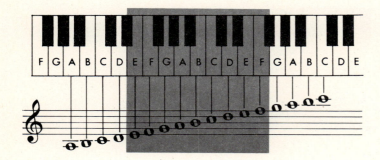

Play each exercise slowly but without hesitating between notes. You may wish to recite the note names as you play to reinforce your pitch reading skills.

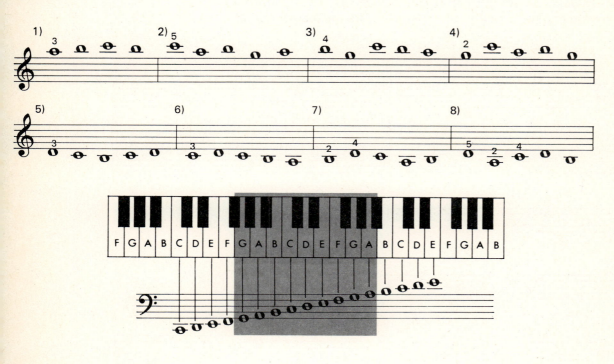

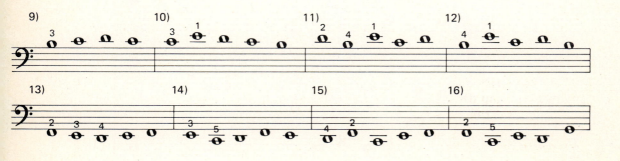

Piano (Frames 42–48)

Great staff notation requires combined visual and physical familiarity with a large, central position of the keyboard.

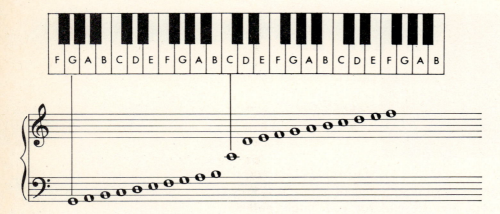

Maintain a steady pace as you play these exercises. Do not hesitate as the notes move from one hand to the other. Recite note names as you play if you wish.

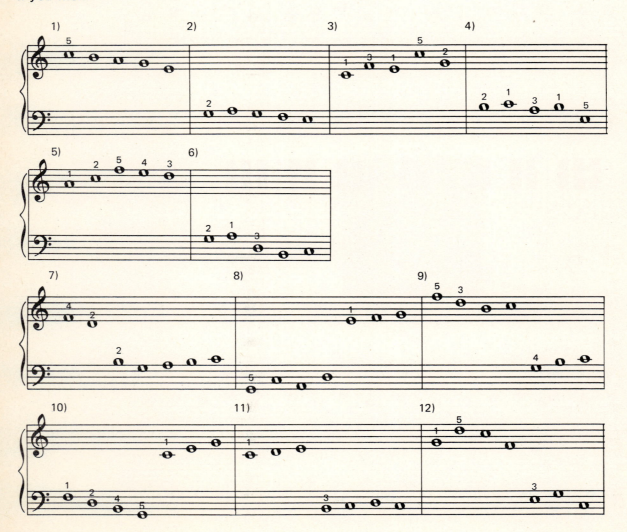

SUPPLEMENTARY ACTIVITIES

1. Identify note and rest types found in the Song Supplement.

2. Identify pitch names in songs found in the Song Supplement. Either drill may be performed by writing in your text or by reciting aloud.

3. Practice notating both the treble and bass clef symbols.
    The various steps in drawing each are as follows:

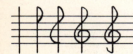

Duration and Meter

2

1

Relative durations, represented by the various note and rest values, create the feeling of motion in music that we call **rhythm.** When you tap your foot or clap your hands to a piece of music, you are *responding* to its rhythm. (Your tapping or clapping probably does not coincide with every note, but it is your physical response to the rhythmic motion of the composition.)

The feeling of motion that we experience in listening to

rhythm

a musical composition is called _____.

2

We perceive rhythm as a foreground of flexible or variable motion against an inflexible and recurring background called pulse or **beat.** Tapping or clapping as described above usually coincides with this background pulse or beat.

We perceive the flexible motion of rhythm in relation to

beat

an inflexible pulse or _____.

3

Rhythm is the flexible (foreground/background) _____

foreground

_____ of motion in a musical composition.

4

The recurring background against which rhythm moves is

pulse (or) beat
(Any order.)

called _____ or _____.

You should feel some beats as carrying more weight than others in this piece. If you did not, repeat this exercise being very careful to evaluate the relative emphasis given to each syllable of the text.

As you listen to a composition and tap the beats, you will probably notice that some beats assume more weight or emphasis than others. These are called accented or strong beats.

Sing this familiar song to yourself and tap or clap the beats.

My coun - try, 'tis of thee,
Sweet land of lib - er - ty,
Of thee I sing;
Land where my fa - thers died,
Land of the Pil - grims' pride,
From ev - 'ry moun - tain side
Let_____ free - dom ring.

Can you sense that some beats in this piece are stronger than others? _____.

My coun - try, 'tis of thee,
x   x
Sweet land of lib - er - ty,
   x   x
Of thee I sing;
x   x
Land where my fa - thers died,
   x   x
Land of the Pil - grims' pride,
   x   x
From ev - 'ry moun - tain side
   x   x
Let_____ free - dom ring.
   x   x

Now repeat this song and place an x beneath each syllable that represents a strong beat.

My coun - try, 'tis of thee,

Sweet land of lib - er - ty,

Of thee I sing;

Land where my fa - thers died,

Land of the Pil - grims' pride,

From ev - 'ry moun - tain side

Let_____ free - dom ring.

7

Sing *America* to yourself again. This time in addition to placing an x under each strong syllable, place a dash under each weak syllable.

My coun - try, 'tis of thee,

Sweet land of lib - er - ty,

Of thee I sing;

Land where my fa - thers died,

Land of the Pil - grims' pride,

From ev - 'ry moun - tain side

Let_____ free - dom ring.

My coun - try, 'tis of thee,
x   —   —   x   —   —

Sweet land of lib - er - ty,
  x   —   —   x   —   —

Of thee I sing;
x   —   —   x

Land where my fa - thers died,
  x   —   —   x   —   —

Land of the Pil - grims' pride,
  x   —   —   x   —   —

From ev - 'ry moun - tain side
  x   —   —   x

Let_____ free - dom ring.
x   —   —   x

8

Each of the strong beats in this song is followed by

_____ weak beats.
(number)

two

9

This regular recurrence of strong beats groups both the strong and weak beats into repeated sets.

How many beats do you feel in each set? _____

three

10

Is the strong beat the first, second, or third of each set?

_____

first

11

In this same song, draw a vertical line before the *beginning* of each repeated set of beats.

|My coun - try,|'tis of thee,

|Sweet land of|lib - er - ty,

|Of thee I|sing;

|Land where my|fa - thers died,

|Land of the|Pil - grims' pride,

|From ev - 'ry|moun - tain side

|Let_____ free - dom|ring.

My coun - try, 'tis of thee,

Sweet land of lib - er - ty,

Of thee I sing;

Land where my fa - thers died,

Land of the Pil - grims' pride,

From ev - 'ry moun - tain side

Let_____ free - dom ring.

12

Vertical lines such as those you provided in Frame 11, when placed on a staff, are called **bar lines.** Bar lines group the patterns of strong and weak beats into **measures** of a fixed number of beats.

measures

Bar lines group the beats into _____ of a fixed number of beats.

13

This organization into measures, each containing the same number of beats, establishes the **meter** of a piece. Depending upon the piece there can be 2, 3, 4, 5 or just about any number of beats per measure.

meters

In other words, many different _____ exist.

14

The meter of a piece is indicated by a **meter signature** or **time signature** found at the beginning of the piece following the clef sign.

A meter signature has been placed on the staff below.

$\frac{3}{4}$

The meter of a piece is indicated by a _____

_____ .

meter signature (*or*) time signature

15

In a meter signature (such as $\frac{3}{4}$), the lower numeral represents a reference note (4 = ♩) while the upper numeral indicates the number of reference notes per measure (three). The meter signature $\frac{3}{4}$ may also be illustrated as

3.
♩

In $\frac{2}{4}$ meter the reference note is _____

♩ (*or*) a quarter note

16

In $\frac{2}{4}$ meter there are _____ quarter notes per measure.

two

17

Explain the meaning of the meter signature $\frac{4}{4}$ $\left(\frac{4}{\text{♩}} \right)$.

_____

_____

There are four quarter notes in a measure. (*Your own words.*)

18

Using quarter notes, write three measures of $\frac{2}{4}$ $\left(\frac{2}{\text{♩}} \right)$ meter on the line below.

$\frac{2}{4}$

$\frac{2}{4}$

19

Using quarter notes, write three measures of $\frac{3}{4}$ $\left(\frac{3}{\text{♩}}\right)$ meter on the line below.

$\frac{3}{4}$ | | |

20

Although the meter signature $\frac{3}{4}$ $\left(\frac{3}{\text{♩}}\right)$ indicates that there are three quarter notes per measure, the measure may in fact be occupied by notes of any value equal to the accumulative value of three quarter notes, such as six eighth notes. The same is true in any meter.

How many eighth notes are there in one measure of $\frac{2}{4}$ $\left(\frac{2}{\text{♩}}\right)$ time? _____

four

21

Using only eighth notes, write two measures of $\frac{2}{4}$ $\left(\frac{2}{\text{♩}}\right)$ meter on the line below. (Refer to the chart in Chapter 1, Frame 52, if necessary.)

$\frac{2}{4}$ | |

(or)

22

Using only sixteenth notes, write two measures of $\frac{2}{4}$ meter on the line below.

$\frac{2}{4}$ | |

23

Using only sixteenth notes, write one measure of $\frac{4}{4}$ meter on the line below.

$\frac{4}{4}$ | |

DEVELOPING PERFORMANCE SKILLS

Basic exercises in rhythmic performance begin on page 56.

24

Any combination of note values may be employed so long as their accumulative value is equal to the measure length indicated by the meter signature.

In the following example brackets have been placed opposite all notes and combinations of notes equal to a quarter note.

Add brackets in a similar fashion to the following example.

25

Continue as in Frame 24.

26

Circle the measure in the following example that does not contain the correct sum of note values.

27

27

Continue as in Frame 26.

DEVELOPING PERFORMANCE SKILLS

Additional rhythmic performance skills appear on page 57.

28

Notes larger than the reference note may also be used to accomplish the accumulative duration of a measure. Consider the following example.

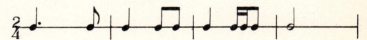

In each measure the total rhythmic value indicated is exactly two quarter notes.

Circle the measure in the following example of $\frac{3}{4}$ meter that does not contain the correct total rhythmic value.

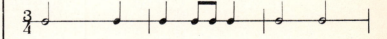

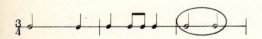

29

Circle the measure in the following example of $\frac{2}{4}$ meter that does not contain the correct sum of note values.

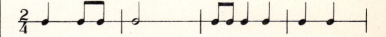

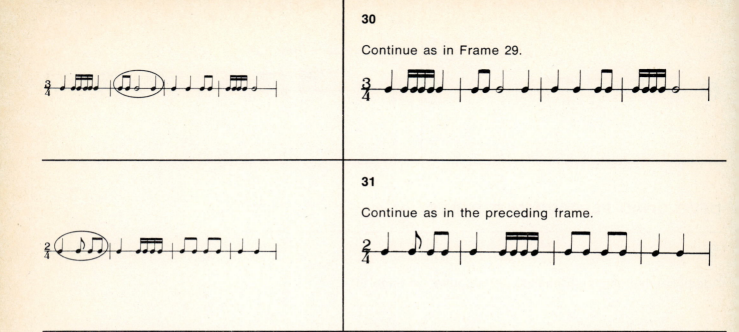

30

Continue as in Frame 29.

31

Continue as in the preceding frame.

DEVELOPING PERFORMANCE SKILLS

Rhythmic performance exercises employing a wider range of note values begin on page 57.

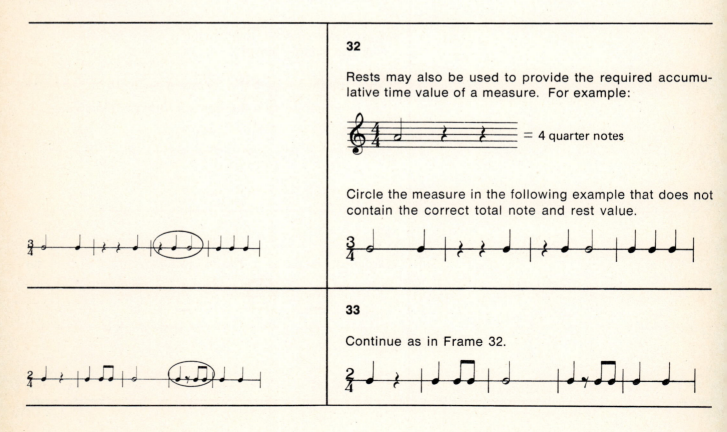

32

Rests may also be used to provide the required accumulative time value of a measure. For example:

= 4 quarter notes

Circle the measure in the following example that does not contain the correct total note and rest value.

33

Continue as in Frame 32.

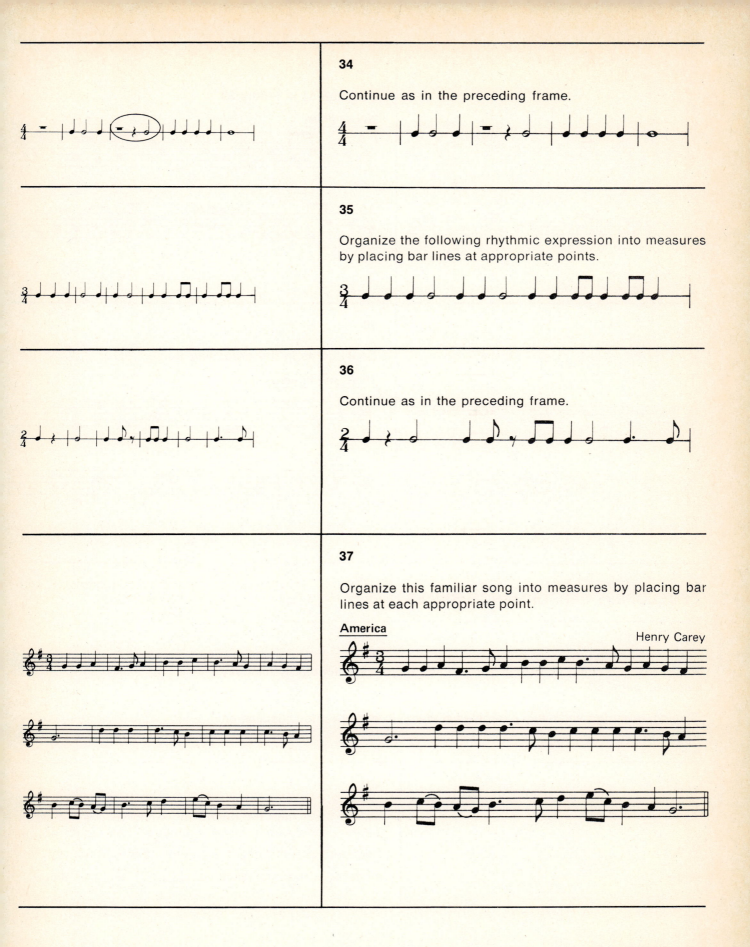

34

Continue as in the preceding frame.

35

Organize the following rhythmic expression into measures by placing bar lines at appropriate points.

36

Continue as in the preceding frame.

37

Organize this familiar song into measures by placing bar lines at each appropriate point.

America

Henry Carey

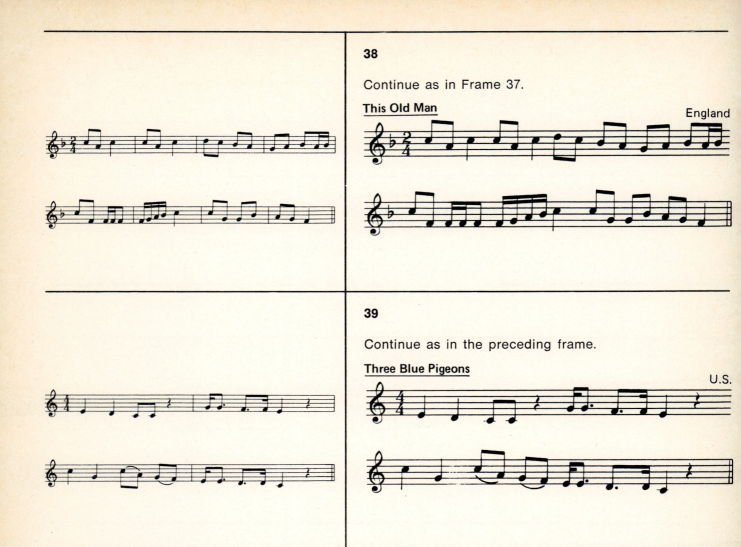

38

Continue as in Frame 37.

This Old Man   England

39

Continue as in the preceding frame.

Three Blue Pigeons   U.S.

DEVELOPING PERFORMANCE SKILLS

Exercises in reciting and singing treble and bass clef pitches rhythmically begin on page 58.

Singing, recorder, and piano exercises in rhythmic interpretation continue on page 58.

40

three

Values other than the quarter note may also serve as the reference note for a meter signature. The eighth note is frequently used. In $\frac{3}{8}$ $\left(\frac{3}{\rlap/\!b}\right)$ meter, the duration of one measure is the equivalent of _____ eighth notes.

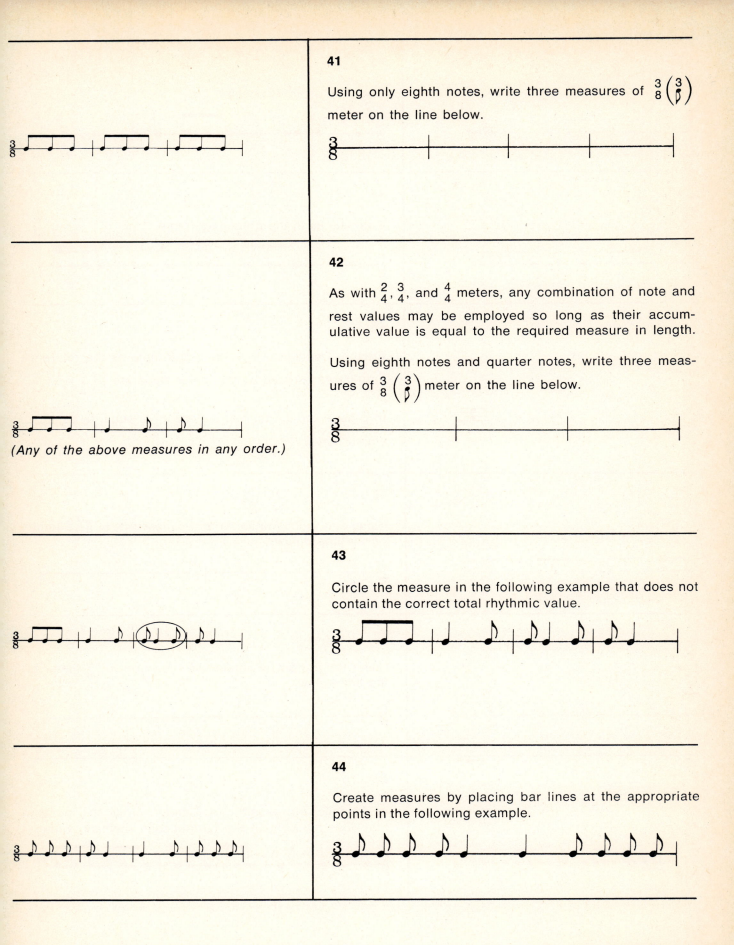

41

Using only eighth notes, write three measures of $\frac{3}{8}$ $\left(\frac{3}{\flat}\right)$ meter on the line below.

42

As with $\frac{2}{4}$, $\frac{3}{4}$, and $\frac{4}{4}$ meters, any combination of note and rest values may be employed so long as their accumulative value is equal to the required measure in length.

Using eighth notes and quarter notes, write three measures of $\frac{3}{8}$ $\left(\frac{3}{\flat}\right)$ meter on the line below.

43

Circle the measure in the following example that does not contain the correct total rhythmic value.

44

Create measures by placing bar lines at the appropriate points in the following example.

(Any of the above measures in any order.)

Continue as in Frame 44.

$\frac{3}{8}$

Continue as in the preceding frame.

$\frac{3}{8}$

Another frequent use of the eighth note as the reference note is represented by the meter signature $\frac{6}{8}\left(\frac{6}{\flat}\right)$.

six

In $\frac{6}{8}$ meter the duration of a measure is equal to _____ eighth notes.

Using only eighth notes, write two measures of $\frac{6}{8}\left(\frac{6}{\flat}\right)$ meter on the line below.

$\frac{6}{8}$

Using the pattern ♩♪ notate two measures of $\frac{6}{8}$ meter on the line below.

$\frac{6}{8}$

In the following example of $\frac{6}{8}$ meter, circle the measure that does not contain the correct total rhythmic value.

$\frac{6}{8}$

51

Continue as in Frame 50.

52

Continue as in the preceding frame.

53

Continue as in the preceding frame.

54

Place bar lines in the following example of $\frac{6}{8}$ meter.

55

Continue as in Frame 54.

56

Place bar lines at each appropriate point in the following song.

Eency, Weency Spider

Action Song

57

Continue as in Frame 56.

Pop, Goes the Weasel

England

58

Continue as in the preceding frame.

Bring a Torch, Jeannette, Isabella   France

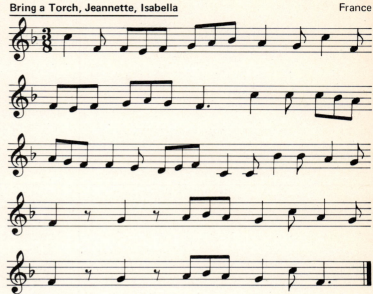

DEVELOPING PERFORMANCE SKILLS

Basic rhythmic performance exercises in $\frac{6}{8}$ meter begin on page 60.

Singing, recorder, and piano exercises in $\frac{6}{8}$ meter begin on page 60.

59

You have learned that some durations not represented by the basic note types may be represented by the addition of a dot, *which is equal to one-half the value of the note to which it is added.*

Example: ♩. = ♩ + ♪

The dot, however, is not capable of expressing durations other than one and one-half times a basic note type. For instance in the duration ♩+♪, a ♪ is not equal to one-half of a ♩. Therefore, it cannot be represented by a dot.

Circle the combinations in the following examples that *cannot* be represented by the addition of a dot.

a. ♩ + ♪   b. 𝅝 + ♩   c. ♩ + ♩   d. 𝅝 + ♩

60

If *one pitch* is to be sustained for a duration such as ♩ + ♪ , a **tie** must be used. A tie is a curved line joining note heads (not stems) as shown in the following example.

Tie ⟶ ♩‿♩

The tie combines the durational value of two or more notes of the same pitch.

The tie 𝅝‿♪ expresses a duration of 𝅝 + _____ .

♪

61

The tie combines the durational value of two or more notes of the same _____ .

pitch

62

When two notes are joined by a tie, only the first note is sung or played. The duration of the note to which the tie is connected is "added" to the value of the first note.

Example: ♩‿♩

The total duration of the above tied note is equal to a _____ note.

whole

63

The total duration of the tied notes below is equal to a _____ note.

♩‿♩

half

64

The total duration of the tied notes below is equal to a _____ note.

♪‿♪

quarter

65

Add the note required to complete the following measure rhythmically without adding a new pitch.

66

Add the note required to complete the following measure rhythmically without adding a new pitch.

67

Continue as in Frame 66.

68

Continue as in the preceding frame.

69

Continue as in the preceding frame.

70

Ties may also be used in cases where dotted notes can be used.

Notate the following dotted notes using ties.

a. 𝅝 ⌣ 𝅗𝅥

b. 𝅘𝅥 ⌣ 𝅘𝅥𝅮

c. 𝅗𝅥 ⌣ 𝅘𝅥

d. 𝅘𝅥𝅮 ⌣ 𝅘𝅥𝅯

a. 𝅝· = 𝅝 ⌣ 𝅗𝅥

b. 𝅘𝅥· =

c. 𝅗𝅥· =

d. 𝅘𝅥𝅮· =

71

Notate the following tied notes using dotted notes.

a. 𝅘𝅥·

b. 𝅗𝅥·

c. 𝅝·

d. 𝅘𝅥𝅮·

a. 𝅘𝅥 ⌣ 𝅘𝅥𝅮 =

b. 𝅗𝅥 ⌣ 𝅘𝅥 =

c. 𝅝 ⌣ 𝅗𝅥 =

d. 𝅘𝅥𝅮 ⌣ 𝅘𝅥𝅯 =

CHECK YOUR UNDERSTANDING

1. The feeling of motion that we experience in listening to a musical composition is called _____.

2. The recurring background against which rhythm moves is called _____.

3. Bar lines group the beats into _____ of a fixed number of beats.

4. The meter of a piece is indicated by a _____ or _____.

5. Explain the meaning of the meter signature $\frac{4}{4}$. _____ _____.

6. One measure of $\frac{3}{4}$ meter may contain _____ quarter notes.

7. One measure of $\frac{2}{4}$ meter may contain _____ eighth notes.

8. The durational values of two or more notes of the same pitch may be combined by joining the two notes with a _____.

(Answers may be found on page 356.)

APPLY YOUR UNDERSTANDING

Identify the musical symbols indicated by the arrows.

Add bar lines to the following songs.

(Answers may be found on page 357.)

7. The Tailor and the Mouse

England

8. Oats, Peas, Beans

England

Add the appropriate meter signature to the following examples.

9. Sourwood Mountain

Appalachia

10. On Top of Old Smoky

U.S.

11. Dame Get Up

England

12. The Riddle Song

Kentucky

For additional drill identify each note by letter name below the staff in songs 5-8 above.

(Answers may be found on page 357.)

DEVELOPING PERFORMANCE SKILLS

Rhythmic Performance (Frames 15–23)

Understanding the intellectual principles on which Western musical rhythm is based is certainly necessary to recognize and interpret musical notation. Accurate and fluent rhythmic performance however, is more a matter of feeling rhythmic relationships kinesthetically than of mentally decoding musical symbols. The following exercises explore some basic aspects of this physical interaction.

Tapping your hands on a table or your knees, first establish the reference note pattern of each example with your left hand. Recognize the strong beat (first note) of each measure with a louder tap. After two or three repetitions of the left-hand pattern, add the rhythmic pattern notated for the right hand. Repeat each exercise several times without pause. Keep a steady pace and perform the notes evenly. Repeat the entire group of exercises several times in different orders. See how quickly you can adjust to different metric patterns of strong and weak beats.

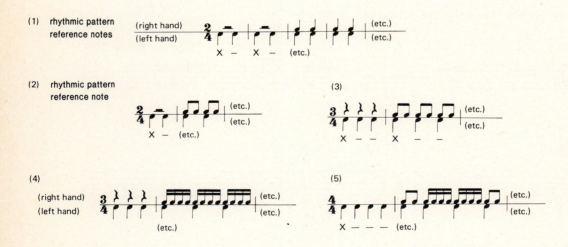

Invent additional exercises like these to further develop your rhythmic coordination.

Rhythmic Performance (Frames 24–27)

Continue as in the previous exercises. Repeat these drills several times in different orders to develop reading and performance fluency.

(1) rhythmic pattern (right hand)
reference note (left hand)

X x (etc.)

(2) rhythmic pattern
reference note

X x x

(3) (right hand)
(left hand)

X x x x

Rhythmic Performance (Frames 28–31)

When different combinations of note values comprise each beat it is often difficult to execute the relative durations precisely. In such cases measuring against a recurring background of the shortest note value present will enhance your accuracy. To make these exercises more like actual singing or playing an instrument you are asked to say the variable rhythmic patterns out loud with a neutral syllable such as "ta." Tap the background pattern lightly with either hand. Emphasize the beginning of each beat.

ta ta-ta (etc.)

(1) rhythmic pattern
background (tap)

X – X –

(2) rhythm
background

X   X

(3) rhythm
background

X   X   X

(4) rhythm
background

X   X   X   X

Repeat several times in different orders. Perform with a partner as a duet, each taking a turn on each part. Compose similar examples of your own. (You may even wish to write some on the chalk board in class to test your colleagues. You will be testing your aural skill by evaluating their performance.)

Rhythmic Performance (Frames 32–39)

Dealing with pitch and rhythm simultaneously in real musical performance is more complex than the previous, purely rhythmic exercises. Try your skill in combining these two mental and physical processes by clapping the reference note pattern to these songs with your hands while reciting the note names in the correct rhythm.

1. **America** — S. Smith / H. Carey

2. **Three Blue Pigeons** — U.S.

Now try singing the note names to these melodies (in your own vocal register) while clapping the reference note pattern. Use your recorder or the piano to find your starting pitch.

Singing, Recorder, Piano (Frames 24–39)

This process of so called "real musical performance" reaches another level of mental and physical complexity as you move from singing to playing an instrument. Continue beyond the two levels you have just practiced by performing each of the following examples in this four step sequence:

1. Clap the reference note pattern with your hands while reciting the melody in note names in the correct rhythm.

2. Sing each melody with note names while clapping the reference note pattern.

3. Play each treble staff melody on your recorder while tapping the reference note pattern with your foot.

4. Play each treble and bass staff melody on the piano while tapping the reference note pattern with your foot. (Remember to use your right hand for the treble staff and your left hand for the bass staff.)

1. **Pierrot**

2. **Mary Had A Little Lamb**   S. Hale

3. **Melody**   M.W.

4. **Lightly Row**   Germany

5. **London Bridge**   England

6. **Dona Nobis Pacem**   Round

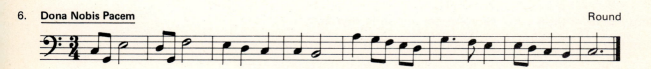

As you become more fluent in rhythmic performance on recorder and piano, try a new exercise eliminating the preparatory reciting and singing steps.

Rhythmic Performance (Frames 40–58)

The following songs apply basic rhythmic skills in $\frac{6}{8}$ meter. Clap the reference note pattern while reciting the note names in the correct rhythm.

1. **Three Blind Mice**   Round

2. **Silent Night**   Franz Gruber

In your own vocal range try to sing the note names to these melodies, while clapping the reference note pattern. Use your recorder or a piano to find your starting pitch.

Singing, Recorder, Piano (Frames 40–58)

Continue developing your performance skills in $\frac{6}{8}$ meter by performing the following pieces. Drill each melody in this four-step sequence:

1.   Clap the reference note: recite note names in rhythm.

2.   Clap the reference note: sing note names in rhythm.

3.   Play on the recorder (treble clef only) while tapping the reference note.

4.   Play on the piano while tapping the reference note.

"Low C" (middle C) is a difficult note for beginning recorder players. Be certain all of the finger holes are completely covered and blow very gently.

1. **Row, Row, Row Your Boat**   U.S.

2. **Oats, Peas, Beans**   England

3. **Pop, Goes the Weasel**   England

4. **Little Tom Tinker**   England

5. **Hey, Diddle, Diddle**   J.W. Elliott

6. **Eency, Weency Spider**   Action Song

Listening

Music truly exists only in the form of sound. Written notation and verbal descriptions are only "codes" for its reproduction. We grasp and identify music as sound through aural discrimination. These listening exercises dealing with the pitch structure of familiar songs utilize your singing, recorder, and piano skills to introduce the process of identifying musical organization by ear rather than from its written notation.

Exercise 1

Step 1: Sing the words of this familiar song by ear. Use your recorder or a piano to locate the starting pitch given.

Starting
Pitch

Twin-kle, twin-kle lit-tle star,
How I won-der what you are.
High a-bove the world so bright,
Like a dia-mond in the night.
Twin-kle, twin-kle lit-tle star,
How I won-der what you are.

Step 2: Sing the song again with a neutral syllable such as "la." Listen carefully to the tune.

Step 3: Now play the exercise several times "by ear" on your recorder and on the piano. Identify the letter name of each note mentally as you play.

Step 4: Write the letter name of each note under the corresponding syllable of the text.

Step 5: Play the song from the letter names you have written. Listen carefully as you play to check the accuracy of what you have written. (The piano will provide a more graphic reference to the pitch names than your recorder.)

Step 6: Sing the song with the correct note names to reinforce the sound of these pitch relationships in your ear.

Repeat these steps in Exercise 2–4.

1. Locate starting pitch on recorder or piano and sing with words to establish tune (melody).

2. Sing again with neutral syllable.

3. Play by ear on recorder and piano, mentally identifying note names as you play.

4. Write letter names below text.

5. Play from letter names to check your answers. (Piano if possible.)

6. Sing with letter names to reinforce.

Starting
Pitch

Exercise 2

Are you sleep-ing, are you sleep-ing,
Broth-er John, Broth-er John?
Morn-ing bells are ring-ing,
Morn-ing bells are ring-ing,
Ding, ding, dong, ding, ding, dong.

As your skill develops you should eliminate some of the drill steps. Can you begin at step 3? Your ultimate goal is to begin singing "mentally" (silently) at step 6 while simultaneously writing the note names (step 4). Always include step 5 to check your answers.

Starting
Pitch

Exercise 3

Row, row, row your boat
Gent-ly down the stream,
Mer-ri-ly, mer-ri-ly, mer-ri-ly, mer-ri-ly
Life is but a dream.

Exercise 4

Jin-gle bells, jin-gle bells,
Jin-gle all the way,
Oh, what fun it is to ride
In a one-horse o-pen sleigh! _____
Jin-gle bells, jin-gle bells,
Jin-gle all the way,
Oh, what fun it is to ride
In a one-horse o-pen sleigh!

SUPPLEMENTARY ACTIVITIES

1. Find familiar songs in the Song Supplement. Sing them while clapping or tapping the meter.

2. Recite the pitches of these melodies in rhythm while clapping or tapping the meter.

3. Using note names, sing these melodies while continuing to clap or tap the meter.

4. Play the following melodies on the recorder and piano:

   Christmas Is Coming, 370
   The Orchestra Song, 374
   Onchimbo, 373
   Michael Finnigan, 377
   Old Dan Tucker, 378
   Tzenza, Tzenza, 382
   Roll on, Columbia, 396
   Barb'ra Allen, 392

Rhythm and Counting

3

1

Knowing the meter of a melody and the relative duration of each note does not in itself enable you to interpret the rhythm of that melody accurately. To locate the notes of a melody precisely in time, it is necessary to identify the starting point and *absolute* duration of each note.

Accurate interpretation of rhythm requires identification

of the _____ _____ and _____

_____ of each note.

starting point (and) absolute duration

2

The precise location of notes requires the use of some scale of measurement. The meter created by the recurring background of beats provides an appropriate scale of measurement to which the starting point and absolute duration of each note may be related.

The notes of a melody may be located precisely in time

by relating each note to the _____.

meter

3

To use the meter of a melody as a scale of measurement for rhythmic interpretation, each beat of a measure is identified numerically by *counting* 1, 2, 3, and so on. The starting point and absolute duration of each note of a melody is then identified by its relationship to one or more of these numbered beats or counts.

Each note of a melody may be related to one or more of

the beats in a measure by _____.

counting

4

When you sang *America* to yourself and tapped the beats you formed a repeated set of three beats, one strong pulse followed by two weak pulses. The three beats of this meter are counted 1-2-3.

Sing the following portion of *America* to yourself while tapping the meter. Circle any syllable which occupies *more* than one beat or count.

My coun - try, 'tis of thee,

Sweet land of lib - er - ty,

Of thee I sing;

My coun - try, ('tis) of thee,

Sweet land of (lib) er - ty,

Of thee I (sing;)

5

Sing and tap the same portion of *America* to yourself again and circle each syllable which occupies *less* than one beat or count.

My coun - try, 'tis of thee,

Sweet land of lib - er - ty,

Of thee I sing;

My coun - try, 'tis (of) thee,

Sweet land of lib - (er) - ty,

Of thee I sing;

6

Sing *America* to yourself again and locate each beat in relation to the words by writing one or more numerals under *only* those syllables which are sounding *as each beat occurs.*

My coun - try, 'tis of thee,

Sweet land of lib - er - ty,

Of thee I sing;

Land where my fa - thers died,

Land of the Pil - grims' pride,

From ev - 'ry moun - tain side

Let _____ free - dom ring.

My coun - try, 'tis of thee,
1   2   3   12   3

Sweet land of lib - er - ty,
1   2   3   12   3

Of thee I sing;
1   2   3   123

Land where my fa - thers died,
1   2   3   12   3

Land of the Pil - grims' pride,
1   2   3   12   3

From ev - 'ry moun - tain side
1   2   3   12   3

Let _____ free - dom ring.
1   2   3   123

three

7

Since the meter of *America* is a pattern of three beats, this melody is organized into measures of _____ beats each.

three

8

This melody is usually notated as follows:

etc.

The meter signature indicates that there are _____ quarter notes (or equivalent) in each measure.

9

Since there are three beats and the equivalent of three quarter notes in each measure of *America* the duration of one quarter note is one beat. It follows that any note longer than a quarter note will occupy more than one beat and any note shorter than a quarter note will sound for less than one beat.

Locate each beat in the following example by writing one or more numerals under *only* those notes which are sounding *as each beat occurs.*

two

10

Sing *Twinkle, Twinkle Little Star* to yourself while tapping the meter. How many beats occur in each measure?

_____

quarter

11

The usual meter signature of *Twinkle, Twinkle Little Star* is $\frac{2}{4}$, meaning that each measure contains the equivalent of two _____ notes.

12

Since each measure of *Twinkle, Twinkle Little Star* contains two beats as well as two quarter notes (or equivalent) each quarter note has a duration of _____ beat.

one

13

Write the appropriate count or counts under each note of *Twinkle, Twinkle Little Star.*

14

In *America* and *Twinkle, Twinkle Little Star,* the reference note of the meter signature has a duration of one beat. This is true of many meters including $\frac{2}{4}$, $\frac{3}{4}$, $\frac{4}{4}$ and $\frac{3}{8}$. Because the reference note has a duration of one beat, these meters are classified as **simple meters.**

A simple meter is one in which the reference note has a duration of _____.

one beat

15

Another feature of simple meters is that the upper number of the meter signature identifies the number of beats per measure.

In the simple meter $\frac{4}{4}$ there are _____ beats per measure.

four

beats	**16** In simple meter the upper number of the meter signature indicates the number of _____ per measure.
b. and c.	**17** Because not all meter signatures signify simple meter, you must be able to recognize those which do. Any meter signature in which the upper number is *NOT* a *multiple of three other than one,* signifies simple meter. Which of the following represent simple meter? a. $\frac{6}{8}$ b. $\frac{2}{4}$ c. $\frac{4}{8}$ d. $\frac{9}{8}$ Answer: _____
True	**18** is a simple meter. The upper number of this meter signature is equal to 3×1. The expression "multiple of three other than one" means 6 (2×3), 9 (3×3), or higher multiples of three. $\frac{3}{8}$ is a simple meter. (True/False) _____.
False	**19** $\frac{6}{4}$ is a simple meter. (True/False) _____.
quarter	**20** In $\frac{3}{4}$ meter, one beat represents the duration of a _____ note.
three	**21** In $\frac{3}{4}$ meter, there are _____ beats per measure.

22

Fast moving melodies in $\frac{3}{4}$ meter are sometimes interpreted as having one beat per measure. This is an intellectual compromise employed for performance purposes and does not invalidate the common identification of $\frac{3}{4}$ as simple meter.

(No response necessary.)

23

The number of beats per measure and the note value equivalent to one beat combine to indicate the placement of counts.

Write the counting below each line of the following example. Be sure to identify beats that occur during, as well as at the beginning of, each note.

The Sidewalks of New York   C. B. Lawlor
                                                       J. W. Blake

24

Continue as in Frame 23.

Go Tell Aunt Rhody   U. S.

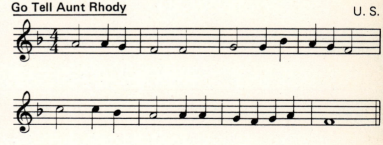

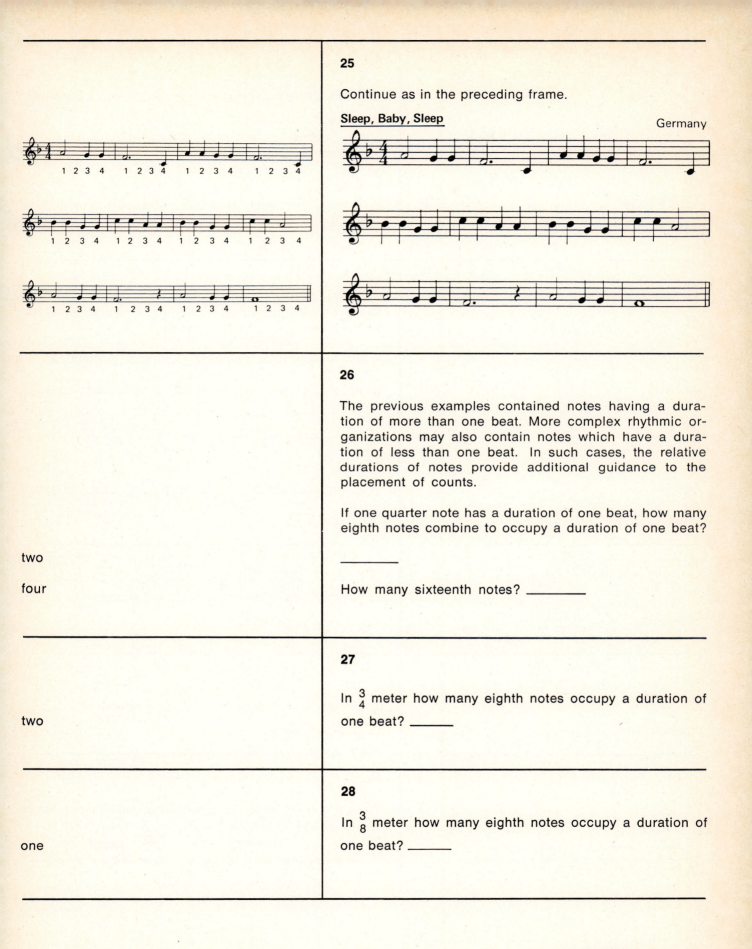

25

Continue as in the preceding frame.

Sleep, Baby, Sleep   Germany

26

The previous examples contained notes having a duration of more than one beat. More complex rhythmic organizations may also contain notes which have a duration of less than one beat. In such cases, the relative durations of notes provide additional guidance to the placement of counts.

If one quarter note has a duration of one beat, how many eighth notes combine to occupy a duration of one beat?

two

_____

four

How many sixteenth notes? _____

27

In $\frac{3}{4}$ meter how many eighth notes occupy a duration of

two

one beat? _____

28

In $\frac{3}{8}$ meter how many eighth notes occupy a duration of

one

one beat? _____

four	**29** In $\frac{4}{4}$ meter how many sixteenth notes occupy a duration of one beat? _____
two	**30** In $\frac{3}{8}$ meter how many sixteenth notes occupy a duration of one beat? _____
one-half	**31** The duration of individual eighth and sixteenth notes may be expressed as fractions of beats. If two eighth notes combine to form a duration of one beat, one eighth note has a duration of _____ of a beat.
four	**32** In $\frac{3}{4}$ meter one beat may contain _____ sixteenth notes.
one-fourth	**33** In $\frac{3}{4}$ meter one sixteenth note has a duration of _____ _____ of a beat.
one-half	**34** In $\frac{3}{8}$ meter a sixteenth note has a duration of _____ _____ of a beat.
	35 Place a bracket under each note or group of notes having a duration of one beat.

36

As you may have noticed in the previous frame the task of grouping eighth and sixteenth notes by beats was already accomplished by the beams used in the notation.

Beams

This is common in instrumental music. Eighth and sixteenth notes are written with flags when they occur singly or in vocal music when each note is associated with a different word or syllable of the text.

(No response necessary.)

37

This grouping of relative values by beats indicates where beats occur in more complex rhythmic organizations. The correct placement of beats is necessary in counting any rhythm.

Write the appropriate count below each note in the following example which coincides with a beat. (Identify beat durations with brackets first if you wish.)

38

Continue as in Frame 37.

39

Continue as in the previous frame.

40

To properly interpret notes that do not coincide with beats, counting systems are expanded to identify every note in a rhythmic context. The point of occurrence of each beat is identified by a number as in the previous frames. The point at which the *second half* of each beat occurs is identified by a neutral syllable such as "and" (written "&").

Write the counting under this example using numerals and "&" as appropriate.

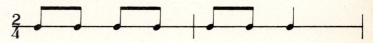

INSTRUCTOR'S CHOICE

Various systems of counting exist. Your instructor may prefer a choice other than "and." Substitute your instructor's preference in subsequent frames.

41

Write the counting below the notes of this melody.

Lightly Row

Little 'Liza Jane

42

Continue as in Frame 41.

74   Rhythm and Counting

43

Continue as in the preceding frame.

Santa Lucia

Teodoro Cottrau

1 & 2 & 3 & 1 & 2 3 & 1 & 2 & 3 & 1 & 2 & 3 &

44

The second half of a beat may be occupied by a note having a duration greater than one half beat. This is illustrated at points marked with an * in example (a) which follows.

a.

1 & 2 & 3 & 4 & 1 & 2 & 3 & 4 &

Example b. has precisely the same rhythm as example a. The use of ties at points corresponding to * in example a. illustrates visually how notes which begin on the syllable "and" extend through the occurrence of the next beat number.

b.

1 & 2 & 3 & 4 & 1 & 2 & 3 & 4 &

Write the counting below the notes of this melody.

In this and some following answer frames, some silent syllables appear in parentheses for clarification. Only syllables that correspond to notes (those not in parentheses) are required in your answers.

45

The counting of quarter beats (usually encountered as sixteenth notes) requires the use of additional syllables. In the following example each quarter of each beat is identified by adding the syllables "e" and "ah."

Write the counting below the notes of this melody.

This Old Man   England

INSTRUCTOR'S CHOICE

Counting systems vary even more in dealing with sixteenth notes. Substitute the system preferred by your instructor in the following frames.

46

Continue as in Frame 45.

Skip to My Lou   Southern U. S.

47

This system of counting will accommodate all of the rhythmic situations you are likely to encounter in simple meter including dotted notes. Consider this rhythm:

The duration of the dotted quarter note is _____ and _____ beats.

The dot represents the first half of the _____ beat.

The eighth note coincides with the _____ half of the second beat.

one (and) one-half

second

second

48

Write the counting below the notes of this example.

49

In the rhythm the dotted quarter note begins on the second half of the _____ beat of the measure.

first

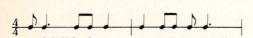

1 & (2 &) 3 & 4 | 1 2 & 3 & (4 &)

1 2 3 (&4) & 1 2 3 4 1(&2)&3(&4)& 1 23 4

1 &(2&) 3 &4)& 1 & 2 3(&4)& 1 2 3(&4)& 1 234

50

Write the counting below the notes of this example.

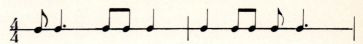

51

Write the counting below the notes of this melody.

52

Dotted notes may also involve quarter beats as in this example.

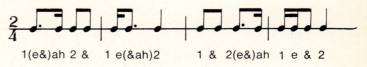

1(e&)ah 2 &   1 e(&ah)2   1 & 2(e&)ah 1 e & 2

Write the counting below the notes of this melody.

Nelly Bly   Stephen C. Foster

1   2 &   1   2 &   1 e(&ah)2(e&) ah 1   2 &

1 & 2   1 & 2 (e&) ah   1 & 2(e&) ah   1 2

53

The rhythm of many melodies requires that they *not* begin on the first beat of a measure. To count a rhythm that begins with a partial measure, you may wish to first count backwards from the first bar line to determine the count on which the first note occurs.

This rhythm begins on count _____.

three

54

This rhythm begins on count _____.

three

55

Write the counting below each note of this melody.

Lullaby

Brahms

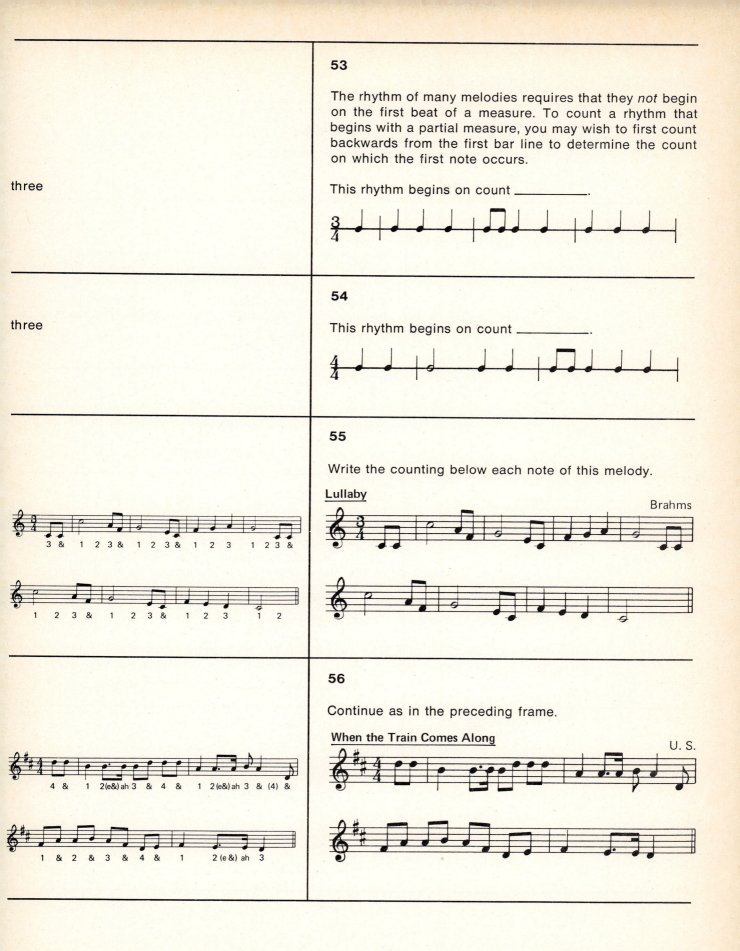

56

Continue as in the preceding frame.

When the Train Comes Along

U. S.

DEVELOPING PERFORMANCE SKILLS

Exercises in simple meter for singing, recorder, and piano are found on page 91.

	57 This study of counting so far has been limited to simple meters. In simple meter the reference note of the meter signature has a duration of _____ beat and the upper number of the meter signature indicates the number of _____ per measure.
one beats	
three	**58** Simple meters all utilize meter signatures in which the upper number is *not* a multiple of _____.
	59 Meters that do not conform to the identity of simple meter are called **compound meters.** The most obvious identity feature of a compound meter is that the upper number of the meter signature *is* a multiple of three other than one. The most frequently used compound meter is $\frac{6}{8}$. Other examples are $\frac{9}{8}$, $\frac{6}{4}$ and $\frac{12}{8}$. The upper number of a compound meter signature is always a _____ of three other than one.
multiple	
b. and d.	**60** Which of the following meter signatures identify compound meters? a. $\frac{3}{4}$ c. $\frac{4}{8}$ b. $\frac{6}{8}$ d. $\frac{9}{8}$ Answer: _____

61

Unlike simple meter signatures, compound meter signatures do not directly represent the note value equivalent to one beat or the number of beats per measure unless the tempo is very slow. Dividing the top number of the meter signature by three will identify the number of beats per measure in most cases.

How many beats usually occur in one measure of $\frac{6}{8}$ meter? _____

two

62

A very *slow* melody in $\frac{6}{8}$ meter *may* be felt as having six beats per measure, but the rhythmic flavor of most $\frac{6}{8}$ melodies is more suggestive of two rhythmic pulses or beats per measure. A similar feeling may also occur in *slow* melodies in other compound meters.

(No response necessary.)

63

In most cases, the number of beats per measure in compound meter is determined by dividing the upper number of the meter signature by _____.

three

64

$\frac{6}{4}$ meter is usually counted in reference to _____ beats per measure.

two

65

$\frac{12}{8}$ meter is usually counted in reference to _____ beats per measure.

four

66

$\frac{9}{8}$ meter is usually counted in reference to _____ beats per measure.

three

67

Having identified the number of beats per measure in the above manner, the same proportion must then be used in calculating the note value equivalent to one beat. This note will have a relative duration of three reference notes.

For instance, in $\frac{6}{8}$ meter, the note having a duration of one beat is usually equivalent to three eighth notes.

Circle the note below that is equivalent to three eighth notes.

a. ♩ b. 𝅗𝅥 c. ♪. d. 𝅗𝅥.

d.

68

In $\frac{6}{4}$ meter the duration of one beat is usually equivalent to _____ quarter notes.

three

69

Notate the note having a duration of one beat in $\frac{6}{8}$ meter.

_____

♩.

70

Notate the note having a duration of one beat in $\frac{6}{4}$ meter.

_____

𝅗𝅥.

71

Since our system of relative note values accepts each basic note type as equal to two of the next shortest relative duration, the fact that compound meters contain beats equal to three times the reference note means that the beat in compound meter is always equal in duration to a *dotted note.* (Except at a slow tempo.)

Which of the following notes are capable of representing a duration of one beat in a compound meter?

a. ♩. b. 𝅗𝅥 c. ♪ d. 𝅗𝅥.

Answer: _____

a. and d.

72

Knowing that each beat in $\frac{6}{8}$ meter has a duration of three eighth notes will serve as a guide to the placement of beats in $\frac{6}{8}$ rhythms.

Indicate the placement of beats by writing numbers below the appropriate notes in the following melody.

Blow the Winds Southerly

England

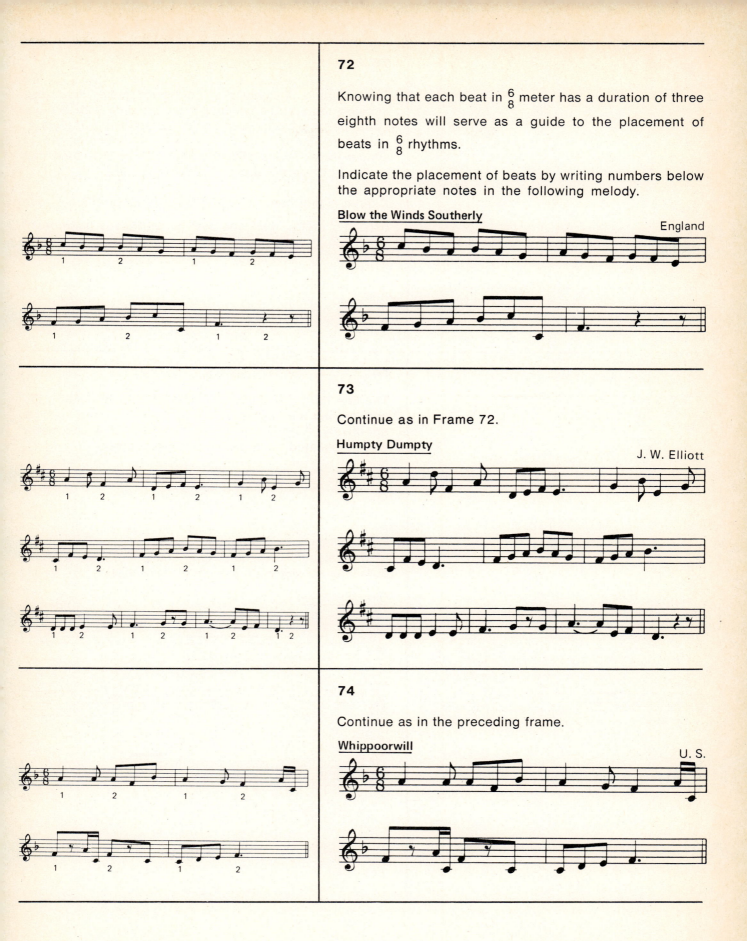

73

Continue as in Frame 72.

Humpty Dumpty

J. W. Elliott

74

Continue as in the preceding frame.

Whippoorwill

U. S.

one-third

75

The counting of rhythms in compound meter must also accommodate notes which do not coincide with the occurrence of a beat. Here again the relative durations of notes provide an additional guide to counting. As in simple meter, notes having a duration of less than one beat may be expressed as fractions of beats.

If three eighth notes combine to form the duration of one beat in $\frac{6}{8}$ meter, then one eighth note has a duration of _____ of a beat.

76

The first third of each beat is identified by a number, the second and third by syllables such as "ah" and "la" respectively. A series of eighth notes in compound meter can be counted as in the following example.

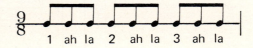

Write syllables to locate each eighth note in this melody. Identify eighth note equivalents that occur within longer durations as well as individual eighth notes.

One More River

Spiritual

INSTRUCTOR'S CHOICE

Substitute the counting system preferred when dealing with compound meters.

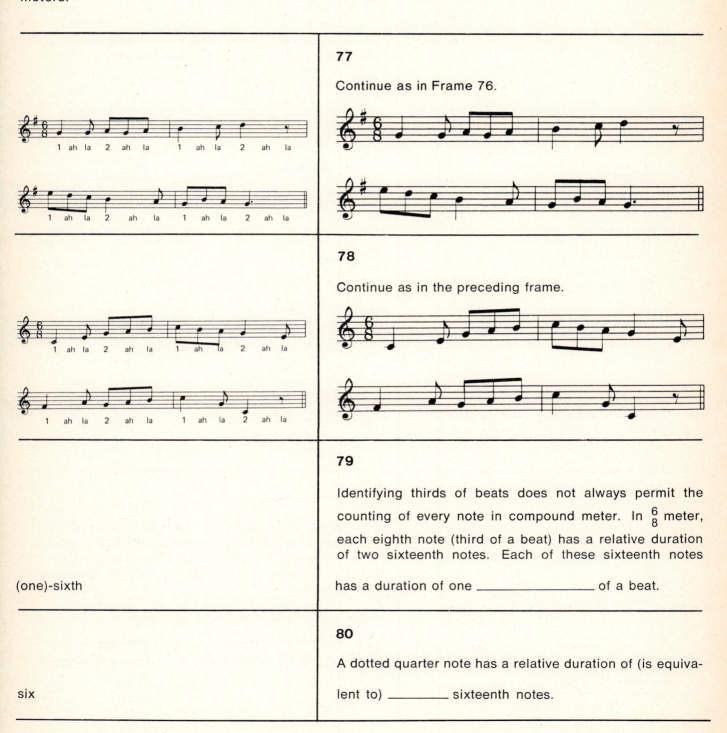

77

Continue as in Frame 76.

78

Continue as in the preceding frame.

79

Identifying thirds of beats does not always permit the counting of every note in compound meter. In $\frac{6}{8}$ meter, each eighth note (third of a beat) has a relative duration of two sixteenth notes. Each of these sixteenth notes

(one)-sixth

has a duration of one _____ of a beat.

80

A dotted quarter note has a relative duration of (is equiva-

six

lent to) _____ sixteenth notes.

81

When counting sixths of beats in compound meter, a syllable such as "de" is inserted after each third of a beat to create a pattern of six syllables as in this example.

Write the counting below the notes of this melody.
Use the counting system preferred by your instructor.

Whippoorwill

U. S.

82

Continue as in the preceding frame.

Home on the Range

Cowboy

83

This approach to counting in compound meter will accommodate very intricate rhythmic organization, such as in the following example, simply by adopting the set of syllables necessary to identify the shortest relative duration present.

Write the counting below this example.

84

Write the counting below each note of this melody. Notice that it begins with a partial measure.

Susie, Little Susie

E. Humperdinck

DEVELOPING PERFORMANCE SKILLS

Melodies in compound meters for singing, recorder, and piano may be found on page 93.

CHECK YOUR UNDERSTANDING

1. Which of the following meter signatures identify simple meters?

   a. $\frac{6}{8}$ b. $\frac{2}{4}$ c. $\frac{3}{8}$ d. $\frac{12}{8}$

   Answer: _____

2. In $\frac{4}{4}$ meter there are _____ beats per measure.

3. In $\frac{2}{4}$ meter there are _____ beats per measure.

4. If one quarter note has the duration of one beat, how many eighth notes combine to occupy a duration of one beat? _____

5. In $\frac{2}{4}$ meter how many sixteenth notes occupy a duration of one beat? _____

6. If two eighth notes combine to form a duration of one beat, one eighth note has a duration of _____ beat.

7. In $\frac{3}{8}$ meter a sixteenth note has a duration of _____ beat.

8. Which of the following meter signatures identify compound meters?

   a. $\frac{3}{4}$ b. $\frac{6}{8}$ c. $\frac{4}{8}$ d. $\frac{9}{8}$

   Answer: _____

9. In compound meter the numerals of the meter signature directly identify neither the number of beats per measure nor the note having a duration of one beat. (True/False) _____

10. $\frac{6}{8}$ meter is usually counted in reference to _____ beats per measure.

(Answers may be found on page 358.)

APPLY YOUR UNDERSTANDING

Write the counting under the notes in the following songs.

1. **The Glendy Burk**   Stephen C. Foster

2. **The Riddle Song**   Kentucky

3. **Clementine**   U.S.

(Answers may be found on pages 358-60.)

4. **Sumer Is Icumen In**   England

5. **Dancing Doll**   E. Poldini

(Answers may be found on pages 359-60.)

DEVELOPING PERFORMANCE SKILLS

Singing, Recorder (Frames 13–56)

Perform the following drills on these songs:

1. Write the counts below the notes.
2. Sing each song with the counting you have written.
3. Play each song on your recorder.

1. **The Woodchuck** U.S.

2. **Lavender's Blue** England

3. **Bring A Torch, Jeannette Isabella** France

Singing, Piano (Frames 13–56)

Perform these songs in the following sequence:

1. Sing with counting at sight. (Your counting skill in easy rhythmic con-figurations should now be sufficiently developed that you do not need to write the counting below the notes.)

2. Play these melodies on the piano. Count aloud as you play if you ex-perience any difficulty.

1. **Choral Theme from the Ninth Symphony**   Beethoven

2. **Marine's Hymn**   U.S. Military

3. **Three Cornered Hat**   Camp Song

Singing, Recorder (Frames 58–83)

Perform the following drills on these songs:

1. Write the counts below the notes.

2. Sing each song with the counting you have written.

3. Play each song on your recorder.

1. **Barcarolle** — Offenbach

2. **The Reaper's Song** — Schumann

3. **Down In The Valley** — Kentucky

Singing, Piano (Frames 58–83)

Perform these songs in the following sequence:

1. Sing with counting at sight.

2. Play these melodies on the piano. Count aloud as you play if you experience any difficulty.

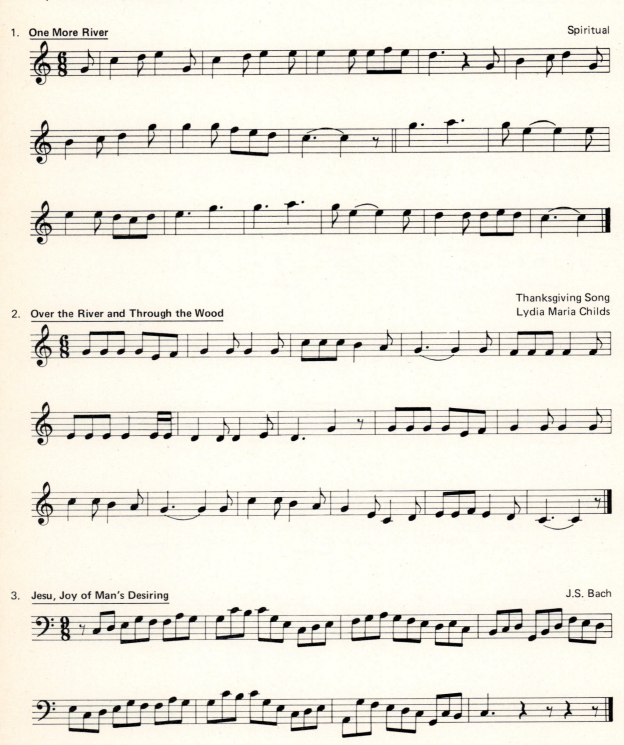

1. **One More River**
    Spiritual

2. **Over the River and Through the Wood**
    Thanksgiving Song
    Lydia Maria Childs

3. **Jesu, Joy of Man's Desiring**
    J.S. Bach

Listening, Rhythmic Performance: Simple meter (Frames 13–56)

These exercises require the participation of two or more persons. One claps or taps each exercise from the text; another listens and "echos" back the same rhythmic statement by ear without looking at the notation. The initial performer must listen carefully to the "echo" while following the text. If errors occur the exercise is repeated immediately; if not, proceed immediately to the next exercise. Perform an entire group of exercises in a given meter several times without pause. Vary the order of individual exercises as groups are repeated. (i.e., a, b, c, d, e, b, a, d, e, c, b, e, d, etc.) Each participant should experience both roles in each group of exercises. Establish the meter of each group by counting two measures aloud, then proceed into the exercises without pause.

Group 1 - clap or tap

Group 2

Group 3

Group 4

Group 5

Group 6

Listening, Rhythmic Performance: Compound meter (Frames 58–83)

Continue as in the previous exercises.

Group 1 - clap or tap

Group 2

Group 3

Group 4

Group 5

Group 6

Listening, Writing: Simple and compound meters (Frames 13–83)

As one individual performs each of these rhythmic statements, others notate that rhythm in the space provided. Cover the answer frames before beginning. The performer will count two measures aloud in the appropriate meter, then proceed immediately with each exercise. Each statement should be performed as many times as any listener requires, with an appropriate pause for writing between each performance. Check the accuracy of each response before going on to the next exercise.

Clap or tap

1

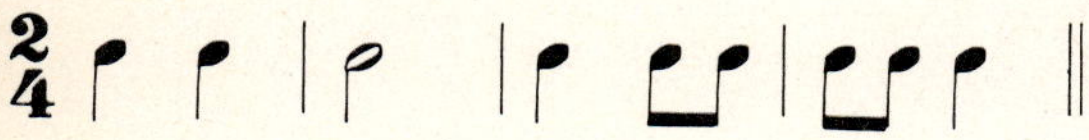

1

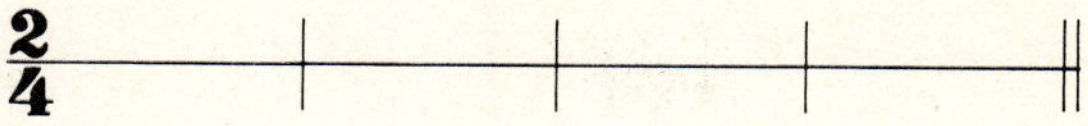

2

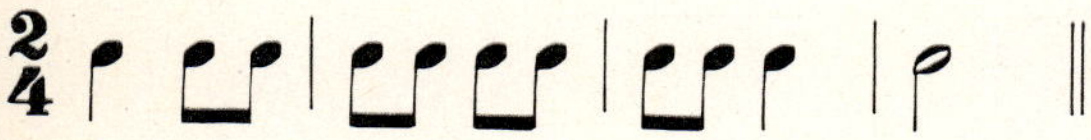

2

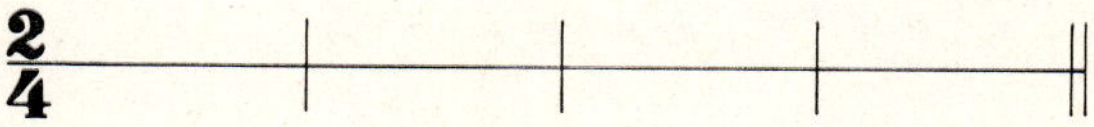

3

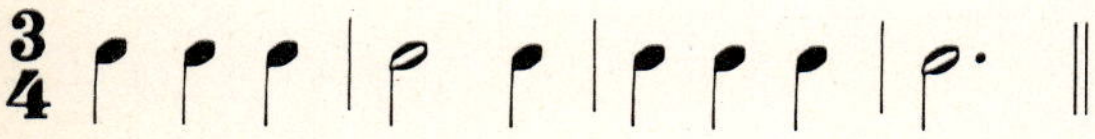

3

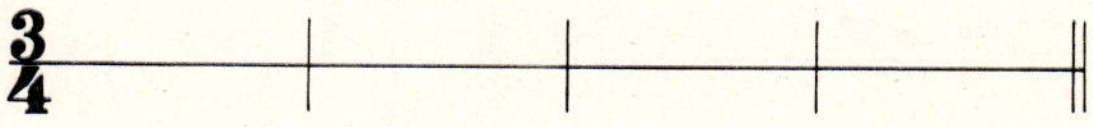

4

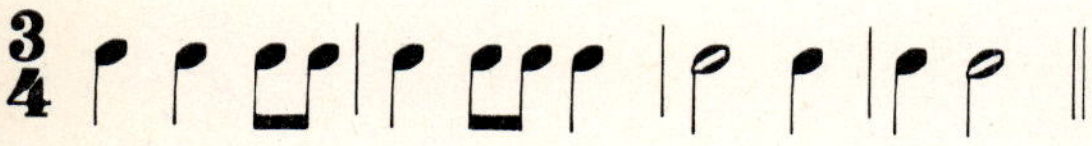

4

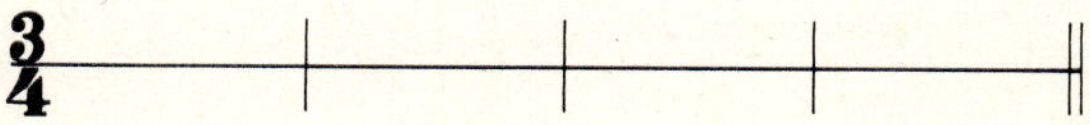

5

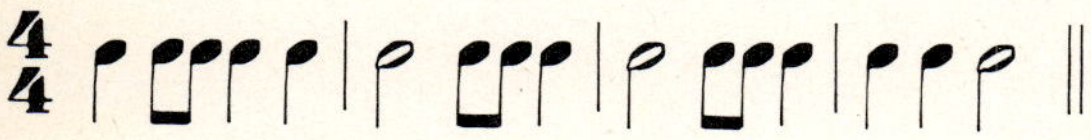

5

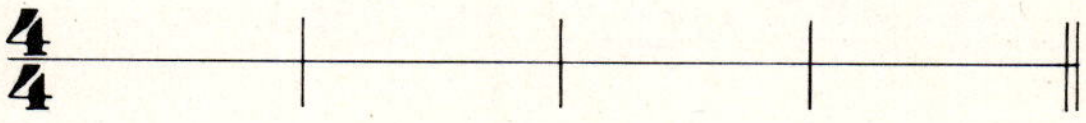

6

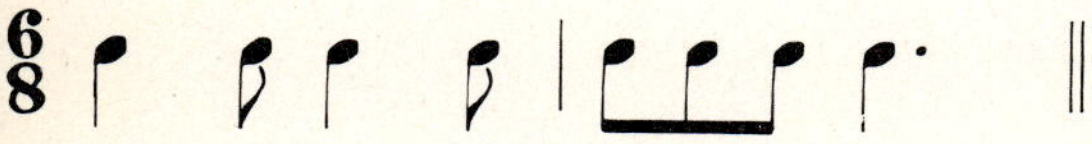

6

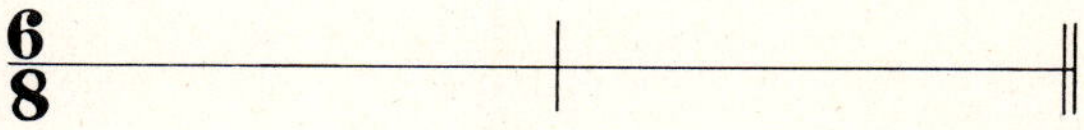

7

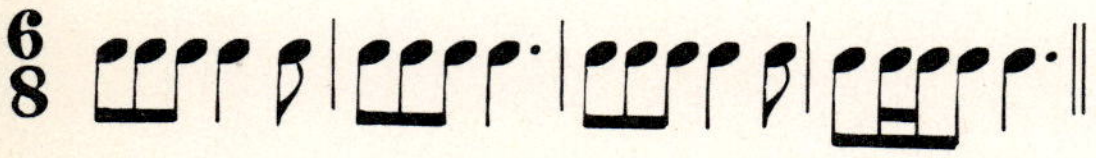

7

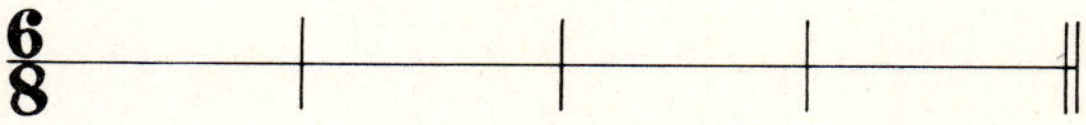

Play on recorder or piano

8

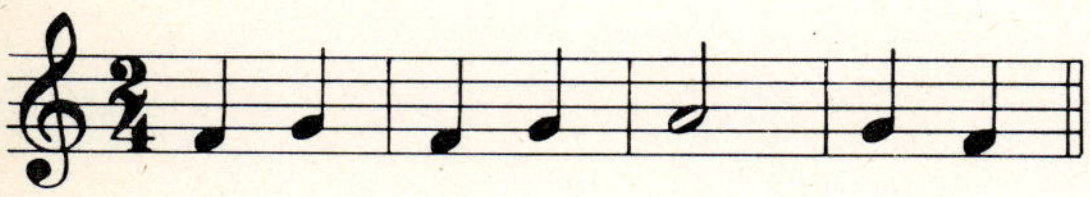

8

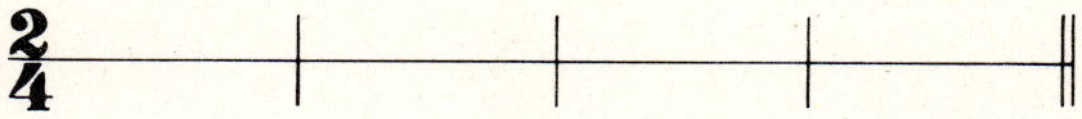

9

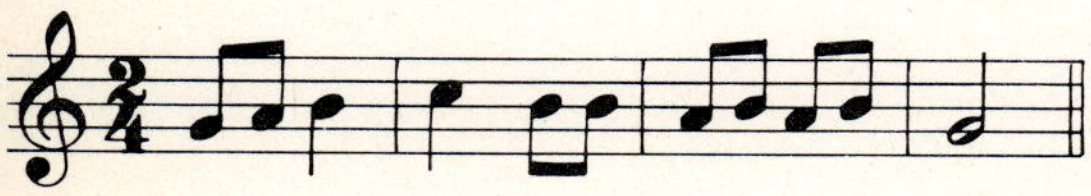

9

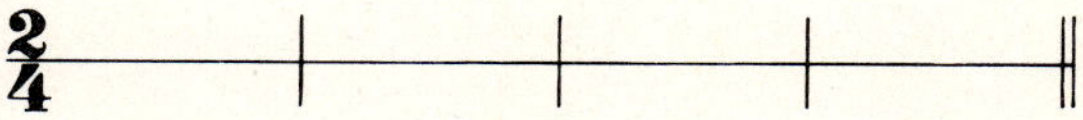

SUPPLEMENTARY ACTIVITIES

1. Examine various meter signatures used in the Song Supplement. Identify which are simple meters and which are compound.

2. Practice counting the rhythm of various songs in the supplement. You may write the counts below the notes or recite aloud.

3. Turn to the conducting patterns illustrated in the Appendix. Practice conducting various songs in the Song Supplement. Sing the words, recite pitch letters, or count aloud as you conduct.

4. Clap the rhythm of various songs in the supplement.

5. Tap the meter of a song with one hand on a desk top while tapping the rhythm with your other hand.

6. Sing and/or play additional songs from the supplement on the piano or recorder.

Basic Intervals and Accidentals

4

1

The term **interval** refers to the relationship of one pitch to another. This relationship can be measured scientifically by computing the difference in the frequencies of two pitches. Musicians identify pitches by letter name, rather than by frequency, and identify pitch *relationships* as intervals.

Interval

The relationship of one pitch to another is called an

_____.

interval

2

Frequency differences between various pitches range from small to large. Therefore, several different *interval names* are employed to express various pitch relationships in comparative terms.

Pitch relationships may be compared by using **different**

interval _____.

names

3

The smallest interval identified in our musical system is the **half step.** Two half steps combine to form the next largest interval, the **whole step.** These are the two basic intervals.

The smallest interval in our musical system is the _____ step.

half

4

Two half steps combine to form a _____ step.

whole

5

The piano keyboard offers a simple visual illustration of various pitch relationships. The white keys of the piano represent the fundamental pitches with which you are already familiar. They are identified in the keyboard in the following example. The black keys represent other pitches presented later in this chapter.

Is each pair of adjacent white keys separated by a black key? ____

no

6

Each pair of adjacent white keys that is *not* separated by a black key represents the smallest interval in our musical system, the half step.

Half steps occur between the fundamental pitches ____ and ____ and between ____ and ____.

E (and) F
B (and) C

7

Which of the following intervals is a half step?

a. F to G

b. D to E

c. B to C

Answer: _____

c.

8

Which of the following intervals is a half step?

a. A to B

b. E to F

c. G to A

Answer: _____

---

b.

9

B to C and E to F represent the smallest intervals in our pitch system because no other pitch occurs between these pairs of notes. The keyboard illustrates that an additional pitch (located by a black key) does occur between all other adjacent fundamental pitches such as C to D, or G to A, and so on. Adjacent white keys separated by a black key illustrate the interval of a whole step.

Identify the other whole steps that occur between fundamental pitches by joining the appropriate white keys in the manner of G-A and C-D in the following example.

10

whole

The interval between F and G is a _____ step.

11

half

The interval below is a _____ step.

12

whole

The interval below is a _____ step.

half

13

The interval below is a _____ step.

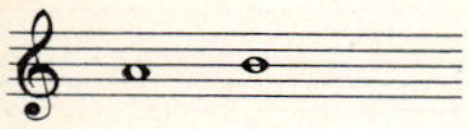

14

On the staff below notate the pitch located a whole step above A.

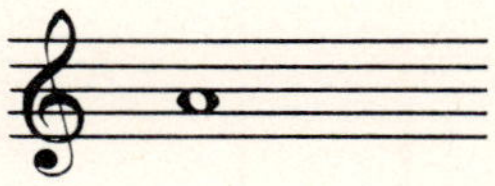

15

Notate a whole step above the given pitch.

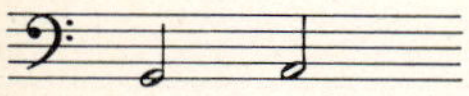

16

Continue as in the previous frame.

17

On the staff below notate the pitch located a half step above B.

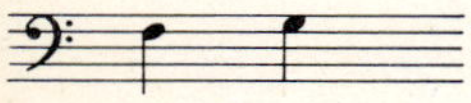

18

Notate a whole step above the given pitch.

19

In the example below place a caret (∧) between adjacent notes which are a half step apart.

20

Continue as in Frame 19.

21

All of the pitches mentioned so far can be called fundamental or unaltered pitches. These are identified simply by the letters A through G. These seven letters (fundamental pitches) do not accommodate all of the pitches used in our musical system, as illustrated by the fact that they represent only the white keys of the piano. The remaining pitches in our musical system, those illustrated by the black keys of the piano, are created by altering fundamental pitches through the use of **accidentals.**

Accidentals

_____ are used to alter fundamental pitches.

22

There are three basic accidentals. They are:

      sharp ♯

      flat ♭

      natural ♮

The three basic accidentals are the _____, the _____, and the natural.

sharp, flat, (any order.)

23

♯

The symbol for a sharp is _____.

flat	**24** ♭ is the symbol for a _____.
	25 Which is the symbol for a natural? a. ♪ b. ♮ c. ♯
b.	Answer: _____
	26 A **sharp** placed *before* a fundamental pitch (on the same line or space) will *raise* that pitch one half step.
above	 F-sharp is one half step (above/below) _____ F.
raise	**27** A sharp placed before a fundamental pitch will _____ that pitch one half step.
  (Be certain each sharp is on the same line or space as the note.)	**28** Mark the notes below to raise the pitch of each one half step.

DEVELOPING PERFORMANCE SKILLS

Turn to page 119 for piano, singing, and recorder exercises involving sharps.

29

A **flat** is placed before a fundamental pitch (on the same line or space) to *lower* that pitch one half step.

B-flat is one half step (above/below) _____ B.

below

30

A flat placed before a fundamental pitch will (raise/lower)

_____ that pitch one half step.

lower

31

Mark the notes below to lower the pitch of each one half step.

(Be certain each flat is on the same line or space as the note.)

DEVELOPING PERFORMANCE SKILLS

Turn to page 121 for piano, singing, and recorder exercises involving flats.

a. F-sharp

b. C-sharp

c. D-flat

d. A-flat

e. G-sharp

32

Identify the following altered fundamental pitches.

a.  _____

b. _____

c. _____

d. _____

e. _____

33

A **natural** cancels a previous sharp or flat.

C-sharp   C (natural)

Use a natural to cancel the accidental applied to the first note in each measure. (A natural is also placed *before* the note.)

natural	**34** A _____ cancels a previous sharp or flat.
raises lowers cancels	**35** Complete the following statements. A ♯ _____ a fundamental pitch one half step. A ♭ _____ a fundamental pitch one half step. A ♮ _____ a previous sharp or flat.
	36 The alteration of fundamental pitches with accidentals makes possible the creation of many additional intervallic relationships. For example, there is no fundamental pitch located a whole step above E. The note a whole step above E is created through the use of a sharp. half step whole step Convert the following half step to a whole step by altering the second note.

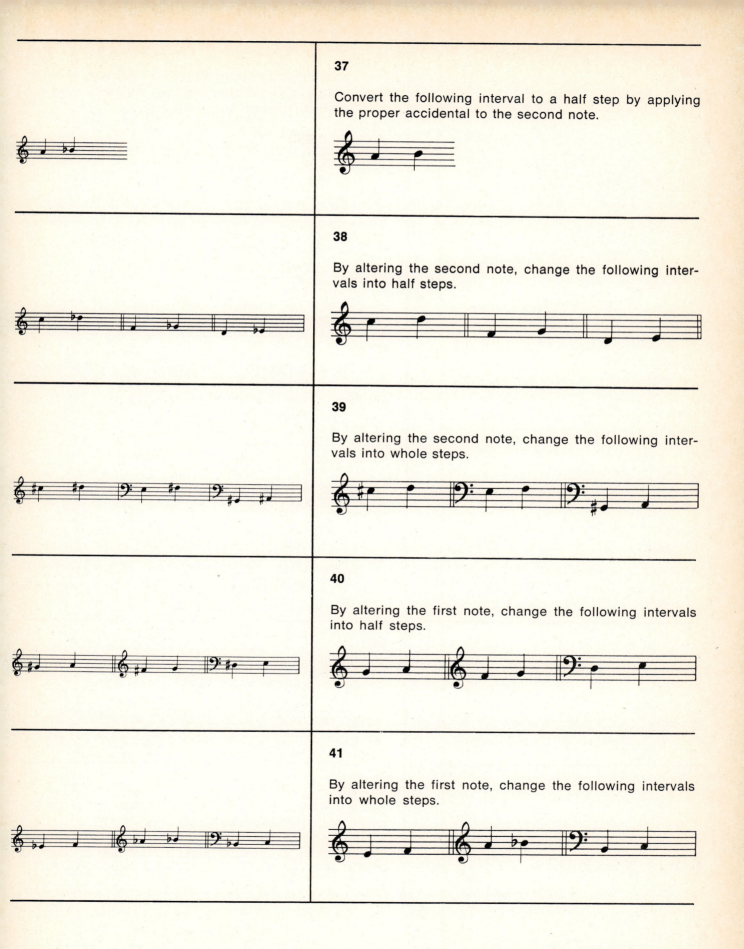

37

Convert the following interval to a half step by applying the proper accidental to the second note.

38

By altering the second note, change the following intervals into half steps.

39

By altering the second note, change the following intervals into whole steps.

40

By altering the first note, change the following intervals into half steps.

41

By altering the first note, change the following intervals into whole steps.

42

In the space provided, renotate these half steps as whole steps using the same basic pitches. Add a ♯, ♭, or ♮ to the first note to convert the interval size.

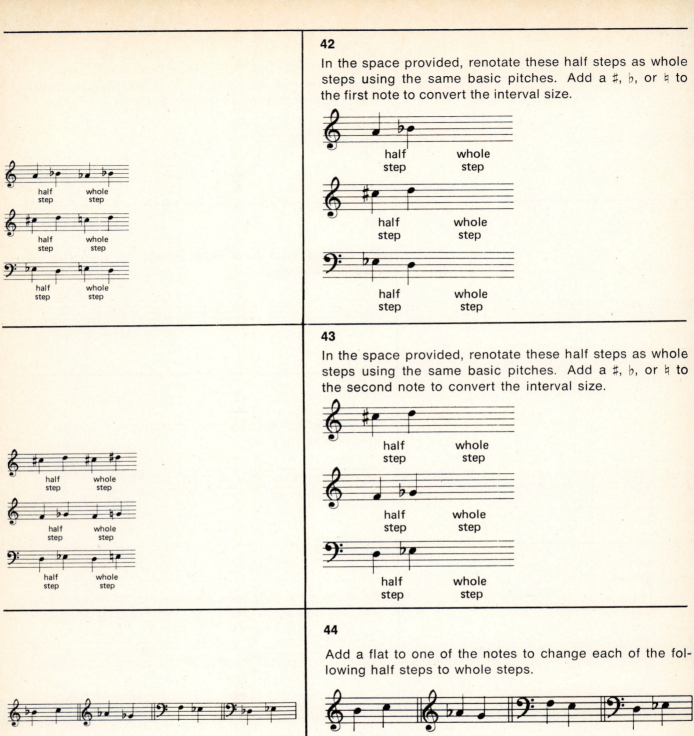

43

In the space provided, renotate these half steps as whole steps using the same basic pitches. Add a ♯, ♭, or ♮ to the second note to convert the interval size.

44

Add a flat to one of the notes to change each of the following half steps to whole steps.

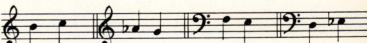

45

Add a sharp to one of the notes to change each of the following half steps to whole steps.

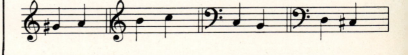

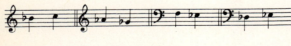

46

Add a flat to one of the notes to change each of the following whole steps to half steps.

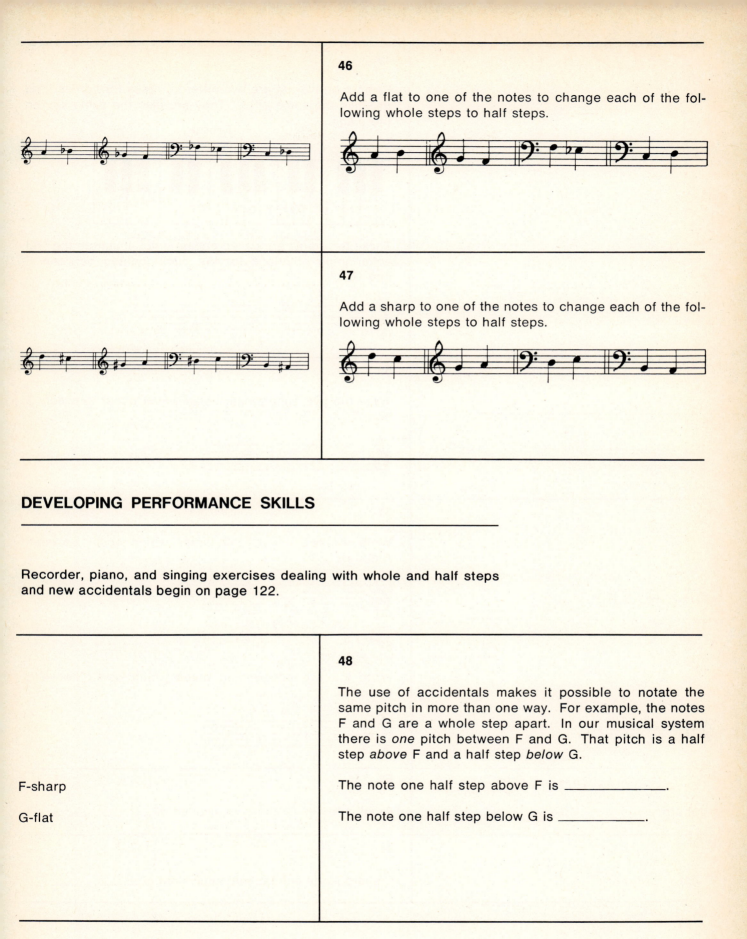

47

Add a sharp to one of the notes to change each of the following whole steps to half steps.

DEVELOPING PERFORMANCE SKILLS

Recorder, piano, and singing exercises dealing with whole and half steps and new accidentals begin on page 122.

48

The use of accidentals makes it possible to notate the same pitch in more than one way. For example, the notes F and G are a whole step apart. In our musical system there is *one* pitch between F and G. That pitch is a half step *above* F and a half step *below* G.

F-sharp

The note one half step above F is _____.

G-flat

The note one half step below G is _____.

49

F-sharp and G-flat are two different notes (or names) that produce the same pitch. They are also the same key on the piano.

These two notes are called **enharmonic.** Illustrate the two enharmonic notations for the pitch located between F and G.

50

Write the two enharmonic notes which occur between G and A.

51

Write the two enharmonic notes which occur between A and B.

52

Write the two enharmonic notes which occur between C and D.

53

A-flat is the enharmonic equivalent of _____.

G-sharp

54

C-sharp is the enharmonic equivalent of _____.

D-flat

Complete the following table of enharmonic notes.

 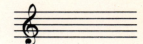

 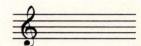

 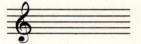

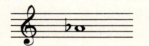 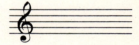

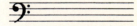

 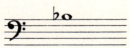 

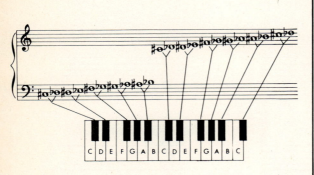

56

Notate the two enharmonic equivalents corresponding to each black key of the piano keyboard.

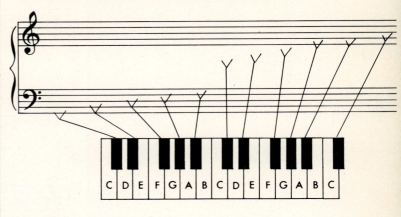

DEVELOPING PERFORMANCE SKILLS

Listening exercises dealing with whole and half steps and songs with accidentals for recorder, piano, and singing begin on page 124.

CHECK YOUR UNDERSTANDING

1. The relationship of one pitch to another is called an _____.

2. The smallest interval in our musical system is the _____ step.

3. Two half steps combine to form a _____ step.

4. Half steps occur between by the fundamental pitches _____ and _____

   and between _____ and _____.

5. Identify the following whole and half steps.

   a. _____ step b. _____ step c. _____ step d. _____ step e. _____ step.

6. _____ are used to alter fundamental pitches.

7. A sharp placed before a fundamental pitch will _____ that pitch one half step.

8. A _____ is placed before a fundamental pitch to lower that pitch

   one half step.

9. A _____ cancels a previous sharp or flat.

10. Two different notes (or names) for the same pitch, such as F-sharp

    and G-flat, are known as _____ equivalents.

(Answers may be found on page 360.)

Circle and identify all accidentals.

2. Identify all whole steps ♩♩ and all half steps ♩♩ .

Children's Prayer

E. Humperdinck

(Answers may be found on page 361.)

DEVELOPING PERFORMANCE SKILLS

Piano, Singing (Frames 26–28)

The most common use of the sharp is probably the note F♯. It is easy to find on the piano as the lowest of each group of three black keys. Play the following melodies on the piano, then sing them with letter names. Be sure to ennunciate "f sharp" in rhythm when you sing that pitch.

*Once an accidental is indicated it is maintained for *every* note of that letter name until the next barline. *All* Fs in each of these measures is performed as an F sharp (unless the accidental is cancelled by a natural sign, as in *Chorale* above).

Vive L'amour

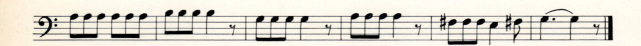

Recorder (Frames 26–28)

F♯ is a new fingering on the recorder. Practice these exercises to develop coordination in playing F♯.

Now play the treble staff melodies in the previous piano and singing exercises on your recorder for further practice in playing F♯.

NOTE: The above F♯ is from the Baroque fingering system, which was the authentic fingering of recorders from the Baroque period until the early 1900s. The German fingering system is closer in relationship to orchestral woodwind fingerings.

Piano, Singing (Frames 29–31)

B♭ is probably the most often used flat. It is also easy to find on the piano as the highest of each group of three black keys. Play the following melodies on the piano, then sing them with letter names. Remember to sing "b flat" when you encounter that pitch.

Good Night   Round

The Blue Tail Fly   U.S.

Lovely Evening   Round

Recorder (Frames 26–28)

B♭ is also a new recorder fingering. These exercises will develop your finger coordination in playing B♭.

Now play the treble staff piano and singing exercises involving B♭ on your recorder.

Recorder, Piano, Singing (Frames 32–47)

The exercises below combine instrumental performance and singing to develop your familiarity with the sound of the whole step and half step. Use either your recorder or the piano. Perform each exercise in this sequence:

Exercise as printed / Your performance

Play | G G A whole step up | Play
Sing with letters, then words

Exercise as printed / Your performance

Play | D D C half step down | Play
Sing with letters, then words

Listen carefully during the second playing to determine if you sang the interval correctly. Immediately repeat any exercises not sung accurately. After the first few exercises you must also identify each interval.

The following new notes on the recorder and piano are found in these exercises:

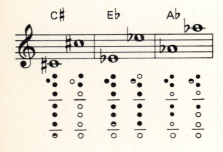

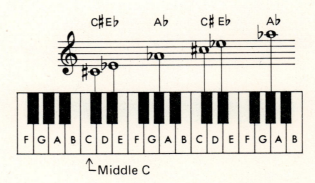

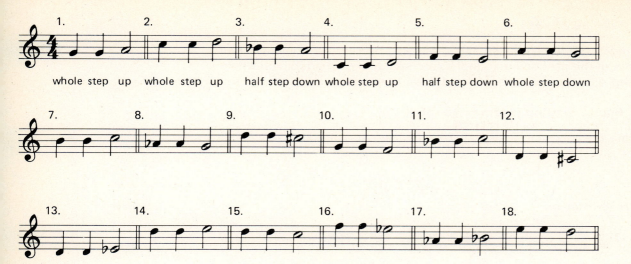

whole step up   whole step up   half step down   whole step up   half step down   whole step down

Perform these exercises as you did the previous set, using the piano. Be sure to play these intervals with your left hand.

The following new piano notes will be required.

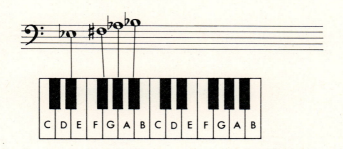

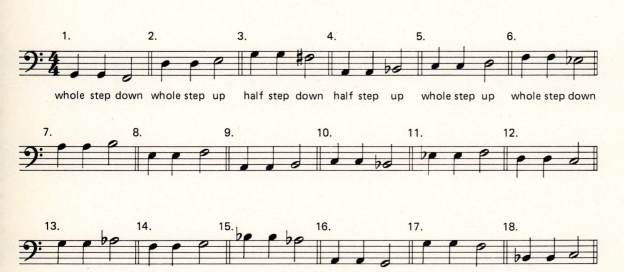

whole step down   whole step up   half step down   half step up   whole step up   whole step down

Listening (Frames 32–56)

With a partner, take turns playing and identifying by ear, the whole and half steps in both of the preceding sets of exercises. Make up additional whole and half step exercises incorporating different pitches.

Recorder, Piano, Singing (Frames 48–56)

Play and sing the following compositions involving accidentals.

Recorder

Now Is The Month of Maying   T. Morley

The Bear Song

Piano

Refer to Frame 56 on page 116 to locate accidentals you have not previously encountered on the piano.

Pomp and Circumstance E. Elgar

Frog He Would A-Wooing Go England

*Remember, an accidental remains in effect for the entire measure in which it appears unless canceled by a natural sign.

There Was A Jolly Miller

England

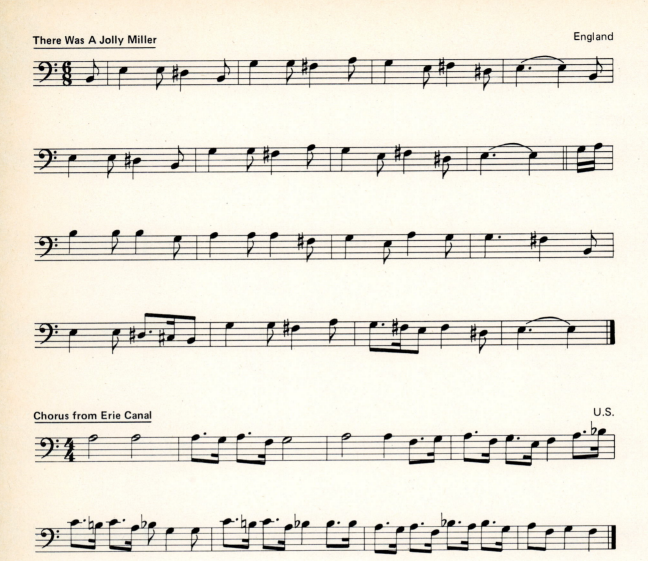

Chorus from Erie Canal

U.S.

SUPPLEMENTARY ACTIVITIES

1. Turn to the Song Supplement and locate half steps and whole steps in several songs. Locate and identify accidentals.

2. Play patterns such as F to F♯ and B to B♭ and listen to the pitch difference. Work at the piano, or with individual tone bells, or with a xylophone to *see* the difference.

3. With a partner, play this song as a recorder duet and as a piano duet. Sing the song as a duet with the words. Identify each whole and half step.

Tell Me Why

College Song

Tell ____ me why ____ the stars do shine. Tell ____ me why ____ the
i - vy twines. Tell ____ me why ____ the skies are
blue, And I will tell you why I ____ love you.

Major Scales

1

In our Western musical system the organization of pitches into a stepwise or alphabetic order is called a **scale.**

A scale is the organization of pitches into alphabetic or

_____ order.

stepwise

2

A scale may be an ascending or descending succession of pitches and may begin on any pitch.

A scale may ascend or _____ from the pitch on which it begins.

descend

3

Which of the following examples represent scale-wise motion?

a. A   C   B   D

b. A   C   G   A

c. A   B   C   D

Answer: _____

c.

4

Which of these examples represent scale-wise motion?

a.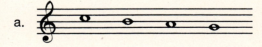

b.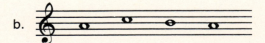

c.

Answer: _____

a.

5

The most common scales in traditional Western music consist of eight pitches, *two* of which (the first and last) are identified by the *same letter-name* but have different frequencies.

Such scales may be easily represented in terms of fundamental pitches.

A	B	C	D	E	F	G	__
1	2	3	4	5	6	7	8

The final pitch of the above scale will be identified by the

letter _____.

A

6

The second A has the same letter-name as the note on which the scale began, but it is *not* the same pitch (frequency). The interval (difference) between these two A's is an **octave.**

or

octave

Proceeding upward or downward from any pitch to the next recurrence of the same letter-name spans the interval of an _____.

octave

POINT OF REFERENCE

If you have been doing the DEVELOPING PERFORMANCE SKILLS singing exercises in this book, you have already experienced this octave phenomenon. When men sing this written pitch *in their own voice range,*

they usually sing one octave *lower.* Conversely, when women

sing written *in their own voice range,* they usually sing one

octave *higher* on

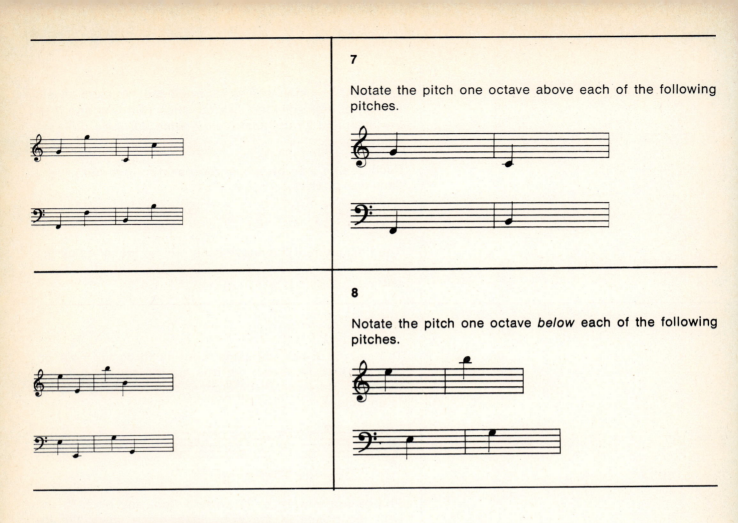

7

Notate the pitch one octave above each of the following pitches.

8

Notate the pitch one octave *below* each of the following pitches.

DEVELOPING PERFORMANCE SKILLS

Exercises for singing, recorder, and piano dealing with octaves may be found on page 144.

C D E F G A B (C)

9

The common eight-note scale utilizes each pitch letter within the interval of an octave.

For study purposes, scales are usually arranged in ascending order.

Write an ascending scale in fundamental pitches beginning on C.

— — — — — — — C̲

E F G A B C D (E)

(E) D C B A G F E

10

Write a scale in fundamental pitches beginning on E, ascending *and* descending, one octave.

—   —   —   —   —   —   —   <u>E</u>

<u>E</u>   —   —   —   —   —   —   —

11

A scale takes its name from the note on which it begins and ends.

Using whole notes place the ascending E scale from the previous frame on the staff provided.

12

In Western musical tradition, two scale forms have been preferred. One of these is the **major scale.** The sound of the major scale may be identified by its pattern of whole steps and half steps. The location of half steps in the major scale below is identified by a caret (∧). (Since this major scale begins and ends on C, it is called the C major scale.)

3 (and) 4

7 (and) 8

In a major scale, half steps occur between scale degree

numbers ____ and ____, and scale degree numbers ____

and _____.

13

The other scale form prevalent in Western musical usage is the *minor* scale you will study in Chapter 7. The older *modal* scales of early Western music are still found in some sacred and folk music. The system of musical structure they represent is now of significance primarily to music historians. Your instructor can tell you more about modes if desired.

Two scale forms of Eastern cultural origin have also been adopted in some Western folk and art music; the *pentatonic* (five-note) and *whole-tone* (no half steps) scales.

The *pentatonic* scale is represented by only the black keys of the piano. Experiment, by yourself and with friends, improvising in this scale. Even sounding many pitches simultaneously usually fails to produce "wrong notes."

The *whole-tone* scale of seven notes (including the octave) is produced by this sequence of 3 white and 3 black keys (plus the octave). In enharmonic terms it contains only whole steps.

1   2   3   4   5   6   7

Try improvising in the whole-tone scale also, including sounding several notes simultaneously. You may recognize this musical "flavor" as well.

(No response necessary.)

14

The interval between *all* adjacent major scale degrees *other than* 3–4, and 7–8 is a _____.

whole step

15

The interval between the first and second degrees of a major scale is a _____.

whole step

16

The interval between the fifth and sixth degrees of a major scale is a _____.

whole step

half step	**17** The interval between the third and fourth degrees of a major scale is a _____.
(No response necessary.)	**18** A song may use the notes of the major scale in any order or the notes may occur in straightforward, scale-wise order. In either case, such songs embody the "sound flavor" of the major scale. Sing *Twinkle, Twinkle Little Star* and *America* to yourself. Each is built upon the major scale and demonstrates its "sound flavor."
	19 The C major scale is the only major scale consisting entirely of fundamental pitches since the appropriate half steps occur only between the fundamental pitches E and F, and B and C. The "sound flavor" of the major scale can be recreated beginning on other fundamental pitches by recreating the same pattern of whole and half steps ascending from any fundamental pitch. Review the pattern of whole and half steps found in the major scale by completing the following table.

	Scale Degrees	Interval
(whole step)	Between 1 and 2 —	whole step
whole step	Between 2 and 3 —	_____
half step	Between 3 and 4 —	_____
whole step	Between 4 and 5 —	_____
whole step	Between 5 and 6 —	_____
whole step	Between 6 and 7 —	_____
half step	Between 7 and 8 —	_____

20

Is the following scale a *major* scale?

Answer: _____

Why? _____

_____

No.

Because it does not contain the correct pattern of whole and half steps.

(Your own words.)

21

Use the letters W (for whole step) and H (for half step) to identify each interval in this scale.

W   __   __   __   __   __   __

W   W   H   W   W   H   W

22

By using an accidental, in this case a sharp, one of the fundamental pitches in the previous example can be altered to maintain the pattern of whole and half steps required to form a G major scale.

By placing a sharp before the F, a _____ step was formed between the sixth and seventh degrees and a

_____ step was formed between the seventh and eighth degrees.

---

whole

half

Yes.

Because it has the correct pattern of whole and half steps.

(Your own words.)

---

b.

---

a.

Is the following scale a major scale?

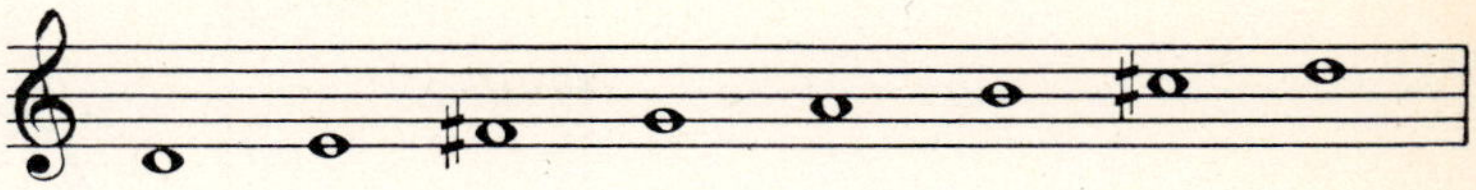

Answer: _____

Why? _____

_____

24

Which of the following examples is an F major scale?

a.

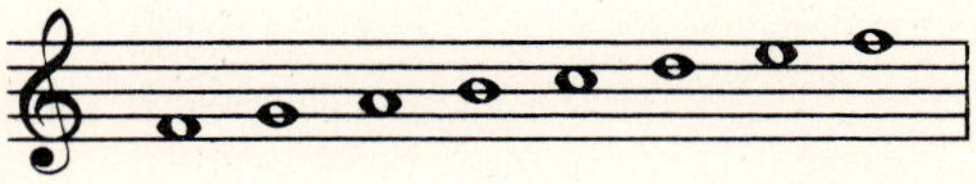

b.

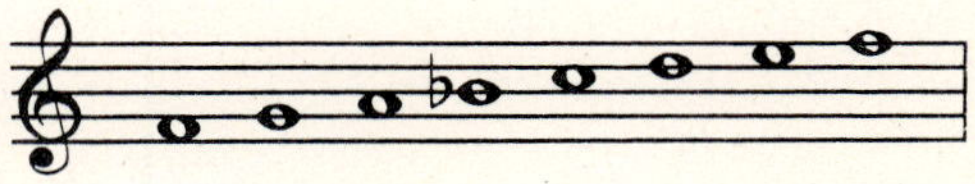

Answer: _____

25

Which of the following examples is an A major scale?

a.

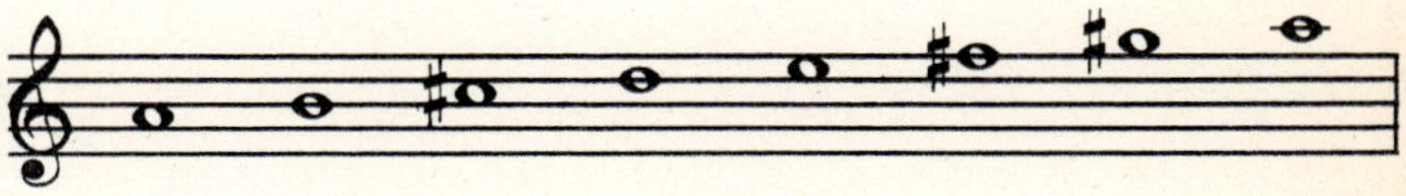

b.

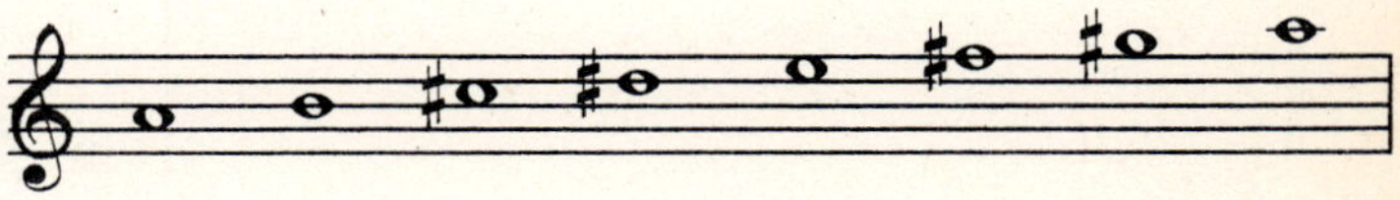

Answer: _____

Which of the following examples is a G major scale?

a.

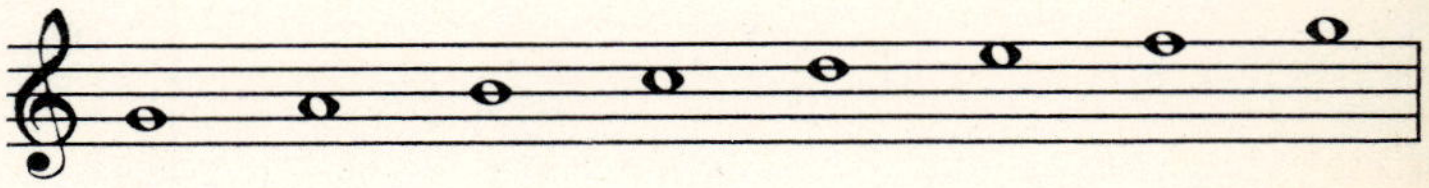

b.

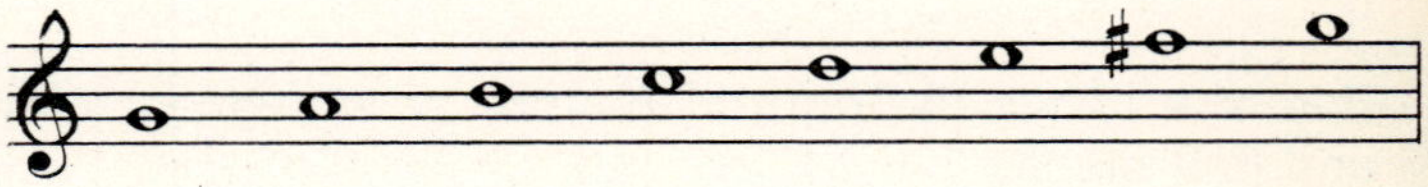

Answer: _____

b.

27

Which of the following examples is a D major scale?

a.

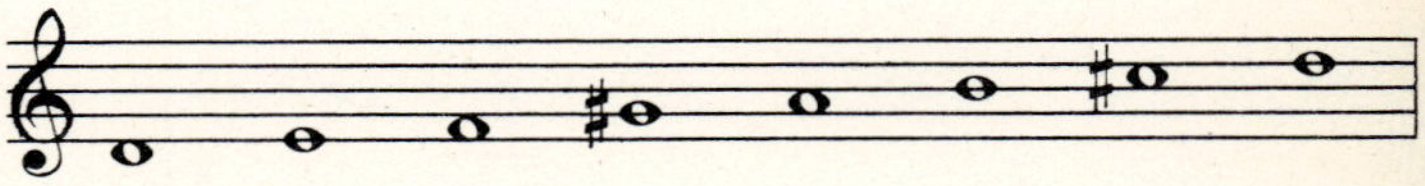

b.

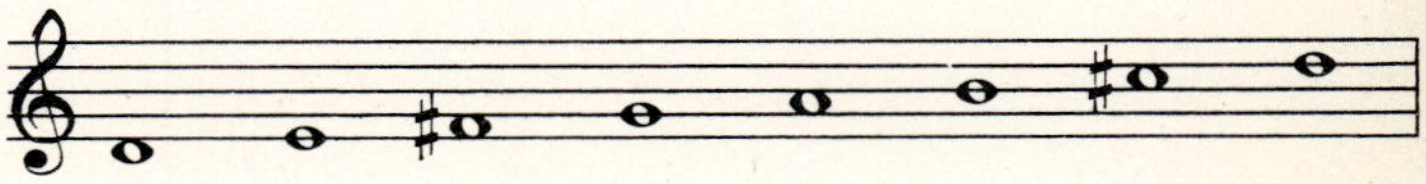

Answer: _____

b.

28

Which of the following examples is an E major scale?

a.

b.

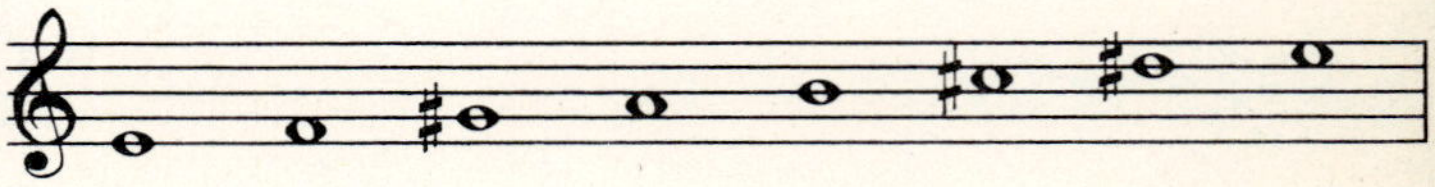

Answer: _____

a.

29

Using the appropriate pattern of whole steps and half steps, add accidentals to the following scale to create a G major scale.

30

Continue as in Frame 29 forming a D major scale.

31

Write the notes of the A major scale on the staff that follows. Be sure to include all necessary accidentals.

32

Notate the E major scale.

33

Notate the F major scale.

34

A major scale may also begin on a note that has been altered by an accidental, such as B-flat.

A second flat (E-flat) is also necessary to maintain the half step between scale degrees three and four. Repetition of the initial B-flat as the eighth degree creates the second necessary half step between degrees _____ and _____.

7 (and) 8

35

Analyze the pattern of whole steps and half steps in each of the following scales. Which of the following is an E-flat major scale?

a.

b.

Answer: _____

b.

36

Which of the following examples is an A-flat major scale?

a.

b.

Answer: _____

a.

Answers column (left)

a.

Questions column (right)

37

Which of the following examples is a B-flat major scale?

a.

b.

Answer: _____

38

Applying the proper sequence of whole and half steps, add accidentals to the following scale to construct the E-flat major scale. Be sure to begin on E-flat.

39

Notate the A-flat major scale.

40

Notate the B-flat major scale.

41

Notate the C major scale in the *bass clef.*

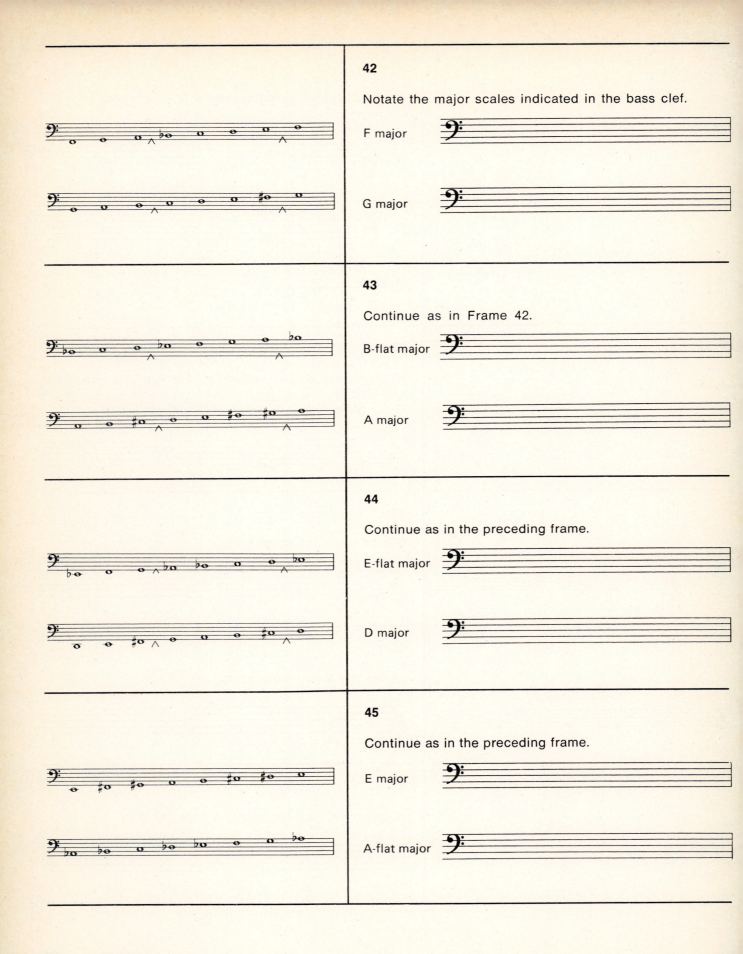

42

Notate the major scales indicated in the bass clef.

F major

G major

43

Continue as in Frame 42.

B-flat major

A major

44

Continue as in the preceding frame.

E-flat major

D major

45

Continue as in the preceding frame.

E major

A-flat major

DEVELOPING PERFORMANCE SKILLS

Singing, recorder, piano, and listening exercises involving major scales begin on page 145.

46

There are six additional major scales in our musical system. These six require more than four sharps or flats in their notation and are found less frequently than those you have already learned.

These additional major scales are:

B major

F-sharp major

C-sharp major

D-flat major

G-flat major

C-flat major

(No response necessary.)

CHECK YOUR UNDERSTANDING

1. The organization of pitches into alphabetic or stepwise order is called

   a _____.

2. Proceeding upward or downward from any pitch to the next recurrence

   of the same letter-name spans the interval of an _____.

3. Notate the pitch one octave above each of the following pitches.

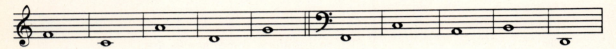

4. In a major scale, half steps occur between scale degree numbers ____

   and ____, and between ____ and ____.

5. Locate the half steps in the following major scale.

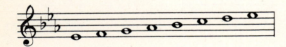

6. Which of the following is a major scale?

   a.

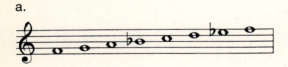

   b.

   Answer: _____

   (Answers may be found on page 361.)

APPLY YOUR UNDERSTANDING

Notate each of the following scales.

1. B-flat major

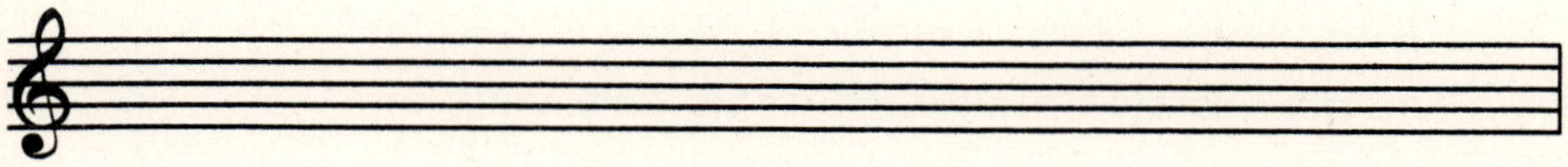

2. A major

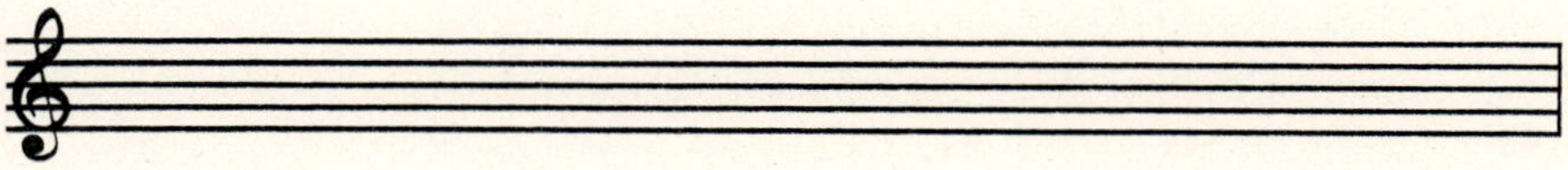

3. E-flat major

4. D major

(Answers may be found on page 362.)

DEVELOPING PERFORMANCE SKILLS

Recorder, Piano, Singing (Frames 6–8)

Group 1

On your recorder and the piano play **up** an octave and back, beginning on each of the following pitches.

(play) piano only (left hand)

Sing as many of the exercises in Group 1 as your vocal range will allow.

Group 2

On your recorder and the piano play **down** an octave and back, beginning on each of the following pitches.

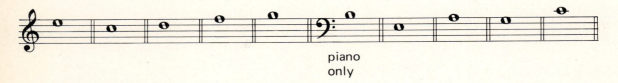

piano only

Sing as many of the exercises in Group 2 as your vocal range will allow. If you experience any difficulty, play through the exercises more than once. Invent similar exercises using other starting pitches and try different rhythmic patterns to increase your technical agility on the recorder and piano.

Listening (Frames 6–8)

Group 1

Ask a partner to play the following drills on the recorder or piano. As you listen, identify which intervals are octaves.

PERFORMER: You will indicate correct and incorrect responses. Play through Group 1 several times in different orders. Then invent additional exercises like these involving other pitches. Add additional rhythmic patterns to expand your instrumental technique as your partner develops listening accuity.

Group 2

Continue as above using the piano. It is important to develop your listening skill in reference to various pitch registers.

PERFORMER: You will again indicate correct and incorrect responses. Play through Group 2 several times in different orders. Play these with your left hand. Then invent additional exercises like these involving other pitches. Add additional rhythmic patterns to expand your instrumental technique as your partner develops listening accuity.

Recorder (Frames 23–45)

Play these ascending and descending major scales on your recorder. Play slowly thinking the complete name of each pitch (i.e., f-sharp, etc.). Listen carefully as you play to instill the tonal character of the major scale in your mind. Do not hesitate excessively between notes so that you learn the pitch continuity of the major scale sound.

New recorder fingerings

Piano (Frames 23–45)

Playing scales on the piano introduces a higher level of keyboard technique. These exercises are designed to increase your familiarity with the keyboard and with the tonal character of major scales, not to develop advanced piano facility.

1. Play the lower voice (bass staff) of these exercises alone and **slowly** with your **left hand,** ascending and descending. Adhere to the fingering indicated below the notes. Practice the left hand alone several times on each scale.

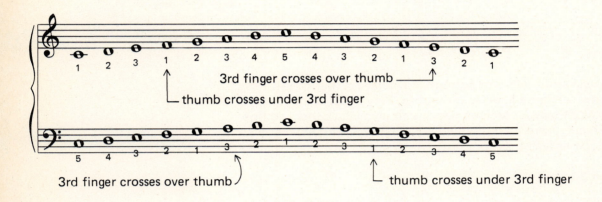

3rd finger crosses over thumb

thumb crosses under 3rd finger

3rd finger crosses over thumb

thumb crosses under 3rd finger

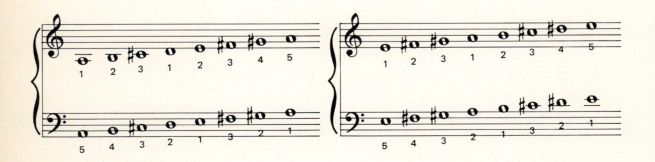

2. Now play the upper voice of each exercise above **slowly** with your right hand alone. Use the fingering given. Practice each scale several times.

Challenge

3. You may wish to try the more difficult skill of playing major scales with both hands together. Maintain a slow but steady pace. Watch carefully for correct fingering.

4. Here are some additional major scales you may wish to try on the piano. These fingerings are more difficult so exercise particular care to learn them correctly. Practice each scale in the sequence presented in drills 1, 2, and 3 above.

Singing and Listening (Frames 23–45)

In your vocal range sing the ascending/descending major scales specified below. (Do not turn back to the scales as written out for recorder and piano.)

1. Sing each scale first with numbers: 1 2 3 4 5 6 7 8 7 6 5 4 3 2 1. Use your recorder or the piano to find each starting pitch.

2. Immediately sing each major scale again with the appropriate note names (including accidentals). Repeat each scale as necessary to develop total fluency.

3. Take turns with a partner on these exercises. Evaluate each other's accuracy aurally.

Major scales: C, G, D, A, F, B♭, E♭

Recorder, Piano, Singing (Frames 23–45)

Play the following major scale songs on your recorder and on the piano. Sing each song with letter names. Be sure to observe accurate performance of rhythm as well as pitch. You may wish first to clap, tap, or recite the note names of each melody rhythmically while clapping the meter to establish an accurate rhythmic interpretation.

Recorder

1. **Scale Song**   M.W.

2. **Evening Bells**   Nursery Song

3. **Joy To The World**   G.F. Handel

Piano

1. **Soldier's March**   R. Schumann

2. **Menuet**   J.S. Bach

3. **Excerpt from The French Suite No. 6**   J.S. Bach

4. **Waltz**

F. Schubert

5. **Yankee Doodle**

U.S.

6. **The First Noel**

Carol

SUPPLEMENTARY ACTIVITIES

1. Play and listen to various major scales on other instruments such as tone bells or xylophone. Build the major scales using individual tone bells.

2. The following songs found in the supplement are in major keys. Sing and play them on various instruments to gain an aural appreciation of major tonality.

    May Day Carol, 384
    Roll On. Columbia, 396
    This Old Man, 373
    Waltzing Matilda, 371
    Funny Shape, 402
    Bingo, 377
    You're A Grand Old Flag, 395

Major Key Signatures

6

1

The ordering of whole and half steps in the major scale creates a feeling of gravitation toward the note on which the scale began.

You may experience this "feeling" by singing or playing the following example.

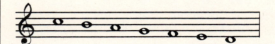

You should feel that the last note (D) wants to continue down to a C. (You are entitled to your own opinion.)

Do you feel that you have arrived at a point of rest acoustically when you reach the last note? _____

2

This feeling of gravitation toward an acoustic point of rest is a central phenomenon of traditional Western music. It is usually called "key feeling" or **tonality.**

Tonality describes the ability of the first note of a major

rest

scale to function as a point of _____ toward which the other scale degrees gravitate.

3

Since the first degree (or tone) of a major scale identifies the tonality which that scale creates, it is called the *tonal center* or *keynote.* The proper musical term for this keynote is **tonic.**

G

The tonic of the G major scale is _____.

4

C

The tonic of the C major scale is _____.

5

The proper musical term for tonal center or keynote is

tonic

_____.

6

The phenomenon of tonality is expressed in compositions that utilize the notes of one scale exclusively, or at least predominantly. The identity of that scale, the feeling of tonality, is expressed in the music itself.

The following melody expresses its tonality by employing the notes of a particular major scale. Identify that scale.

Yankee Doodle   U.S.

G major scale

Answer: _____

7

The use of accidentals to notate pieces based on scales or tonalities which contain sharps or flats can quickly clutter the staff unnecessarily. Consider this melody in the key of A-flat major.

Rock-a-bye, Baby   Mother Goose Rhyme

Count the total number of notes in this example and the number of notes prefaced by an accidental.

23
37

Accidentals are required for _____ of the _____ notes in this melody.

8

To avoid this excessive use of accidentals, the necessary sharps or flats are notated only at the beginning of each line of music. Returning to the G major melody of Frame 6, the F-sharp is placed immediately after the clef sign. (The G major scale contains only one altered note, F-sharp.) This indication is called a **key signature.**

The key signature is located at the beginning of _____

_____ of a piece immediately following the _____ sign.

each line

clef

9

The key signature [music notation] indicates that all pitches notated as an F will be sung or played F-sharp. This key signature therefore indicates which scale is used predominantly in the piece.

In which major scale is F-sharp the only altered note?

_____.

G major scale

	10
	This identification of the predominant scale used in a composition identifies the tonality or key of the piece. Since F-sharp indicates the G major scale, we say that the piece is in the *key of G major*.
	What major scale is identified by the following key signature?
F major scale	Answer: _____
	11
F major	A key signature of one flat indicates the key of _____ _____.
	12
	The key signature of F major, indicates that all pitches notated as B are to be played or sung as
B-flat	_____.
	13
	Notate the A major scale on the following staff. Use all appropriate accidentals.
	14
three	The A major scale requires the use of _____ sharps. (number)
	15
	These three sharps, in order of occurrence in the scale,
C-sharp, F-sharp, (and) G-sharp	are _____, _____, and _____.

16

When using these three sharps to notate the A major key signature, however, they are *not* placed on the staff in their order of appearance in the scale. By tradition F-sharp is always placed first in any key signature requiring it, C-sharp second, and so forth, in an unvarying order for as many sharps as each key signature requires.

Place a check before the choice that best evaluates each of the following statements.

A. Sharps are notated in a key signature in the order of their appearance in the scale of that key.

B. By tradition F-sharp is always placed first in key signatures requiring sharps.

_____ a. A is correct.

_____ b. B is correct.

_____ c. Both are correct.

_____ d. Neither is correct.

✓ b.

17

In any key signature requiring sharps, the first sharp notated is always _____.

F-sharp

18

The order of the remaining sharps may be constructed by counting the letters of the musical alphabet in overlapping groups of five. The first sharp is F-sharp. Counting 1 2 3 4 5 we locate the second sharp on C.
    F G A B C

Starting again on C as 1 and counting five letters, the third sharp is located on _____.

$$\begin{matrix} & & & G & \\ \left(\begin{matrix} 1 & 2 & 3 & 4 & 5 \\ C & D & E & F & G \end{matrix}\right) \end{matrix}$$

19

Begin again on G. Count five more letters of the musical alphabet. The fourth sharp is _____-sharp.

$$\begin{matrix} & & & D\ (\text{-sharp}) & \\ \left(\begin{matrix} 1 & 2 & 3 & 4 & 5 \\ G & A & B & C & D \end{matrix}\right) \end{matrix}$$

---

	20 The order of four sharps as they appear in a key signature is _____, _____, _____, and _____.
F-sharp, C-sharp, G-sharp, (and) D-sharp	
	21 The actual notation of these sharps to construct a key signature follows a constant graphic order on both the treble and bass staves. This avoids the placement of any accidental of a key signature on a ledger line (or ledger space) whether 2, 3, or 4 sharps are required. Indicate the graphic direction (up or down) from each sharp in the above example to the next.
a. down b. up c. down	a. First sharp to second sharp—_____ b. Second sharp to third sharp—_____ c. Third sharp to fourth sharp—_____
	22 This graphic order may be described as down-up-down. The graphic direction from the first to the second sharp as notated in a key signature is (up/down) _____.
down	
	23 The graphic order of four sharps as they appear in key signatures (in terms of down and up) is _____ _____.
down-up-down	

24

Which of the following key signatures is notated correctly?

a.   b.

Answer: _____

25

Continue as in Frame 24.

a.   b.

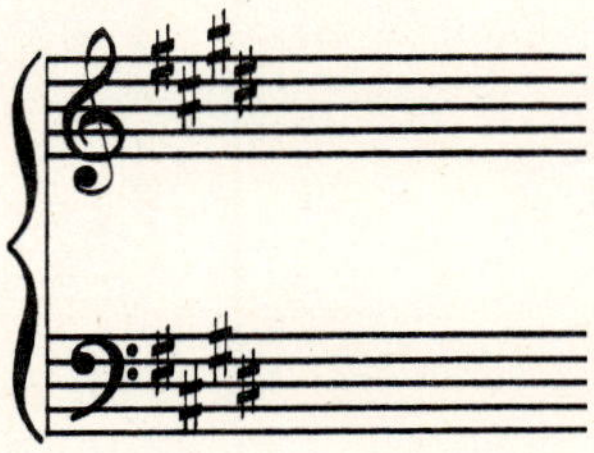

Answer: _____

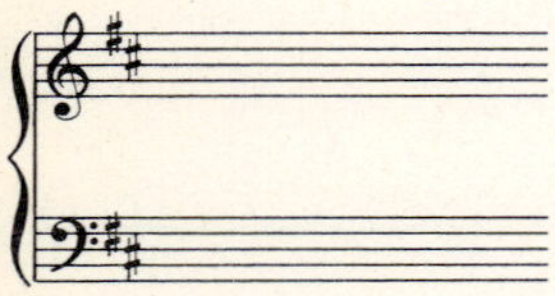

26

Notate a key signature of two sharps on the great staff.

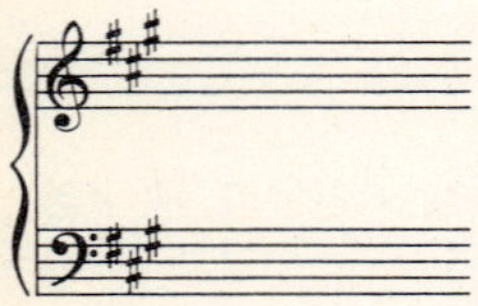

27

Notate the key signatures indicated below. Be sure to follow the proper graphic order.

3 sharps    4 sharps

---

b.

a.

	28 The letter order in which flats appear in key signatures is also invariable, always beginning with B♭. In any key signature requiring flats, the first flat notated B-flat is always _____.
$$\begin{matrix} & & A & \\ \left(\begin{matrix} 1 & 2 & 3 & 4 \\ E & F & G & A \end{matrix}\right) \end{matrix}$$	**29** The order of the remaining flats may be constructed by counting the letters of the musical alphabet in over-lapping groups of *four*. The first flat is B-flat. Counting 1 2 3 4 we locate the second flat on E. Starting B C D E again on E as 1, and counting four letters, the third flat is located on _____.
D (-flat)	**30** Begin again on A. Count four more letters of the musical alphabet. The fourth flat is _____-flat.
B-flat, E-flat, A-flat, (and) D-flat	**31** The order of four flats as they appear in a key signature is _____, _____, _____, and _____.
            a. up b. down c. up	**32** As with the sharps, the actual notation of flats in key signatures follows a constant graphic order. Indicate the graphic direction (up or down) from each flat in the above example to the next. a. First flat to second flat—_____ b. Second flat to third flat—_____ c. Third flat to fourth flat—_____

up	**33** The graphic order of flats as they are notated in a key signature begins (up/down) _____.
up-down-up	**34** The graphic order of four flats as they appear in key signatures (in terms of down and up) is _____ _____
	35 Which of the following key signatures is notated correctly? a. b. Answer: _____
a.	
	36 Continue as in the preceding frame. a. b. Answer: _____
b. 	**37** Notate a key signature that contains two flats. Be sure to follow the correct graphic order.

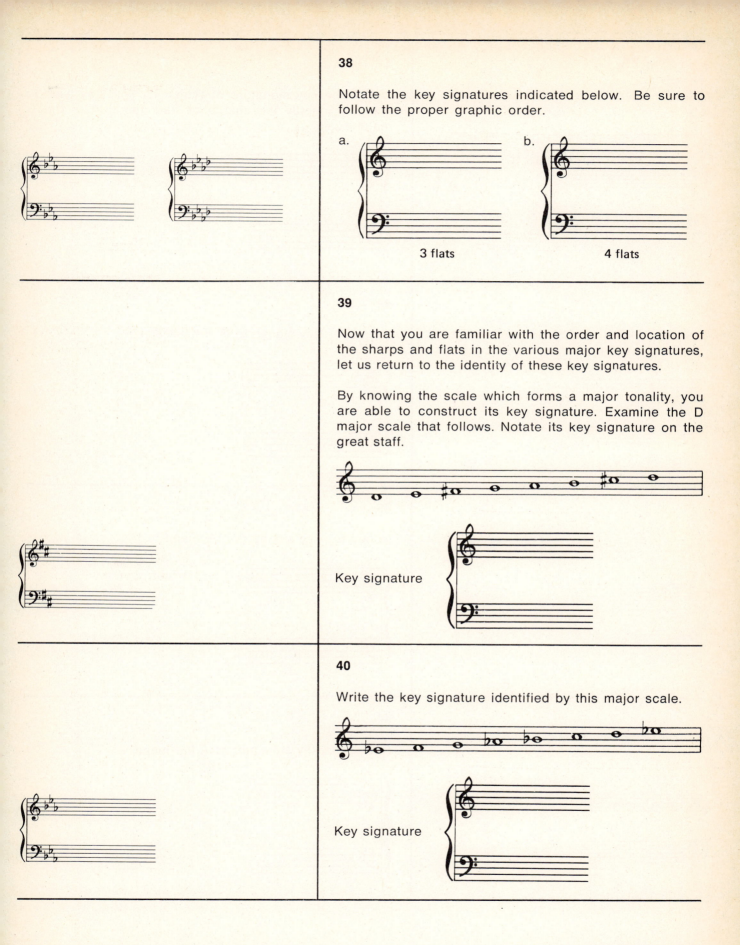

38

Notate the key signatures indicated below. Be sure to follow the proper graphic order.

a.

3 flats

b.

4 flats

39

Now that you are familiar with the order and location of the sharps and flats in the various major key signatures, let us return to the identity of these key signatures.

By knowing the scale which forms a major tonality, you are able to construct its key signature. Examine the D major scale that follows. Notate its key signature on the great staff.

Key signature

40

Write the key signature identified by this major scale.

Key signature

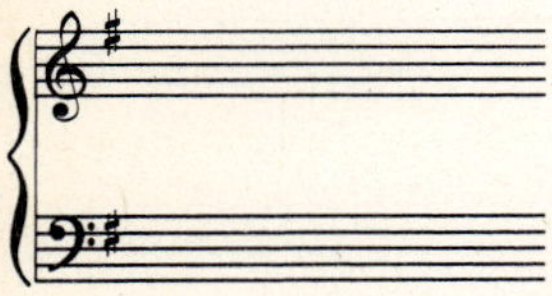

41

Notate the key signature of G major. You may wish to mentally identify the sharps or flats required in the G major scale.

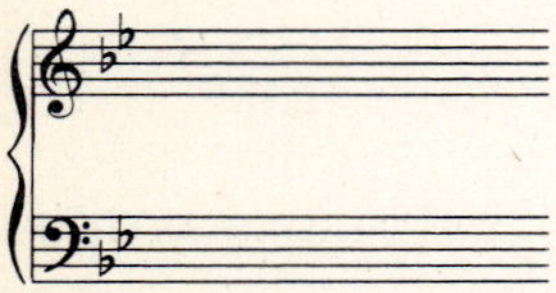

42

Notate the key signature of B-flat major.

43

Notate the key signature of E major.

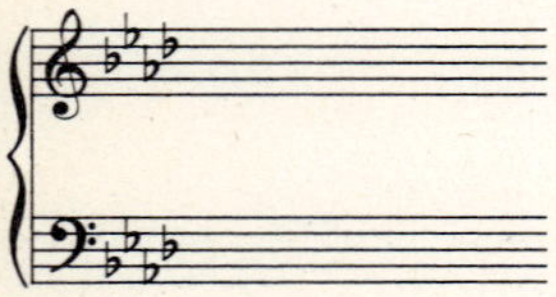

44

Notate the key signature of A-flat major.

45

Notate the key signature of A major.

46

In cases where the key signature is already given and you must identify the major key it represents, one of two simple methods is employed.

If the key signature is notated in sharps, the tonic note of that major key is located one half step *above* the *last* sharp. Consider this example:

The last sharp is C-sharp. One half step above C-sharp

is _____.

D

47

The key signature in Frame 46 identifies the key of _____ major.

D major

48

Identify the following key signatures.

– Key of _____ major

A

– Key of _____ major

G

E

D

49

Continue as in Frame 48.

— Key of _____ major

— Key of _____ major

50

To quickly identify a key signature consisting of flats, count downward *four* scale degrees beginning on the *last* flat.

E-flat

The above key signature identifies the key of _____ major.

51

Notice that the next to the last flat of the key signature identifies the same note name as counting down four scale degrees from the last flat.

1 2 3 4   or

You may use either method to identify key signatures notated in flats.

Identify the following key signatures.

F

— Key of _____ major

B-flat

— Key of _____ major

	52 Continue as in Frame 51. 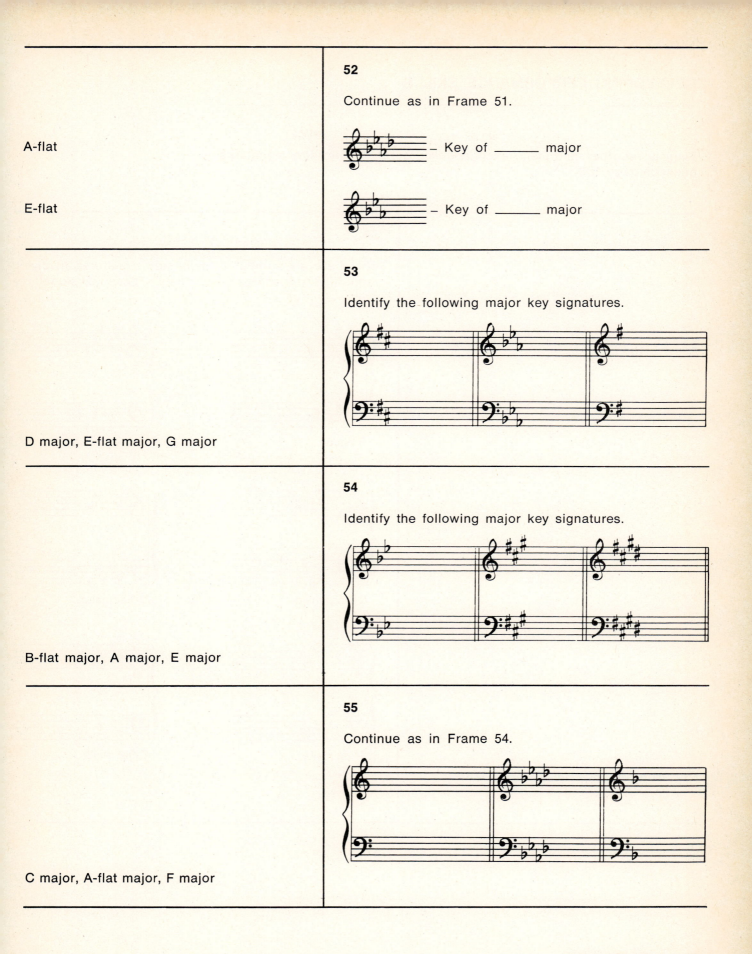– Key of _____ major – Key of _____ major
A-flat E-flat	
	53 Identify the following major key signatures.
D major, E-flat major, G major	
	54 Identify the following major key signatures.
B-flat major, A major, E major	
	55 Continue as in Frame 54.
C major, A-flat major, F major	

DEVELOPING PERFORMANCE SKILLS

Singing, recorder, and piano exercises incorporating major key signatures begin on page 169.

56

There are six additional major key signatures involving more than four sharps or four flats. These key signatures are:

B major

F-sharp major

C-sharp major

D-flat major

G-flat major

C-flat major

(No response necessary.)

CHECK YOUR UNDERSTANDING

1. A key signature represents that feeling of gravitation in music which we call _____.

2. A _____ _____ is used to avoid the excessive use of accidentals throughout a piece of music.

3. The key signature is located at the _____ of each line of a piece immediately following the _____ sign.

4. Which of the following major key signatures is notated correctly?

   a.    b.

   Answer:_____

5. The order of four sharps as they appear in a key signature is ____ _____, _____, _____, and _____.

6. Which of the following major key signatures is notated correctly?

   a.    b.

   Answer: _____

7. The order of four flats as they appear in a key signature is _____, _____, _____, and _____.

8. Notate the following major key signatures.

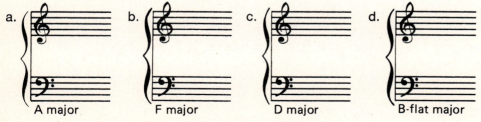

   a. A major   b. F major   c. D major   d. B-flat major

(Answers may be found on page 362.)

APPLY YOUR UNDERSTANDING

Identify the following major key signatures.

a. b. c. d.

Identify the major key signatures in each of the following songs.

1. **Paper of Pins**   British Folk Song

Key of _____

2. **Arietta**   F.J. Haydn

Key of _____

3. **Irish Washerwoman**   Jig

Key of _____

(Answers may be found on page 362.)

DEVELOPING PERFORMANCE SKILLS

Singing, Recorder, Piano (Frames 1–55)

The only additional performance skill required in dealing with key signatures is the use of your *memory.* Before you begin the performance of any composition you must *remember* to look at the key signature. Then as you perform, you must *remember* to apply that key signature consistently unless directed to do otherwise by ♮ or other accidentals. The more sharps or flats a key signature contains, the more you have to remember.

1. Sing this melody *slowly,* enunciating the complete pitch-name of each note (sing "b-flat" etc.).

Prayer of Thanksgiving Netherlands

Now play Exercise 1 on your recorder and the piano. Remember to play all b-flats, e-flats, and a-flats.

2. Enunciating complete pitch names involving accidentals cannot be done in singing most melodies without destroying rhythmic continuity (which is very unmusical and not an acceptable performance practice). In such cases you must *think* and *sing* f-sharp, etc. while enunciating only the letter name to preserve the correct rhythm. Sing this melody with pitch names at a brisk pace. Clap or tap the meter as you sing.

Camptown Races S. Foster

Now play Exercise 2 on your recorder and the piano. Remember to play all f-sharps. Tap the meter with your foot as you play. Test your rhythmic accuracy by asking a classmate or your instructor to listen.

Apply procedures used in the previous exercises as you sing and play the following melodies. Some will tax your vocal range. Some are not well suited to the recorder. Perform them as practical to experience applying several different major key signatures.

3. **Auld Lang Syne**   Scotland

Notice that the complete key signature for B-flat major (the tonality of this melody) is used even though the fourth scale degree, e-flat, never occurs. This is standard practice in tonal music.

4. **Reuben and Rachel**   Traditional canon

5. **Jeanie With the Light Brown Hair**   S. Foster

SUPPLEMENTARY ACTIVITIES

Identify the major key signatures found in the following songs in the Song Supplement.

May Day Carol, 384
Battle Hymn of the Republic, 391
Kum Ba Ya, 394
Shenandoah, 388
Simple Gifts, 379
You're A Grand Old Flag, 395

Minor Scales and Key Signatures

7

1

    The second scale form used prominently in Western music is the **minor** scale. The series of pitches found in each major scale may be arranged above another starting pitch to form a minor scale.

That is to say, each minor scale is *related* to a _____ scale.

major

2

Sounding the notes of any major scale beginning on the sixth degree and continuing for one octave will produce the minor scale which is *related* to that major scale. For example:

C major scale

1   2   3   4   5   6

A minor scale

The minor scale which is *related* to the C major scale is the ____ minor scale.

A

3

The C major and A minor scales illustrated in Frame 2 are related because both employ the same notes although they *begin* on different pitches. The A minor scale is the **relative minor** scale of the C major scale.

The relative major scale of the A minor scale is the ____ _____ scale.

C major

4

Sounding the notes of any major scale beginning on the sixth degree and continuing for one octave will produce its relative minor scale.

Notate the relative minor scale of the G major scale on the staff provided. Use exactly the same notes as those in the G major scale.

G major

E minor

(Be certain that you included F-sharp.)

E minor

5

The relative minor scale of the G major scale is the _____ _____ scale.

G major

6

The relative major scale of the E minor scale is the _____ _____ scale.

E minor

7

Since each major scale and its relative minor share the *same* notes it is logical and proper to conclude that both share the *same* key signature. Just as each major scale creates the sensation of key feeling which we call tonality, each minor scale establishes its first note as the tonal center or tonic.

The relative minor *key* of G major is _____ _____.

---

sharp

8

G major and E minor both have a key signature of one _____.

	9 Evaluate the following statements by placing a check before the appropriate response below. A. Relative major and minor scales share the same pitches. B. Relative major and minor tonalities share the same key signature. ———— a. A is true ———— c. Both are true ———— b. B is true ———— d. Both are false
✓ **c.**	
	10 Keeping in mind this concept of minor scale and minor tonality as two manifestations of the same phenomenon, we may continue the study of minor scales *and* their key signatures.
(No response necessary.)	
	11 The interval between a major tonic and its relative minor tonic may be identified most simply by counting down the major scale from tonic to sixth degree, 8-7-6. The relative minor of F major is identified by the following model: The interval between a major tonic and its relative minor tonic encompasses ————————— letters of the musical alphabet.
three	
	12 The interval from scale degree 8 to degree 7 is a ————————— step.
half (step)	
	13 The interval from degree 7 to degree 6 is a ————————— step.
whole (step)	

three
half (step)
whole (step)

14

The tonic of a relative minor scale may be identified by counting down the major scale _____ letter-names in the sequence of a _____ step followed by a _____ step.

15

Apply the procedure stated in Frame 14 to locate the relative minor of D major on the staff below.

a.   Notate the three pitches required.

b.   Write letter-name (including accidental, if any) below each note.

c.   Use ∧ (half step) and ⏑ (whole step) to identify intervals between adjacent notes.

B

16

The relative minor of D major is _____ minor.

17

Notate the key signature of B minor.

18

Notate the B minor scale.

19

Locate the relative minor of B-flat major through the procedure described in Frame 15.

<table>
<tr>
<td>

G

</td>
<td>

20

The relative minor of B-flat major is _____ minor.

</td>
</tr>
<tr>
<td>

</td>
<td>

21

Notate the G minor scale using accidentals rather than a key signature.

</td>
</tr>
<tr>
<td>

whole (step)
half (step)

</td>
<td>

22

The procedure you applied in the preceding frames may be reversed to identify the relative major tonic of any minor key. This may be done by counting upward three letter-names, begining on the minor tonic, being sure to include any accidentals required to produce the sequence of intervals for a minor scale.

For instance, the C minor scale begins C, D, E-flat. These three ascending notes will form the intervallic sequence

of a _____ step followed by a _____ step.

</td>
</tr>
<tr>
<td>

Yes.

</td>
<td>

23

The following model demonstrates this method of locating the relative major of F-minor.

Study the letter-names and intervallic sequence found in the above model. Do these notes correspond to degrees

6, 7, and 8 of the A-flat major scale? _____

</td>
</tr>
<tr>
<td>

</td>
<td>

24

Notate the key signature of F minor.

</td>
</tr>
</table>

25

Apply this procedure to identify the relative major of F-sharp minor. Identify letter-names and accidentals as well as intervals as illustrated in Frame 23.

26

Yes.

Does the answer to Frame 25 correspond to degrees 6, 7, and 8 of the A major scale? _____

27

A

The relative major of F-sharp minor is _____ major.

28

Notate the F-sharp minor scale on the staff provided. Be sure to include all appropriate accidentals.

29

Construct the appropriate model to identify the relative major of C-sharp minor.

30

Notate the C-sharp minor scale on the following staff utilizing the appropriate key signature.

Model [musical staff with treble clef and notes]

Answer [musical staff with treble clef, two flats]

31

You have experienced two methods of identifying minor tonalities and constructing the corresponding scales: (1) by locating the minor tonic of a given relative major key, or (2) by ascertaining the notes or key signature of the major scale relative to a given minor tonic. Practice will enable you to apply either method mentally rather than by writing out each step.

Notate the key signature of G minor on the staff provided. Space is provided for a model if needed.

Model [musical staff with treble clef] **Answer** [musical staff with treble clef]

Model [musical staff with treble clef and notes]

C minor

32

Identify the relative minor tonality of E-flat major. Space is provided for a model if needed.

Model [musical staff with treble clef] **Answer** _____

Model [musical staff with treble clef and notes]

Answer [musical staff with treble clef and notes]

33

Notate the F minor scale without employing a key signature. Use a model if you wish.

Model [musical staff with treble clef] **Answer** [musical staff with treble clef]

Model [musical staff with treble clef and notes]

Answer [musical staff with treble clef, one sharp]

34

Notate the key signature of E minor.

Model [musical staff with treble clef] **Answer** [musical staff with treble clef]

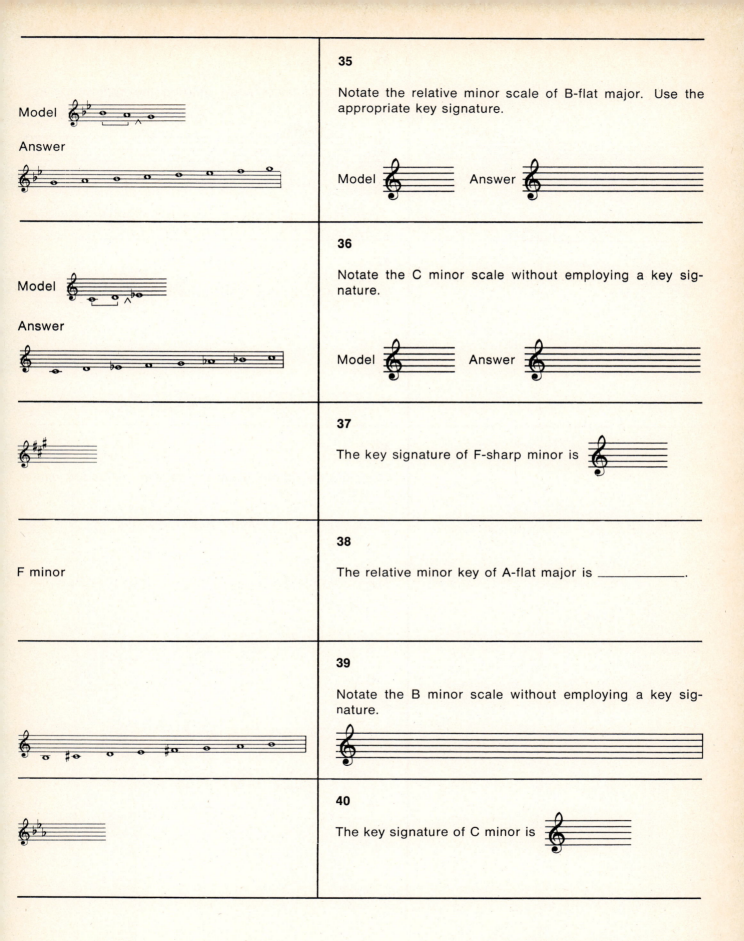

Model

Answer

35

Notate the relative minor scale of B-flat major. Use the appropriate key signature.

Model   Answer

Model

Answer

36

Notate the C minor scale without employing a key signature.

Model   Answer

37

The key signature of F-sharp minor is

F minor

38

The relative minor key of A-flat major is _____.

39

Notate the B minor scale without employing a key signature.

40

The key signature of C minor is

41

Notate the D minor scale utilizing the appropriate key signature.

42

The key signature of C-sharp minor is

43

Complete the following table of relative major and minor tonalities.

A

E

B

F-sharp

C-sharp

D

G

C

F

Major Key	Minor Key
C	_____
G	_____
D	_____
A	_____
E	_____
F	_____
B-flat	_____
E-flat	_____
A-flat	_____

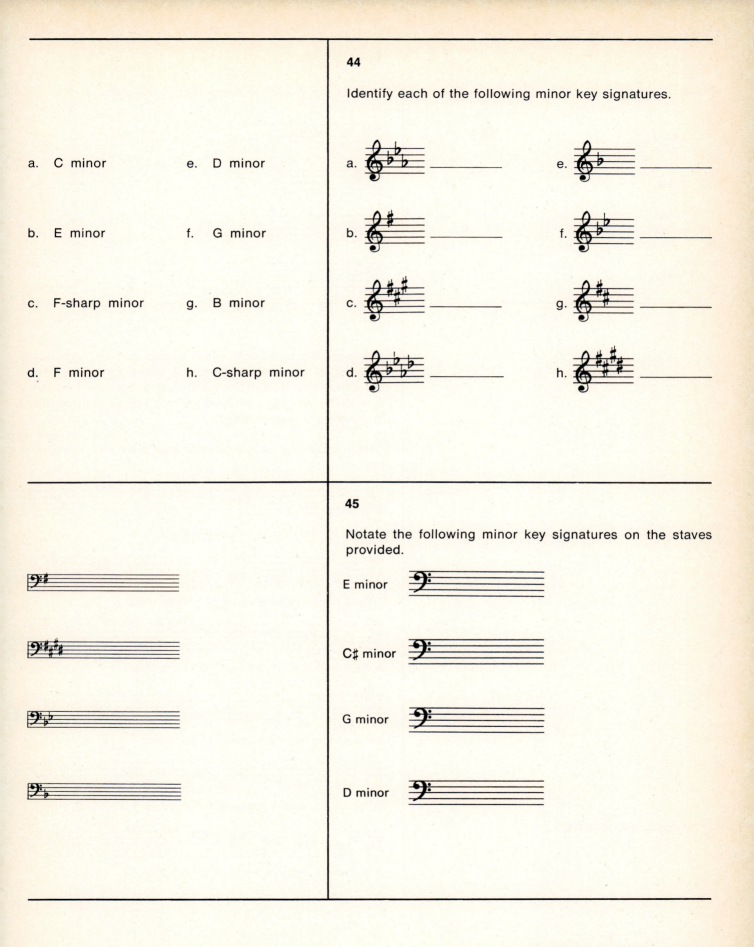

44

Identify each of the following minor key signatures.

a.   C minor   e.   D minor

b.   E minor   f.   G minor

c.   F-sharp minor   g.   B minor

d.   F minor   h.   C-sharp minor

a. _____   e. _____

b. _____   f. _____

c. _____   g. _____

d. _____   h. _____

45

Notate the following minor key signatures on the staves provided.

E minor

C♯ minor

G minor

D minor

46

Identify the following minor key signatures.

C minor

_____

B minor

_____

F minor

_____

F♯ minor

_____

47

There are six additional minor scales and key signatures ranging up to seven sharps and seven flats. Like their corresponding major tonalities, they occur less frequently than those you have learned and are not commonly found in classroom music series.

These additional minor scales and their key signatures are:

G-sharp minor, relative minor of B major

D-sharp minor, relative minor of F-sharp major

A-sharp minor, relative minor of C-sharp major

B-flat minor, relative minor of D-flat major

E-flat minor, relative minor of G-flat major

A-flat minor, relative minor of C-flat major

(No response necessary.)

DEVELOPING PERFORMANCE SKILLS

Recorder, piano, singing, and listening exercises employing minor scales and key signatures begin on page 197.

---

natural

48

Musical compositions in minor keys do utilize more than one form of the minor scale. The minor scale you have just studied is the basic form. It is called the **pure** or **natural** minor scale.

The basic form of the minor scale is called the pure or

_____ minor scale.

√ c.

49

The other forms of the minor scale require accidentals *not* included in the key signature. These may be considered *altered* forms of the minor scale. The most prevalent altered form of the minor scale is the **harmonic** minor scale.

Evaluate the following statements by checking the appropriate choice below.

A. Altered forms of the minor scale require accidentals not included in the key signature.

B. The harmonic minor scale is an altered form of the minor scale.

_____ a. A is true   _____ c. Both are true

_____ b. B is true   _____ d. Both are false

---

b.

50

The harmonic minor scale is formed by raising the seventh degree of the natural minor scale one half step. This alteration is not accommodated by the key signature and requires the use of an accidental.

Which of the following E minor scales is written in the harmonic form?

a.

b.

Answer: _____

seventh

51

The harmonic minor scale is formed by raising the _____ degree of the natural minor scale one half step.

52

Alter the following natural minor scale to form a harmonic minor scale.

53

Continue as in Frame 52. Notice that this natural minor scale is notated using a key signature.

54

Continue as in the preceding frame.

55

Notate the minor scales indicated without using key signatures.

D harmonic minor

C-sharp natural minor

56

Continue as in Frame 55.

F harmonic minor

B harmonic minor

57

Notate the minor scales requested using key signatures. Remember that the harmonic form utilizes exactly the same key signature as the natural minor. Only the altered note requires an accidental.

G natural minor

A harmonic minor

58

Continue as in Frame 57.

C-sharp harmonic minor

F harmonic minor

59

Continue as in the preceding frame.

C harmonic minor

E harmonic minor

60

Continue as in the preceding frame.

B harmonic minor

F-sharp natural minor

61

Continue as in the preceding frame.

G harmonic minor

D harmonic minor

62

Identify the following minor scales by tonic note and scale form (natural or harmonic).

G natural minor

_____

B harmonic minor

_____

E harmonic minor

_____

C harmonic minor

_____

63

Identify the following minor scales on the bass staff by tonic note and scale form (natural or harmonic).

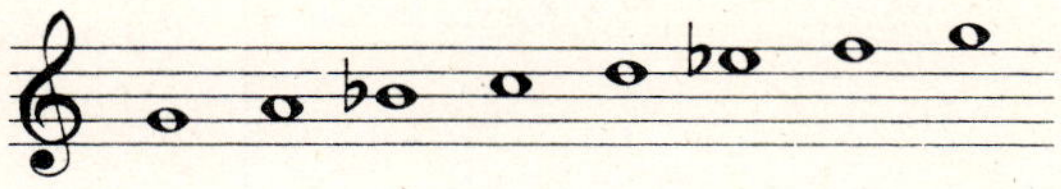

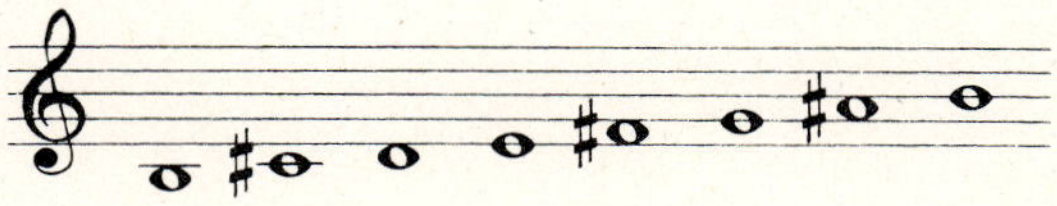

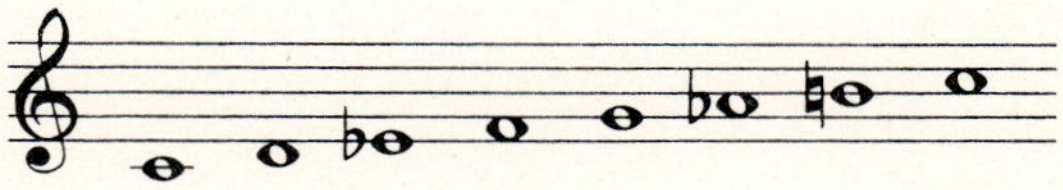

F-sharp natural minor

_____

D harmonic minor

_____

C-sharp natural minor

_____

F harmonic minor

_____

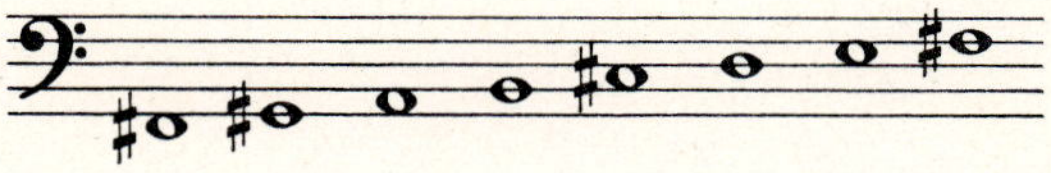

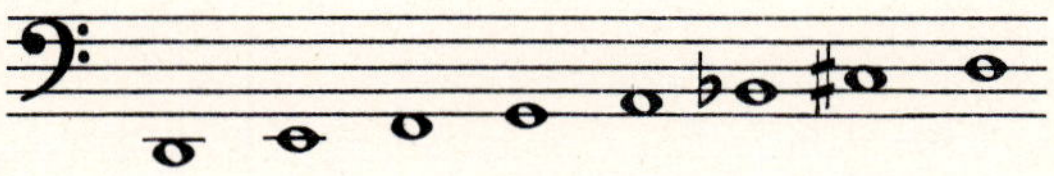

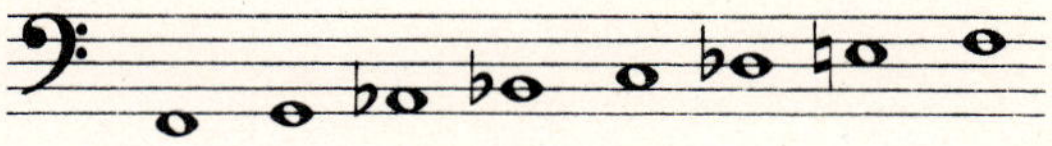

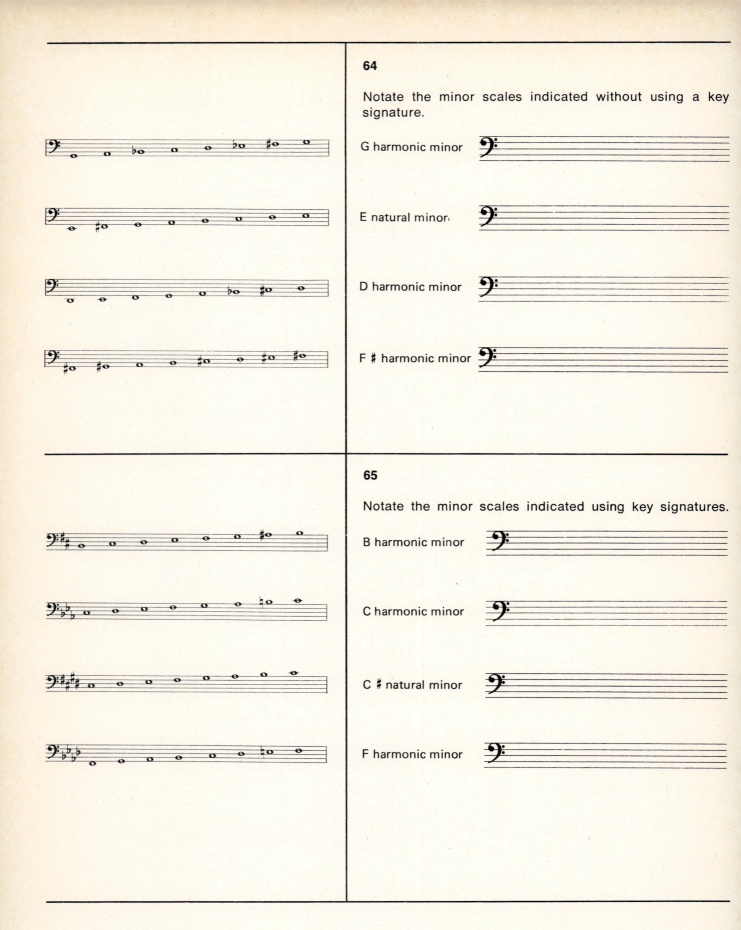

64

Notate the minor scales indicated without using a key signature.

G harmonic minor

E natural minor

D harmonic minor

F♯ harmonic minor

65

Notate the minor scales indicated using key signatures.

B harmonic minor

C harmonic minor

C♯ natural minor

F harmonic minor

DEVELOPING PERFORMANCE SKILLS

Recorder, piano, singing, and listening exercises based on the harmonic minor scale begin on page 200.

66

Perhaps you are wondering why more than one form of minor scale has evolved in Western music. If you have used the Performance Skills exercises thus far in this chapter your ears have probably already led you toward an appropriate decision in that regard. The following experiment provides a closer comparison.

Sing or play these two melodies alternately two or three times.

a.

b.

Does one seem to end with greater finality than the other?

_____ If so, which one?_____

Most people will feel Example a. has a more secure feeling of melodic close.

67

Can you notate and identify the minor-scale form used in each example in Frame 66?

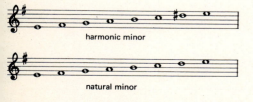

a. _____ _____ (form)

b. _____ _____ (form)

	68
harmonic	The **tonic** or "key note" receives greater tonal emphasis when the _____ form of the minor scale is used.

	69
half whole	The interval between the seventh and eighth degrees of the harmonic minor scale is a _____ step. In the natural minor scale this interval is a _____ step.

	70
	When the minor scale is altered by raising the seventh degree to within a half step of the tonic a greater sense of tonal finality is achieved. Sing the c harmonic minor scale again. Mark where all half steps occur with a caret. (∧)

major

71

The half step from degree 7 to 8 in the harmonic minor

scale is the same relationship found in the _____
scale.

72

Because this half-step relationship in these two scales causes the 7th degree to *lead* strongly to the tonic the 7th degree of the major and harmonic minor scales is called the **leading tone.**

Which of the following scales has/have a leading tone?

a (and) c

Answer _____

DEVELOPING PERFORMANCE SKILLS

Turn to page 202 for performance and listening exercises comparing the natural and harmonic forms of the minor scale.

three	**73** Study the harmonic minor scale in Frame 70 again. How many half steps occur between degree 6 and the leading tone? Answer _____
	74 If you have used the Performance Skills exercises involving the harmonic minor scale, you have had some direct experience in singing this awkward progression. This interval of three half steps has historically proven difficult for many people to sing. Musicians sought a compromise solution to preserve the leading tone in ascending melodies yet eliminate the problem interval from 6 to 7. This is the solution that emerged. 1 2 3 4 5 +6 +7 8 -7 -6 5 4 3 2 1 How does this minor scale differ in ascending and descending directions? _____ _____ _____
Both degrees 6 and 7 are raised one half step when ascending, then lowered one half step when descending. (Your own words.)	
	75 This minor scale that changes structure when it changes direction is called the **melodic** minor scale. Analyze each interval in the c melodic minor scale in Frame 74, both ascending and descending. What is the largest interval
a whole step	you find between adjacent pitches?_____

76

Melodies employing the melodic minor scale are easier to sing, yet preserve the leading tone in ascending passages. Here is an actual melody using the d melodic minor scale. Identify melodic minor activity by placing +6, +7, −6 and −7 below appropriate pitches.

77

No. (Only when the melody ascends to the tonic.)

Is the leading tone *always* present in melodies employing

the melodic minor scale?_____

78

The melodic minor variables of the raised 6th or lowered 7th degree are used only when necessary since both have the temporary effect of destroying minor key tonal flavor to some degree.

Add appropriate accidentals to apply the melodic minor scale *only* to avoid the occurrence of three half steps between degrees 6 and 7 in this melody.

	79
No response necessary.	You should also know that the 6-to-7 interval in the *harmonic* minor scale is easier to play on most instruments than it is to sing. Therefore, much music *does* employ the harmonic minor scale.

DEVELOPING PERFORMANCE SKILLS

Additional exercises involving all three forms of the minor scale may be found on page 205.

CHECK YOUR UNDERSTANDING

1. Each minor scale is related to a _____ scale.

2. Sounding the notes of any major scale beginning on the _____ degree and continuing for one octave will produce its relative minor.

3. The relative minor scale of the G major scale is the _____ scale.

4. Notate the following minor key signatures.

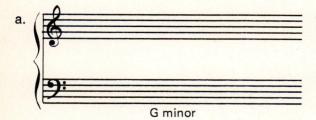

G minor

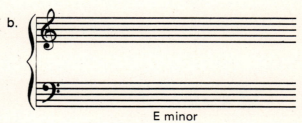

E minor

5. Using the appropriate key signature notate the F♯ natural minor scale.

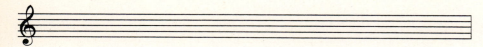

6. The basic form of the minor scale is called the pure or _____ minor scale.

7. The natural minor scale may be altered to form a harmonic minor scale

by raising the _____ degree one _____ step.

8. Using key signatures notate the following harmonic minor scales.

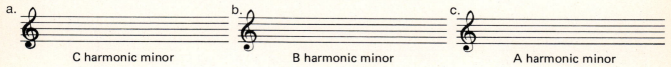

a. C harmonic minor   b. B harmonic minor   c. A harmonic minor

(*Answers may be found on page 363.*)

APPLY YOUR UNDERSTANDING

Identify each of the following minor key signatures.

a. _____ b. _____ c. _____ d. _____

Identify the minor key signatures of each of the following songs.

1. **The Wraggle-Taggle Gypsies**   British Isles

Key of _____

2. **Old King Cole**   Traditional

Key of _____

(Answers may be found on page 363.)

DEVELOPING PERFORMANCE SKILLS

Recorder (Frames 1–47)

Play these minor scales ascending and descending. Think of the complete name of each pitch (including accidentals) as you play slowly, but do not hesitate excessively between notes. Listen carefully as you play each scale to develop your aural recognition of minor tonality.

New recorder fingering

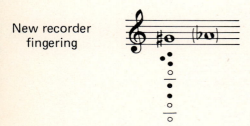

Piano (Frames 1–47)

Minor scales also involve more advanced piano proficiency while presenting additional opportunities to develop your aural recognition of minor tonal relationships.

Practice each of these minor scales **slowly** with each hand separately, ascending and descending. Be attentive to the fingering indicated.

Challenge

If playing scales "hands alone" is not particularly difficult for you, you may wish to attempt these with both hands together.

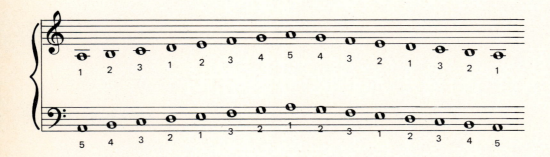

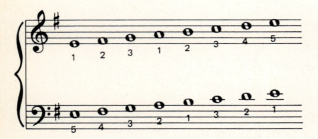 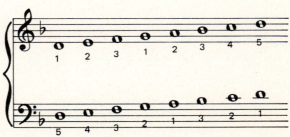

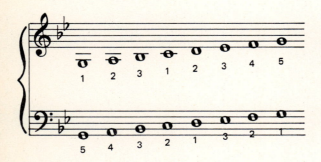 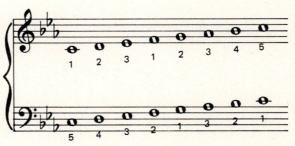

These minor scales involve more difficult fingerings. If you like a challenge, practice them very carefully and slowly.

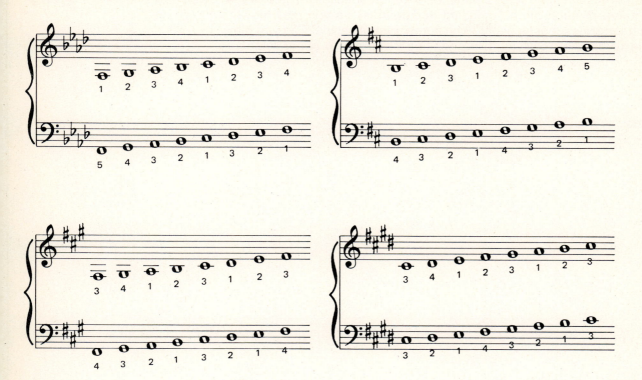

Singing (Frames 1–47)

Sing each minor scale indicated below ascending and descending, first with numbers (1 2 3 4 5 6 7 8 7 6 5 4 3 2 1), then immediately with letter names and accidentals. Repeat each scale as necessary to become fluent in both pitch accuracy and note names. Begin on the correct starting pitch as determined with your recorder or the piano. Take turns with a partner to test your singing and listening accuracy. Minor scales: A E B F♯ C♯ D G C F

Listening (Frames 1–47)

With a partner, take turns playing and singing random major and minor scales and identifying scale form by ear.

Recorder (Frames 48–65)

Play these harmonic minor scales ascending and descending. Think of the complete name of each pitch (including accidentals) as you play slowly, but do not hesitate excessively between notes. Listen carefully as you play each scale to develop your aural recognition of harmonic minor relationships.

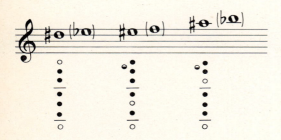

Piano (Frames 48–65)

The addition of an accidental and the wider physical reach between the sixth and seventh notes of the harmonic minor scale add both confusion and technical complexity. If you undertake this challenge begin with each hand separately, (then hands together if you wish) ascending and descending. Be attentive to the fingering indicated.

Challenge

These harmonic minor scales involve more difficult fingerings. Practice them very carefully.

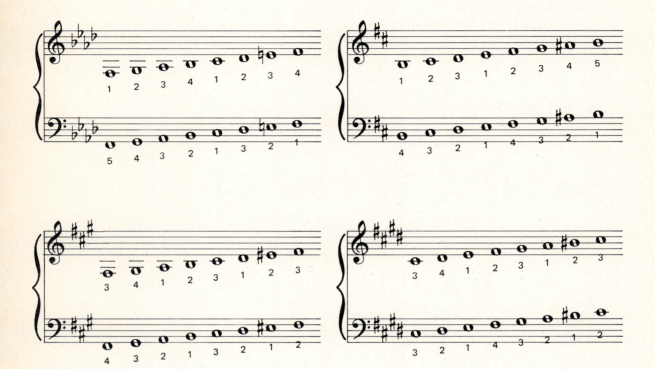

Singing (Frames 1–47)

Sing each harmonic minor scale indicated below ascending and descending, first with numbers (1 2 3 4, etc.), then immediately with letter names and accidentals. Repeat each scale as necessary to become fluent in both pitch accuracy and note names. Begin on the correct starting pitch as determined with your recorder or the piano. Take turns with a partner to test your singing and listening accuracy. Harmonic minor scales: A   E   B F♯ C♯   D   G   C   F

Listening (Frames 66–72)

With a partner, take turns playing and singing natural and harmonic minor scales randomly and identifying each scale from ear.

Now take turns playing the following melodies on recorder and piano and singing them with letter names. Be sure to perform both rhythm and pitch accurately. As one partner performs, the other is to aurally identify the minor scale form (natural or harmonic) on which each melody is based. Compare the tonal flavor of these two scale forms as you perform and listen. Singing will add an important physical recognition of the essential structural difference between natural and harmonic.

Tune of the Tay

England

God Rest You Merry, Gentlemen

England

The Coventry Carol   England

Joshua Fought the Battle of Jericho   Spiritual

Fine

D.C. al Fine*

*D.C. al Fine: Go back to the beginning and repeat until
the word *Fine*.

Recorder (Frames 73-79)

Play these melodic minor scales ascending and descending. Think of the complete name of each pitch (including accidentals) as you play slowly, but do not hesitate excessively between notes. Listen carefully as you play each scale to develop your aural recognition of melodic minor relationships.

Piano (Frames 73–79)

Melodic minor scales are a further challenge to mental and pianistic dexterity. If you undertake these exercises practice each scale first with hands separately, (then together if you wish) ascending and descending. Be attentive to the fingering indicated.

Challenge

These melodic minor scales involve more difficult fingerings. Practice them very carefully.

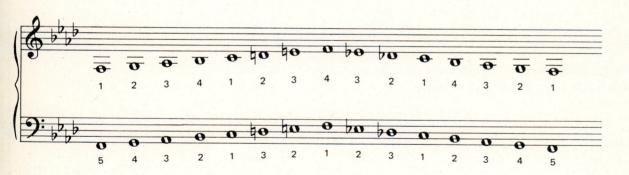

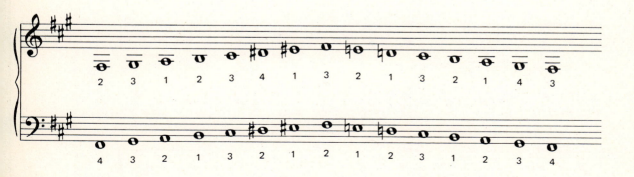

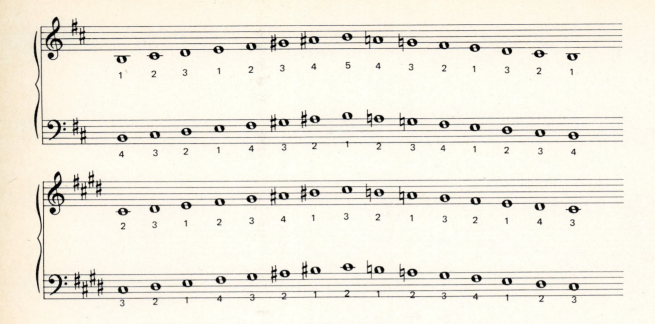

Singing (Frames 73–79)

Sing each melodic minor scale indicated below, ascending and descending, first with numbers, then immediately with letter names and accidentals. Repeat each scale as necessary to become fluent in both pitch accuracy and note names. Begin on the correct starting pitch as determined with your recorder or the piano. Take turns with a partner to test your singing and listening accuracy.

Minor scales: A E B F♯ C♯ D G C F

Listening (Frames 73–79)

Play and sing the following minor melodies with a partner. Take turns aurally identifying the scale form illustrated in each.

Wayfaring Stranger   U.S.

Shalom Chaverim

Jewish Folk Song

The Wild Horseman

R. Schumann

Dame Get Up

England

R.W.

Bell Carol

France

SUPPLEMENTARY ACTIVITIES

1. Build minor scales using individual tone bells.

2. Identify the key of the following songs in the Song Supplement. Play them on your recorder or piano.

   Fum, Fum, Fum, 376
   Pat-a-Pan, 383
   The Tailor and the Mouse, 384
   When Johnny Comes Marching Home, 376
   Zum Gali Gali, 383
   Greensleeves, 390

Perfect, Major and Minor Intervals

8

1

Musical compositions frequently employ other intervals in addition to the whole and half step you have considered in previous chapters. Like the whole and half step, these additional intervals also express the relationship of one

_____ to another.

pitch

2

In our musical vocabulary, intervals are identified by numeric size and quality. We shall first consider numeric size.

Intervals are identified by quality and _____ size.

numeric

3

The easiest method by which to identify an interval is by comparing the higher pitch to the lower pitch. Numeric size is determined by counting each line and space encompassed by an interval including those occupied by each note. Consider the following interval:

Solution

The above interval is called a fourth.

Determine the numeric size of this interval:

Solution

Answer: _____

a fifth

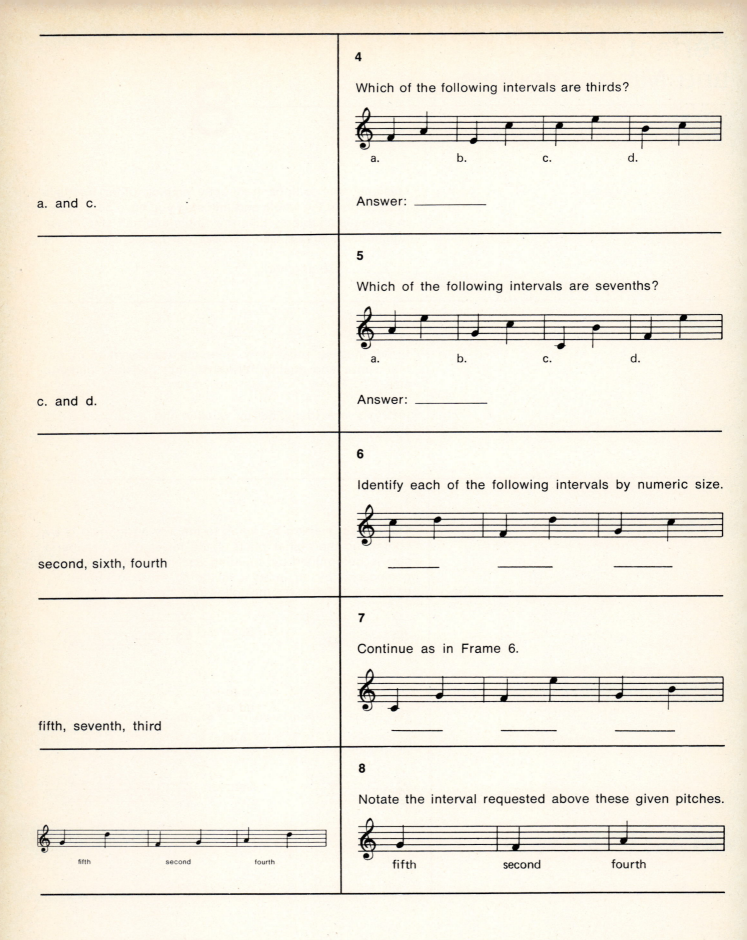

4

Which of the following intervals are thirds?

a.   b.   c.   d.

Answer: _____

a. and c.

5

Which of the following intervals are sevenths?

a.   b.   c.   d.

Answer: _____

c. and d.

6

Identify each of the following intervals by numeric size.

_____   _____   _____

second, sixth, fourth

7

Continue as in Frame 6.

_____   _____   _____

fifth, seventh, third

8

Notate the interval requested above these given pitches.

fifth   second   fourth

fifth   second   fourth

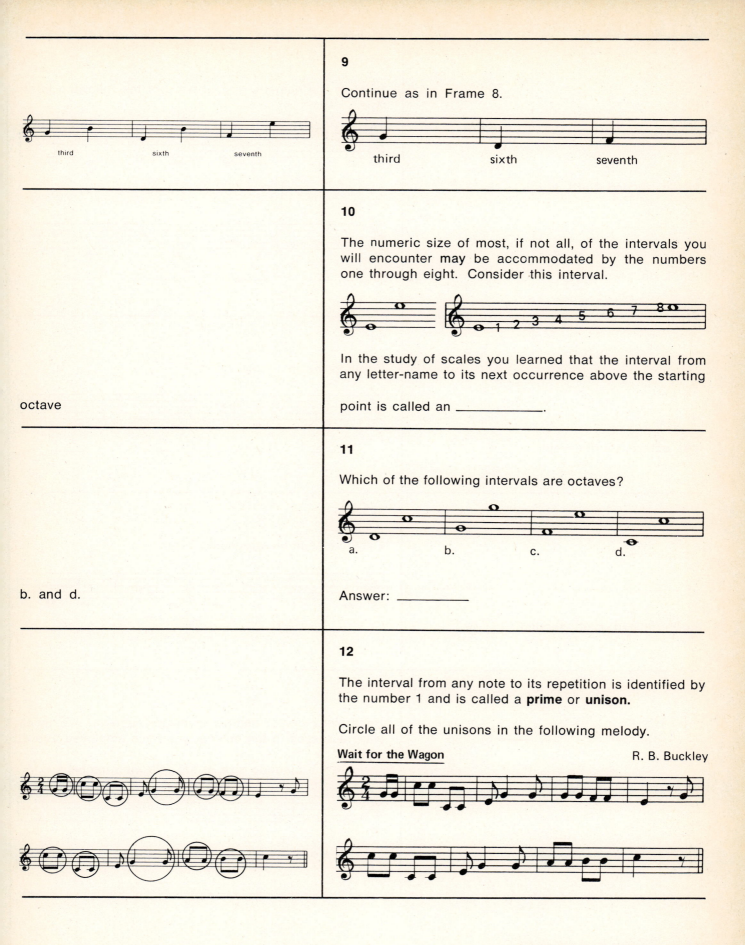

9

Continue as in Frame 8.

third   sixth   seventh

10

The numeric size of most, if not all, of the intervals you will encounter **may** be accommodated by the numbers one through eight. Consider this interval.

In the study of scales you learned that the interval from any letter-name to its next occurrence above the starting point is called an _____.

octave

11

Which of the following intervals are octaves?

a.   b.   c.   d.

Answer: _____

b. and d.

12

The interval from any note to its repetition is identified by the number 1 and is called a **prime** or **unison.**

Circle all of the unisons in the following melody.

Wait for the Wagon   R. B. Buckley

13

Indicate the numeric size of each of the following intervals.

unison, second, third, fourth

_____   _____   _____   _____

fifth, sixth, seventh, octave

_____   _____   _____   _____

14

Continue as in Frame 13.

fifth, octave, third, seventh

_____   _____   _____   _____

15

Continue as in the preceding frame.

fourth, unison, sixth, second

_____   _____   _____   _____

16

Regardless of accidentals involved, numeric size is always assessed in the manner you have employed above.

Indicate the numeric size of the following intervals.

second, seventh, fifth, fourth, third

_____   _____   _____   _____   _____

	17 Continue as in Frame 16. ——— ——— ——— ——— ———
third, fifth, unison, fourth, octave	
	18 Continue as in the preceding frame. ——— ——— ——— ——— ———
second, fourth, sixth, third, seventh	
	19 Do these two intervals have the same numeric size? Answer: ———
Yes.	
No. *(Since A-natural and A-flat are two different pitches, these are not identical intervals.)*	**20** Even though the two intervals in Frame 19 have the same numeric size, do they represent identical pitch relationships? ———
	21 The example in Frame 19 illustrates the need to identify intervals more precisely. This is achieved by identifying *quality* as well as numeric size. In other words, F to A-natural and F to A-flat have the same numeric size (both are thirds) but are different in
quality	————————.
	22 While the numeric size depends only upon letter-names (or lines and spaces encompassed), quality is affected by
accidentals	the presence of————————.

	23 The terms for interval qualities required in this study are **perfect, major,** and **minor.** Additional interval qualities do exist but these are the most prevalent in music that you will encounter. The three most prevalent interval qualities are _____, _____, and _____.
perfect, major, (and) minor *(Any order.)*	
	24 You may determine the quality of an interval by considering the lower note as the first degree of a major scale. The quality of this interval may be determined in reference to the _____ major scale.
D	
	25 The quality of this interval may be determined in reference to the _____ major scale.
E-flat	
	26 The first, fourth, fifth, and eighth degrees of a major scale always form **perfect** intervals above the tonic note. F major scale The interval quality of the unison, fourth, fifth, and octave above the tonic note of a major scale is always _____.
perfect	

27

These four are the *only* intervals ever termed perfect in quality.

The only intervals capable of being perfect in quality are the _____, _____, _____, and _____.

unison, fourth, fifth, (and) octave
(Any order.)

28

To complete the identification of interval size and quality consider the upper note as a member of the major scale of the lower note. This reasoning may be applied as follows.

The numeric size of this interval is a _____.

Is G the fifth degree of the C major scale? _____

Therefore, this interval is a perfect fifth.

fifth

Yes.

29

Continue as in Frame 28.

The numeric size of this interval is a _____.

Is B the fourth degree of the F major scale? _____

Therefore, this interval is *not* a perfect fourth.

fourth

No.
(The fourth degree is B-flat.)

30

Perfect unisons and octaves are easy to identify since in each case, both pitches involved will have the same letter-name *and* accidental, if any.

Place a check below all perfect intervals in the following example.

31

Continue as in Frame 30.

P5 _____ _____ P4 P8 P1

32

For interval analysis the term perfect is abbreviated P. The numeric size is represented by an arabic numeral. Perfect fourth, for instance, is abbreviated P4.

Abbreviate the quality and numeric size below each perfect interval in the following example.

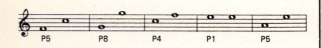

P4 _____ P4 _____ _____ P8 _____

33

Continue as in Frame 32.

P5 _____ P8 _____ P4 _____ P1 _____ P5

34

Notate the intervals indicated above each of the following pitches.

P5 P8 P4 P1 P5

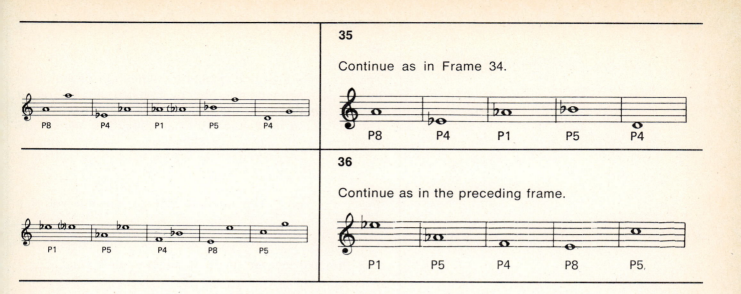

35

Continue as in Frame 34.

36

Continue as in the preceding frame.

DEVELOPING PERFORMANCE SKILLS

Recorder, piano, singing, and listening exercises involving perfect intervals begin on page 231.

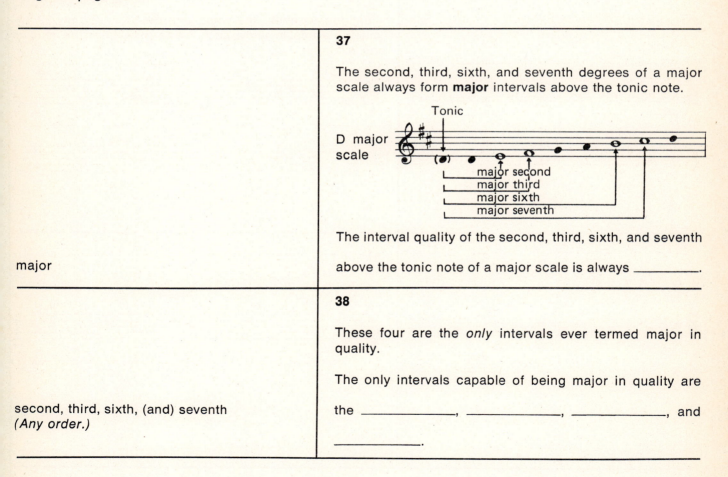

37

The second, third, sixth, and seventh degrees of a major scale always form **major** intervals above the tonic note.

The interval quality of the second, third, sixth, and seventh above the tonic note of a major scale is always _____.

major

38

These four are the *only* intervals ever termed major in quality.

The only intervals capable of being major in quality are the _____, _____, _____, and _____.

second, third, sixth, (and) seventh
(Any order.)

39

The complete size and quality identification of major intervals is also accomplished by considering the upper note as a member of the major scale of the lower note. The reasoning is identical to that applied to perfect intervals.

 The numeric size of this interval is a

sixth

_____.

Yes.

Is A the sixth degree of the C major scale? _____

Yes.

Is this interval a major sixth? _____

40

Continue to apply the logic expressed in Frame 39 by placing a check below each major interval in the following example.

41

Continue as in Frame 40.

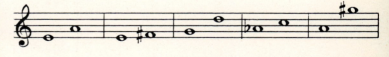

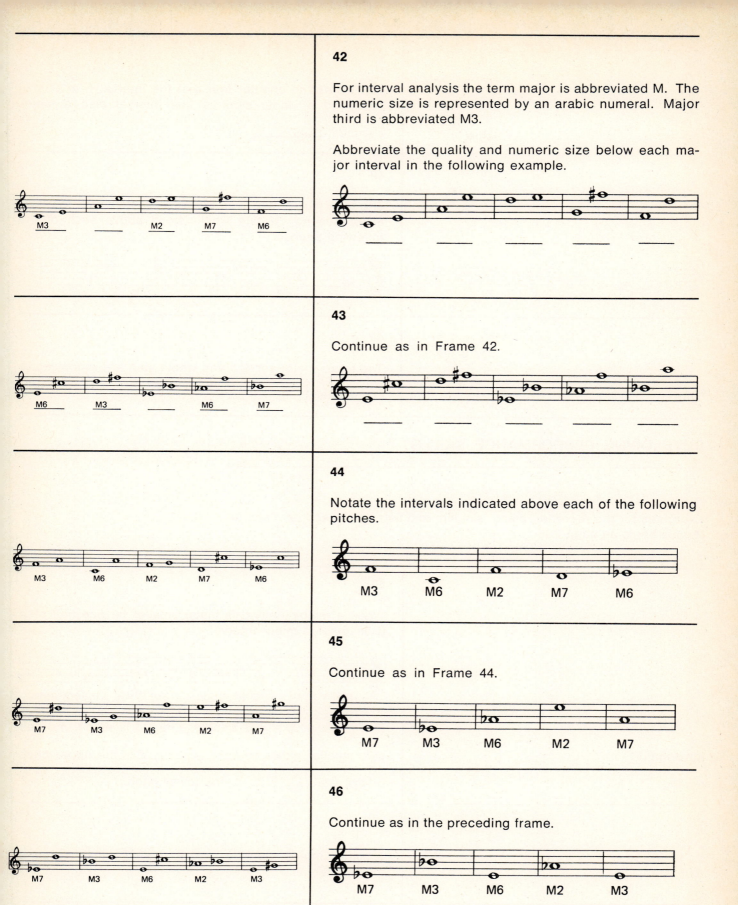

42

For interval analysis the term major is abbreviated M. The numeric size is represented by an arabic numeral. Major third is abbreviated M3.

Abbreviate the quality and numeric size below each major interval in the following example.

43

Continue as in Frame 42.

44

Notate the intervals indicated above each of the following pitches.

M3   M6   M2   M7   M6

45

Continue as in Frame 44.

M7   M3   M6   M2   M7

46

Continue as in the preceding frame.

M7   M3   M6   M2   M3

47

You learned in chapter four that the interval F to G may be called a whole step. Is this interval also a major

Yes.

second? _____

48

The term whole step is in fact synonymous with the term major second. Notate whole steps above each of the following pitches.

49

The terms major second and whole step are synonymous.

True.

(True/False) _____

DEVELOPING PERFORMANCE SKILLS

Exercises for the recorder, piano, singing, and listening based on major intervals begin on page 236.

50

When a major interval is made smaller by one half step it becomes a **minor** interval.

major third   minor third   major third   minor third

In the above example a major interval is made one half

lowering

step smaller either by _____ the upper pitch

raising

or by _____ the lower pitch.

51

A minor interval is one _____ step smaller than a

half (step)

major interval.

52

Only major intervals may be altered to form minor intervals. In other words seconds, thirds, sixths, and sevenths are the only intervals ever termed *minor* in quality.

Place a check before the interval sizes below that are capable of being minor in quality.

_____ unison   _____ fourth

_____ sixth   _____ seventh

_____ third   _____ fifth

_____ octave   _____ second

_____ unison   _____ fourth

✓ sixth   ✓ seventh

✓ third   _____ fifth

_____ octave   ✓ second

53

Only _____ intervals may be altered to form minor intervals.

---

major

54

By adding the appropriate accidental, alter the upper pitch of each of these major intervals to form minor intervals.

55

Continue as in the preceding frame.

56

Continue as in Frame 55. Notice that all of the following examples contain key signatures.

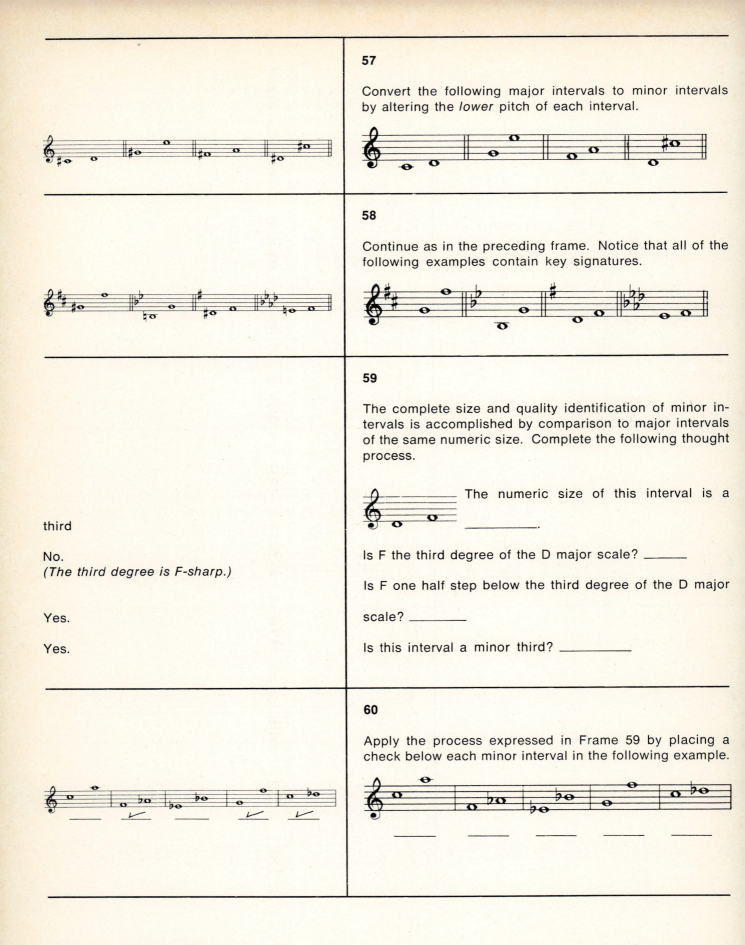

57

Convert the following major intervals to minor intervals by altering the *lower* pitch of each interval.

58

Continue as in the preceding frame. Notice that all of the following examples contain key signatures.

59

The complete size and quality identification of minor intervals is accomplished by comparison to major intervals of the same numeric size. Complete the following thought process.

The numeric size of this interval is a _____.

Is F the third degree of the D major scale? _____

Is F one half step below the third degree of the D major scale? _____

Is this interval a minor third? _____

third

No.
(The third degree is F-sharp.)

Yes.

Yes.

60

Apply the process expressed in Frame 59 by placing a check below each minor interval in the following example.

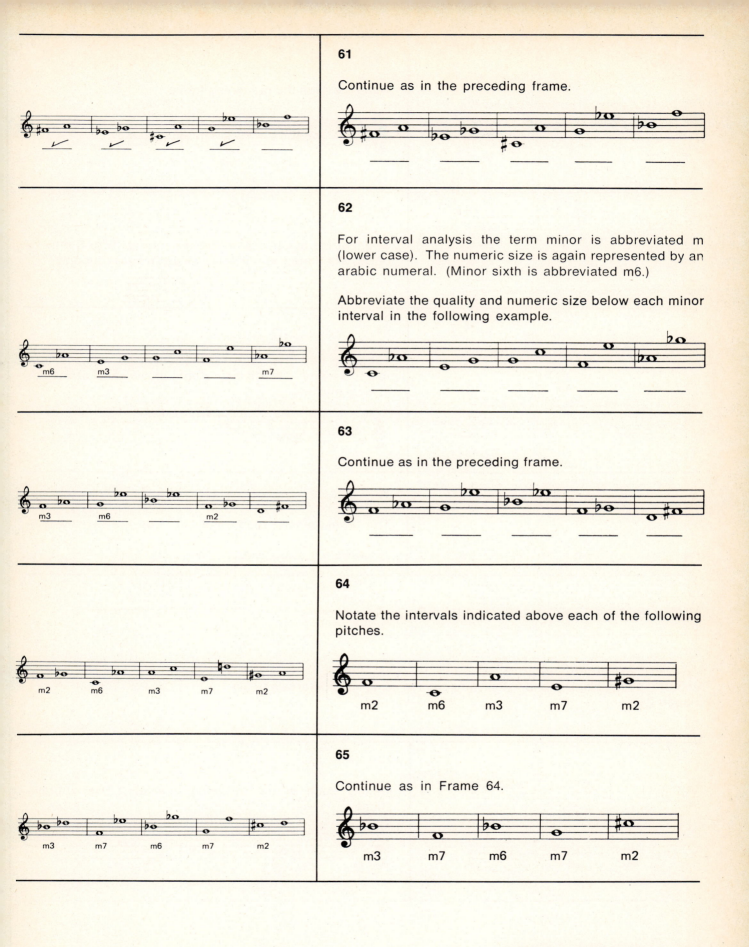

61

Continue as in the preceding frame.

62

For interval analysis the term minor is abbreviated m (lower case). The numeric size is again represented by an arabic numeral. (Minor sixth is abbreviated m6.)

Abbreviate the quality and numeric size below each minor interval in the following example.

63

Continue as in the preceding frame.

64

Notate the intervals indicated above each of the following pitches.

m2   m6   m3   m7   m2

65

Continue as in Frame 64.

m3   m7   m6   m7   m2

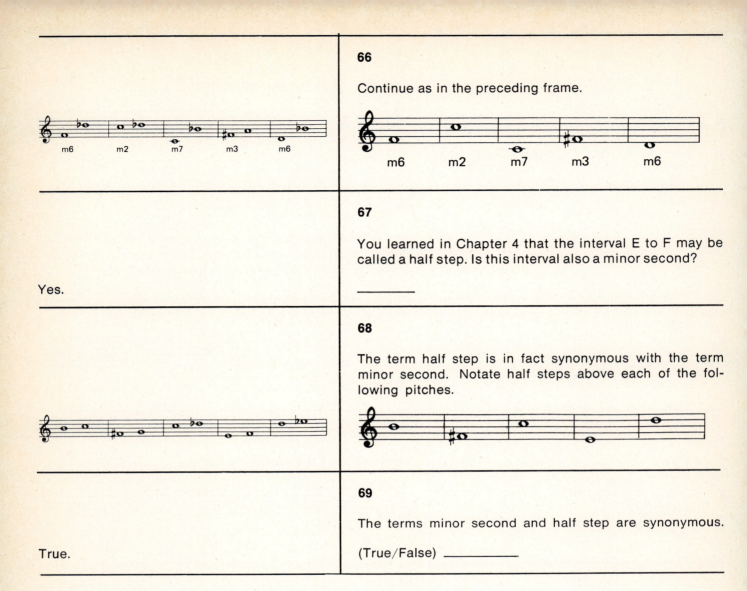

66

Continue as in the preceding frame.

m6   m2   m7   m3   m6

Yes.

67

You learned in Chapter 4 that the interval E to F may be called a half step. Is this interval also a minor second?

_____

68

The term half step is in fact synonymous with the term minor second. Notate half steps above each of the following pitches.

True.

69

The terms minor second and half step are synonymous.

(True/False) _____

DEVELOPING PERFORMANCE SKILLS

Recorder, piano, singing, and listening exercises using minor intervals begin on page 240.

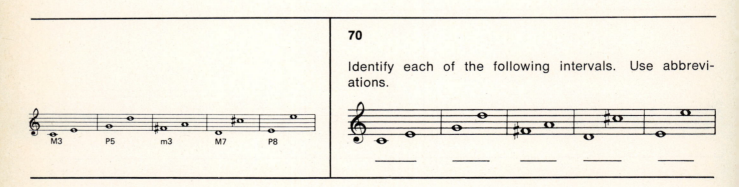

M3   P5   m3   M7   P8

70

Identify each of the following intervals. Use abbreviations.

_____ _____ _____ _____ _____

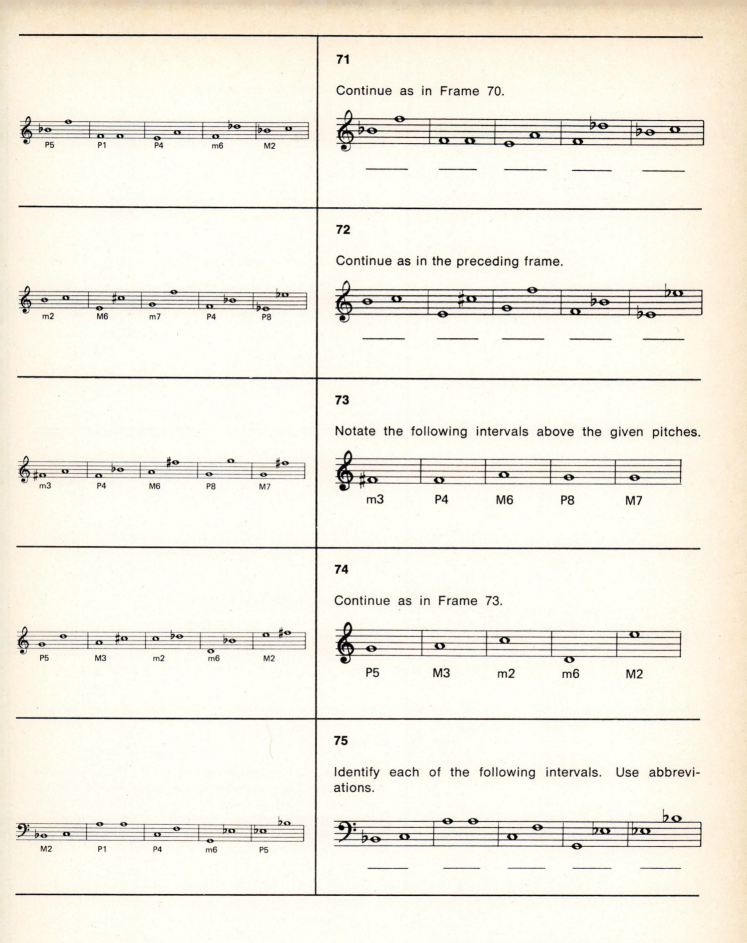

71

Continue as in Frame 70.

72

Continue as in the preceding frame.

73

Notate the following intervals above the given pitches.

m3   P4   M6   P8   M7

74

Continue as in Frame 73.

P5   M3   m2   m6   M2

75

Identify each of the following intervals. Use abbreviations.

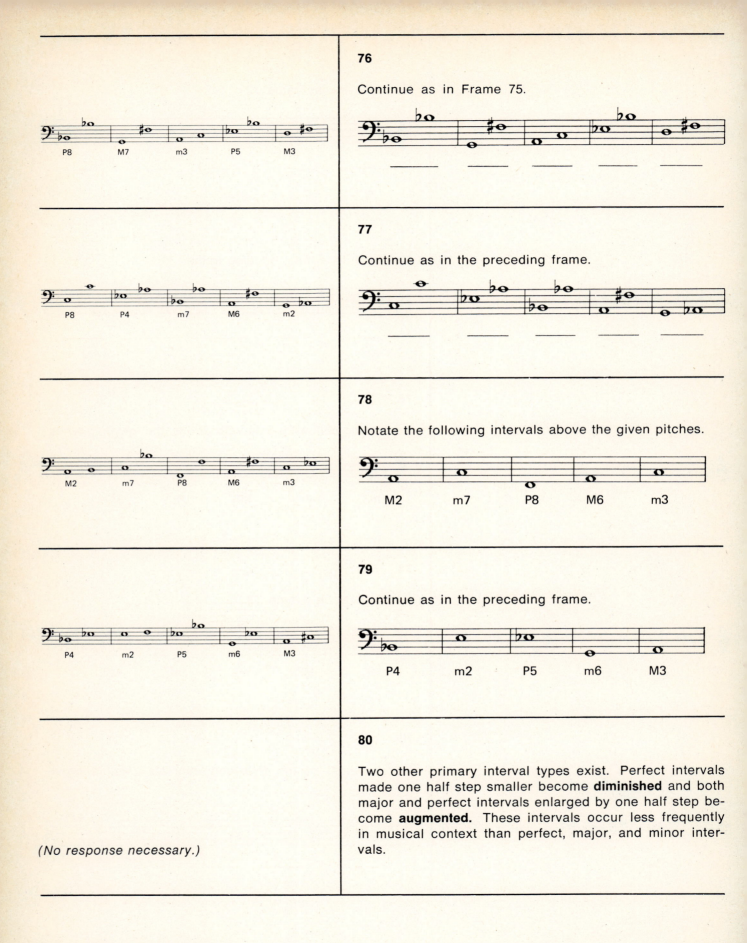

76

Continue as in Frame 75.

77

Continue as in the preceding frame.

78

Notate the following intervals above the given pitches.

M2   m7   P8   M6   m3

79

Continue as in the preceding frame.

P4   m2   P5   m6   M3

80

Two other primary interval types exist. Perfect intervals made one half step smaller become **diminished** and both major and perfect intervals enlarged by one half step become **augmented.** These intervals occur less frequently in musical context than perfect, major, and minor intervals.

(No response necessary.)

CHECK YOUR UNDERSTANDING

1. Intervals are identified by quality and _____ size.
2. Identify the numeric size of each of the following intervals.

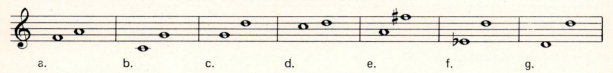

    a.   b.   c.   d.   e.   f.   g.

3. The interval from any note to its repetition is identified by the number

   _____ and is called prime or _____.

4. The three most prevalent interval qualities are _____, _____,

   and _____.

5. The interval quality of the unison, fourth, fifth, and octave above the

   tonic note of a major scale is always _____.

6. The interval quality of the second, third, sixth, and seventh above the

   tonic note of a major scale is always _____.

7. When a major interval is made smaller by one half step it becomes a

   _____ interval.

8. Identify the quality and numeric size of each of the following intervals.

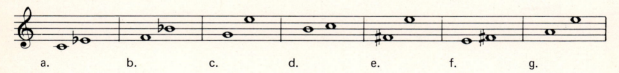

    a.   b.   c.   d.   e.   f.   g.

(Answers may be found on page 363.)

APPLY YOUR UNDERSTANDING

Notate the intervals indicated in each of the following measures.

a. P5   b. m3   c. P8   d. M6   e. m2   f. P4   g. M7

Identify those intervals indicated.

Dixie

Daniel Emmett

(Answers may be found on page 364.)

DEVELOPING PERFORMANCE SKILLS

Recorder (Frames 26–36)

Fluency in thinking, playing, and hearing intervals will greatly expand your ability to recognize and reproduce musical structures quickly, both in terms of written notation and by ear. The perfect unison is an extremely obvious interval since no pitch change is involved at all. The perfect octave is also an interval with which you should be totally familiar. Perfect fourths and fifths require a higher level of discrimination. Practice these drill sequences several times on your recorder. Play each interval in the rhythmic pattern illustrated.

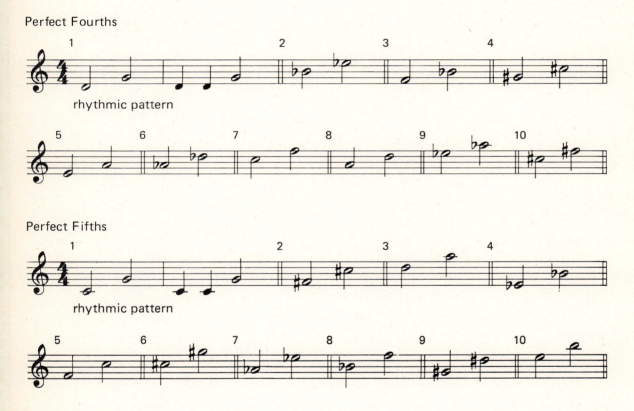

Perfect Fourths

Perfect Fifths

Piano (Frames 26–36)

Fluency in recognizing and reproducing various interval relationships constitutes a basic component of reading, hearing, and performing music on many levels. Gaining command of the complete gamut of interval structure is an extensive task. These exercises offer a sequential exploration of perfect, major, and minor intervals through playing, singing, and listening skills. They may be used selectively to develop skills to various levels of sophistication or in particular performance media.

Practice these sequences several times in the rhythmic pattern illustrated.
Remember to play bass clef exercises with your left hand.

Perfect Fourths

Perfect Fifths

Perfect, Major and Minor Intervals

Singing (Frames 26–36)

These singing drills are designed to reinforce both interval names and spellings as you develop your singing and listening skill. Sing the exercises in groups 1 and 2 in your own vocal range using the words of the appropriate rhythmic sequence. Use an instrument to check your accuracy.

rhythmic sequences

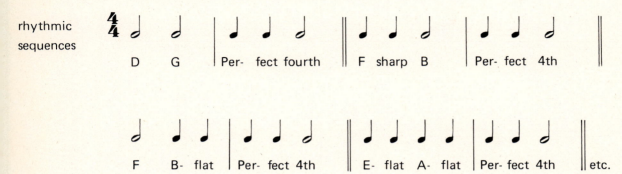

Perfect Fourths

Perfect Fifths

In these exercises only the lower note and interval name are given. You must identify the correct upper pitch name and sing both pitches and the interval name in an appropriate rhythmic pattern as in previous exercises. Again check your accuracy with an instrument as appropriate.

3. Identify and sing a perfect fourth above each of the following pitches.
    G, D, E-flat, F, C, B-flat, F-sharp, E, A-flat, B, A

4. Identify and sing a perfect fifth above each of the following pitches.
    C, A, C-sharp, B, G-sharp, D, F, G, B-flat, E, E-flat

Listening (Frames 26–36)

Listen (without your book) as a partner plays or sings each of the following intervals. Name each interval by ear. Practice these more than once to experience listening critically to various sound sources. Try to develop the ability to identify each interval in *one* hearing. *Performer:* Alternating recorder, piano, and voice randomly as you perform these sequences several times offers the best drill. Repeat each interval immediately as many times as required for your partner to achieve the correct answer. Add rhythmic patterns of your choosing if you wish.

Recorder (Frames 37–49)

Adding the four major intervals places additional demands on mental and aural discrimination. Seconds and thirds occur more frequently than sixths in actual melodies. Sevenths occur least often and are difficult to produce vocally but easy to identify aurally. Practice these drill sequences several times on your recorder. Concentrate on the unique sound of each interval type.

Major Thirds

rhythmic pattern

Major Seconds

rhythmic pattern

Major Sixths

rhythmic pattern

Major Sevenths

rhythmic pattern

Piano (Frames 37–49)

Practice these major intervals several times in the rhythmic pattern illustrated. Remember to play bass clef exercises with your left hand.

Major Thirds

Major Seconds

Major Sixths

Major Sevenths

Singing (Frames 37–49)

The following singing drills are designed to reinforce both the names and spellings of the major intervals as you develop your singing and listening skill. Sing in your own vocal range using the words of the appropriate rhythmic sequence as demonstrated in previous exercises. Use an instrument to check your accuracy.

1. Major Thirds

2. Major Seconds

3. Major Sixths

4. Major Sevenths

5. Identify and sing a major third from each of the following pitches. Sing both pitches plus the interval name as in the previous exercises. Check your accuracy with an appropriate instrument.
F, D, C, B♭, E♭, A, F♯, A♭, E, G

6. Identify and sing a major second above each of the following pitches.
C, E, A, B♭, A♭, E♭, G♯, D, F♯, D♭

7. Identify and sing a major sixth above each of the following pitches.
A, C, E, B, E, F, D, A, C♯, G

8. Identify and sing a major seventh above each of the following pitches.
G, D, C, F, E, B, E, B, A, C♯

Listening (Frames 37–49)

Listen as a partner plays or sings each of the following major intervals. Name each interval by ear. Try to identify each interval in one hearing. *Performer:* alternate recorder, piano, and voice as you perform these sequences. Repeat as required for your partner to achieve a correct answer. Add rhythmic patterns if you choose.

Recorder (Frames 50–69)

Among minor intervals seconds and thirds also occur more frequently in musical contexts and are usually easier to perform. Practice each of these minor interval drill sequences on your recorder. Play each in the rhythmic pattern indicated.

Minor thirds

Minor seconds

Minor sixths

Minor sevenths

Piano (Frames 50–69)

Practice these minor intervals several times in the rhythmic pattern illustrated. Remember to play bass clef exercises with your left hand.

Minor thirds

Minor seconds

Minor sixths

Minor sevenths

Singing (Frames 50–69)

The following drills will help to reinforce both the names and spelling of the
minor intervals as you develop your singing and listening skills. Sing in your
own vocal range, using the words of the appropriate rhythmic sequence.
Check your accuracy with an appropriate instrument.

1. Minor thirds

2. Minor seconds

3. Minor sixths

4. Minor sevenths

5. Identify and sing a minor third from each of the following pitches.
   E, F♯, B, F, C, F, G, C♯, D, A

6. Identify and sing a minor second from each of the following pitches.
   F, G, A, D♯, E, B, F♯, D, C♯, G♯

7. Identify and sing a minor sixth from each of the following pitches.
   E, F♯, G, F, D♯, E, D, C♯, A, G♯

8. Identify and sing a minor seventh from each of the following pitches.
   B♭, C, A♭, G♯, E♭, F♯, C♯, G, D, F

Listening (Frames 50–69)

Name each minor interval as a partner plays or sings them. *Performer:* repeat as required for your partner to achieve a correct answer. If you choose, add rhythmic patterns and alternate recorder, piano, and voice as you perform these sequences.

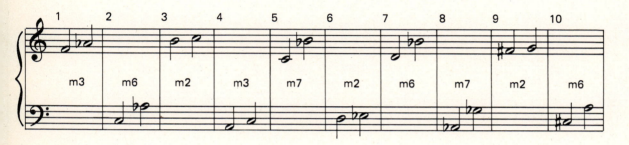

CHALLENGE

Singing (Frames 70–80)

Dealing with more random sequences of mixed intervals (especially vocally) involves rather advanced theoretical skills and also more closely resembles actual melodic structure.

1. Sing these intervals in the note-name-plus-interval-name rhythmic patterns you have used previously. The piano will be the most flexible instrument for determining starting pitches and checking your vocal accuracy. Through repetition, see how fluent you can become in recognizing and adjusting vocally to this more varied series of intervals.

2. Identify the upper pitch and sing both pitches and each interval name rhythmically as in previous exercises. Check your accuracy with the piano. Again, repeat this series of mixed intervals to develop fluency. Example: F (m6) Sing "F–D-flat, minor sixth." etc.

C (P4), E♭ (M3), A (M2), F♯ (P5), D (m3), B♭ (M6), E (m2), A♭ (M3), G♯ (P4), C (m6), F (m7), C♯ (m3), E♭ (M2), B♭ (P5), A♭ (M7), E (M3), F♯ (m6), G (m2), B (P5), F♯ (m3).

Listening, Notation (Frames 70–80)

Listen (without your book) as a partner names the lower note and performs each of these intervals. Your task is to identify and notate (on staff paper or a chalkboard with staff lines) the interval name and upper note. Your partner will repeat each interval as needed for you to complete your response and verify the correct answer. Repeat to develop correct responses in one hearing. *Performer:* add rhythmic patterns if you wish. Create additional exercises in similar fashion.

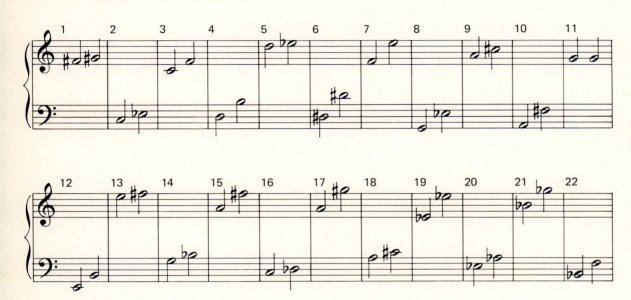

Listening, Performance (Frames 70–80)

A partner will sing and/or play random intervals above each of the following pitches. You will sing/play back the same interval. Repeat intervals "echoed" incorrectly. *Performer:* invent as many different series of intervals as you wish using these starting pitches as the point of reference.

G E D F♯ B A C E G♯ A

C♯ F B D F♯ E G D C D♯

Listening, Notation (Frames 70–80)

Interval and rhythmic relationships combine to form complete melodic gesture. Dealing with both components simultaneously involves very challenging listening experiences. Listen as a partner performs these melodic/rhythmic fragments after telling you the starting pitch. Echo back each example, then notate it in the drill frame provided (or the chalkboard if you wish). Strive to achieve both correct pitch and rhythm in as few repetitions as possible. Verify responses with your textbook or partner. (*Performer:* identify meter, key signature, and starting pitch before starting each exercise if your partner is using a chalkboard rather than the book.) For further drill, invent additional exercises like these. Cover the answer frames before beginning these exercises.

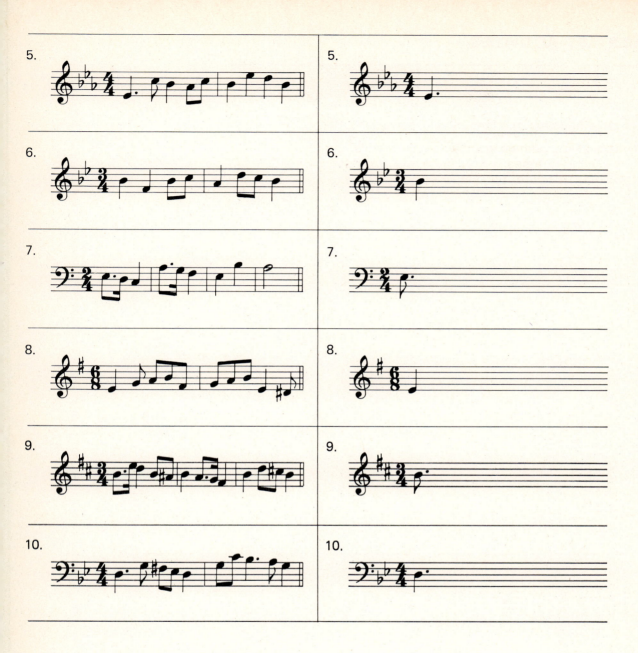

SUPPLEMENTARY ACTIVITIES

1. Select several songs and identify all intervals.
2. Build various intervals using individual tone bells.

Basic Chords

9

1

At this point our study of music has been limited to melody, the horizontal organization of pitch and duration. The addition of other simultaneous pitches and durations to support a melody creates the vertical dimension of music we call **harmony.**

The vertical organization of pitches and durations to support a melody is called _____.

harmony

2

Harmony is generated by the simultaneous sounding of multiple pitches or **chords.**

Three or more pitches sounding together are defined as a chord.

Harmony is generated by _____.

chords

3

A chord is the simultaneous sounding of _____ or more pitches.

three

4

Place a check below each chord in the following series of examples.

5

The most predominant chord type heard in tonal music is the **triad.** A triad consists of *three* notes placed on *consecutive* lines or spaces of the staff.

Triads

Triads consist of _____ notes.

three

6

Triads are easily recognized since *all three* notes are located on adjacent lines or _____ of the staff.

spaces

7

Place a check below each triad in the following series of examples.

8

Using fundamental pitches, construct a triad incorporating each pitch below as the bottom note.

9

The basic triad in any tonal composition is the triad that is constructed on the tonal center or tonic scale degree. This **tonic triad** identifies the harmonic flavor or color of a major or minor key.

The tonic triad in the key of A major is:

This tonic triad consists of the first, _____, and _____ degrees of the A major scale.

third (and) fifth

No.

It does not consist of the first, third, and fifth degrees of the D major scale.

(Your own words.)

A

---

third (and) fifth

10

Is the following triad the tonic triad of the major key in which it is notated?

Answer: _____

Why? _____

_____

11

Notate the tonic triad in each of the following major keys.

12

Each minor key also has a tonic triad. Notate the tonic triad of each of the following *minor* keys.

13

The note on which a triad is constructed is called the **root**.

The root of this triad   is _____.

14

The two upper members of a triad take their identity from the scale degrees which comprise the two upper members of a tonic triad.

A and C are the _____ and

_____ degrees of the F major scale.

A and C are also the *third* and *fifth* of the F major triad.

Basic Chords   **251**

F-sharp	**15** The third of a D major triad is _____.
F	**16** The fifth of a B-flat major triad is _____.
third	**17** Triads and their components may also be identified intervallically. The numeric size of the interval between each pair of adjacent notes in a triad is a _____.
three thirds	**18** A triad consists of _____ notes arranged in consecutive _____.
third	**19** The names already designated for the two upper members of a triad coincide with the numeric interval these notes form above the root. The middle note of a triad is a _____ above the root. *(interval)*
fifth	**20** The upper note of a triad is a _____ above the root. *(interval)*
root, third, (and) fifth	**21** The names of the members of a triad, from lowest to highest, are _____, _____, and _____.
D	**22** The root of this triad is _____.

E	**23** The third of this triad is _____.
D	**24** The fifth of this triad is _____.
third	**25** B-flat is the _____ of this triad.
root	**26** E-flat is the _____ of this triad.
fifth	**27** C-sharp is the _____ of this triad.
major	**28** Triads, like scales, may possess different sound flavors. Just as there are major and minor scales, there are also major and minor (and other) triad qualities. The tonic triad of a major key possesses the same sound flavor we associate with the major scale. This sound or quality is called a major triad. The tonic triad of a major key is always a _____ triad.

29

You may construct a major triad on any pitch by regarding that note as the tonic note of a major key. Then construct the tonic triad in that major key. For example, to construct an E-flat major triad, think of the tonic triad in the key of E-flat major, or the first, third, and fifth degrees of the E-flat major scale.

Notate an E-flat major triad on the staff below. Remember to add the appropriate accidentals.

30

Notate major triads above each note on the staff below. Think of each as a tonic triad in the key of the given note. Be certain to add all necessary accidentals.

31

Place a check below each major triad in the following example.

32

The tonic triad of a minor key possesses the same sound flavor we associate with the minor scale. The quality of this triad is minor.

minor

The tonic triad of a minor key is always a _____ triad.

33

A minor triad may be constructed on any pitch by identifying the tonic triad of that minor key.

The F minor triad contains the first, third, and fifth degrees of the _____ minor scale.

F

34

Notate an F minor triad on the staff below. Remember to add any appropriate accidentals.

35

Notate minor triads above each note on the staff below. Think of each as a tonic triad in the minor key of the given note. Be certain to add all necessary accidentals.

36

Place a check below each minor triad in the following example.

37

Just as a triad may be identified by the numeric intervals between its members, that triad's quality is also indicated by the *interval qualities* between its members.

Identify the interval quality and size from the root to the other members of this triad.

major third

perfect fifth

Root to third _____

Root to fifth _____

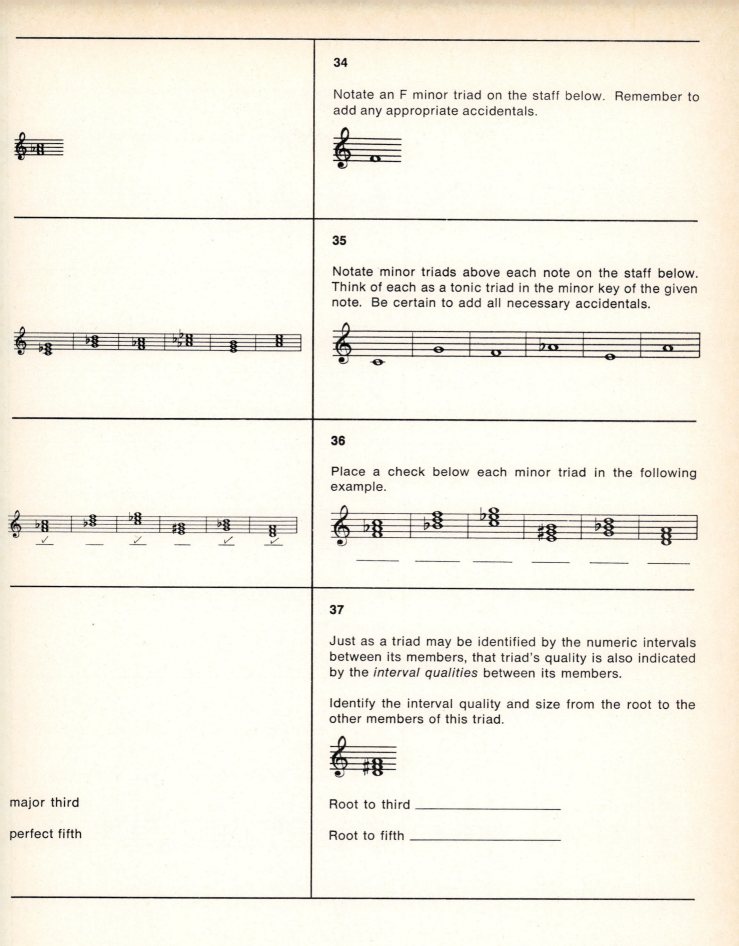

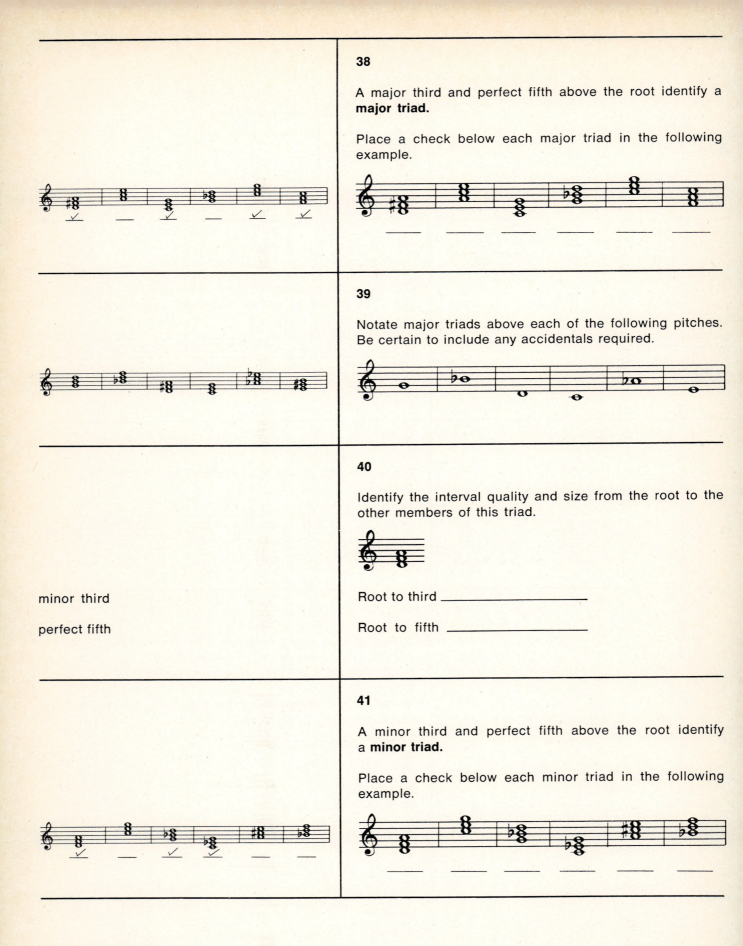

38

A major third and perfect fifth above the root identify a **major triad.**

Place a check below each major triad in the following example.

39

Notate major triads above each of the following pitches. Be certain to include any accidentals required.

40

Identify the interval quality and size from the root to the other members of this triad.

Root to third _____

Root to fifth _____

minor third

perfect fifth

41

A minor third and perfect fifth above the root identify a **minor triad.**

Place a check below each minor triad in the following example.

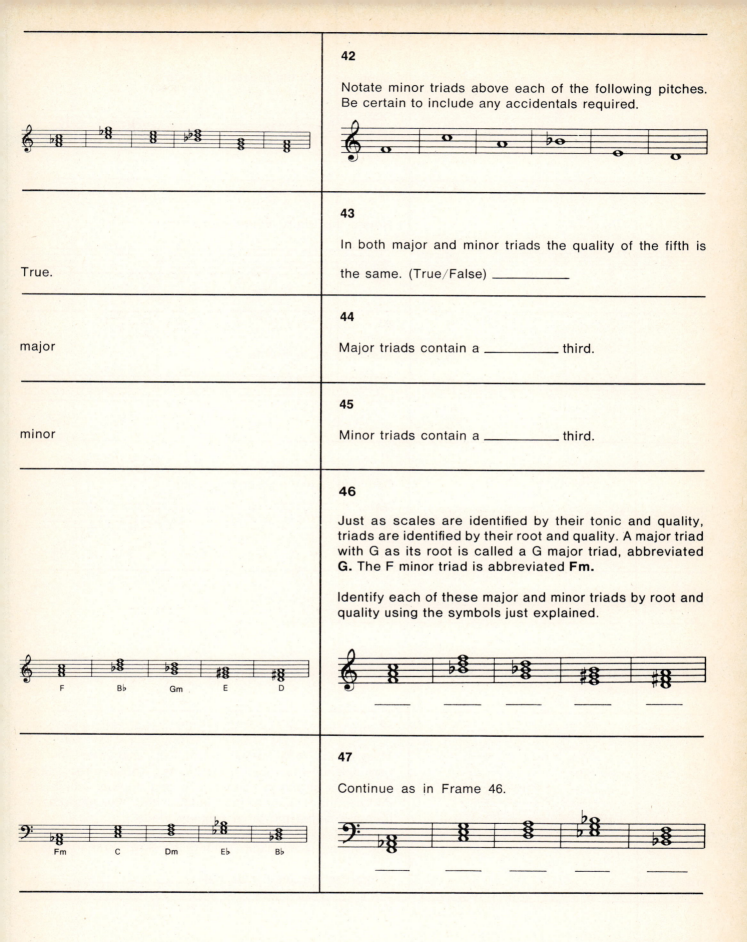

42

Notate minor triads above each of the following pitches. Be certain to include any accidentals required.

43

True.

In both major and minor triads the quality of the fifth is the same. (True/False) _____

44

major

Major triads contain a _____ third.

45

minor

Minor triads contain a _____ third.

46

Just as scales are identified by their tonic and quality, triads are identified by their root and quality. A major triad with G as its root is called a G major triad, abbreviated **G.** The F minor triad is abbreviated **Fm.**

Identify each of these major and minor triads by root and quality using the symbols just explained.

F   Bb   Gm   E   D

47

Continue as in Frame 46.

Fm   C   Dm   Eb   Bb

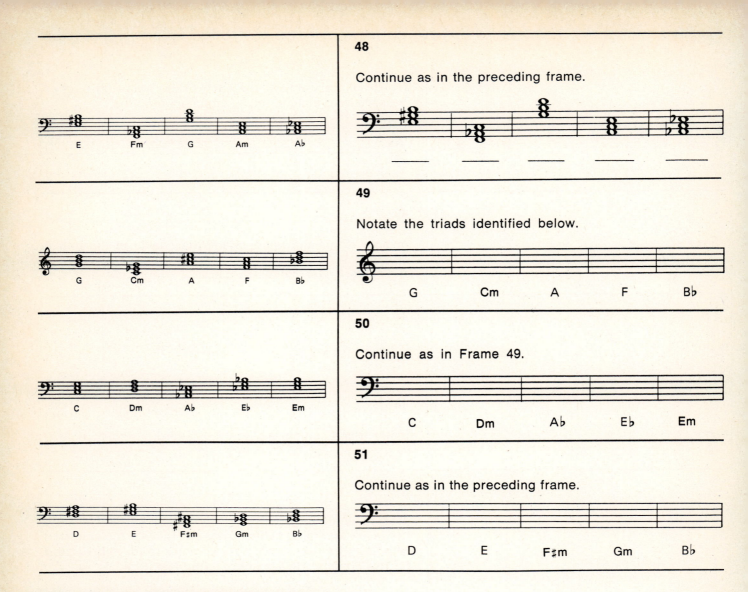

48

Continue as in the preceding frame.

49

Notate the triads identified below.

G   Cm   A   F   B♭

50

Continue as in Frame 49.

C   Dm   A♭   E♭   Em

51

Continue as in the preceding frame.

D   E   F♯m   Gm   B♭

DEVELOPING PERFORMANCE SKILLS

Turn to page 291 for piano, singing, and listening exercises involving major and minor triads.

52

Most of the tonal melodies you will encounter can be harmonized with three basic triads. These three triads possess a strong relationship to one another which reinforces the identity of their tonal center. For this reason they are called the three **primary triads.**

The strong relationship among the three primary triads

reinforces the identity of their _____ _____.

tonal center

53

The three primary triads are constructed upon the first, fourth, and fifth scale degrees of a key.

In the key of C major, the primary triads are constructed

C, F, (and) G

upon the pitches _____, _____, and _____.

54

In the key of A major the roots of the primary triads are

A, D, (and) E

_____, _____, and _____.

55

In the key of F major the roots of the primary triads are

F, B-flat, (and) C

_____, _____, and _____.

56

Collectively the three primary triads of a major key utilize all of the scale degrees of the key in which they function (with some duplications). No altered tones are employed. This explains in part their ability to define a key harmonically.

Notate the primary triads in the key of C major.

57

Do the primary triads in the key of C major utilize each

Yes.

note of the C major scale at least once? _____

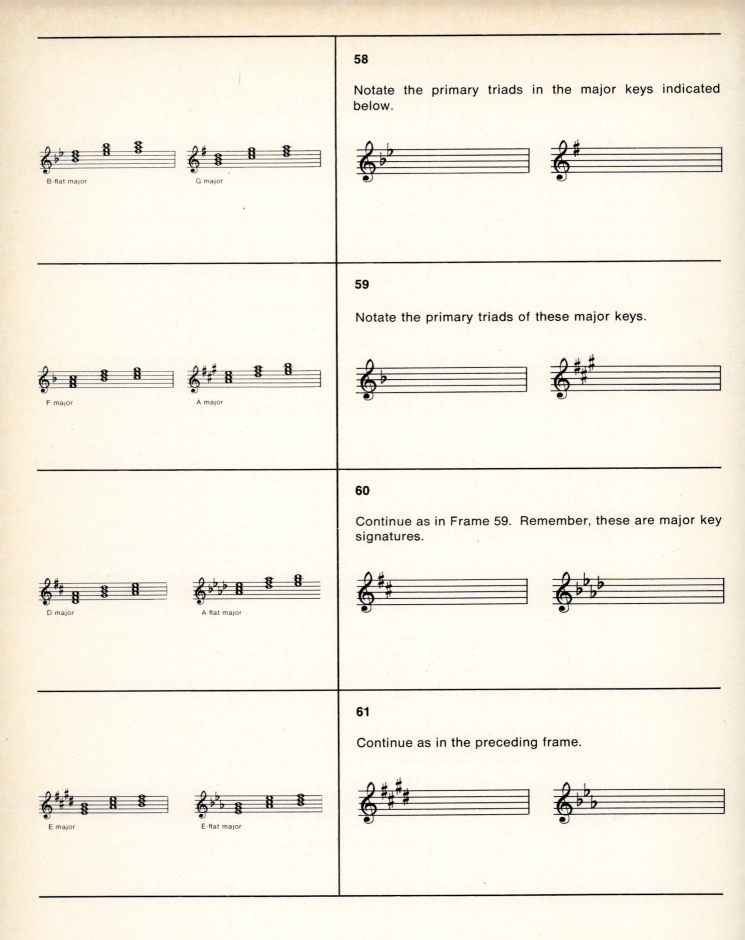

58

Notate the primary triads in the major keys indicated below.

59

Notate the primary triads of these major keys.

60

Continue as in Frame 59. Remember, these are major key signatures.

61

Continue as in the preceding frame.

B-flat major   G major

F major   A major

D major   A-flat major

E major   E-flat major

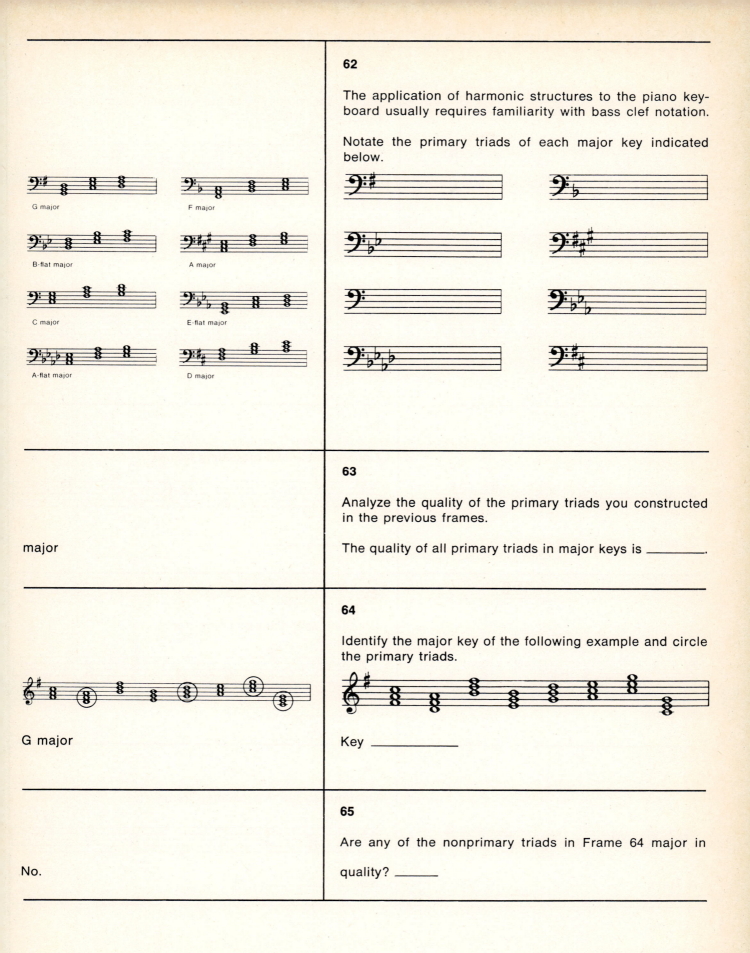

62

The application of harmonic structures to the piano keyboard usually requires familiarity with bass clef notation.

Notate the primary triads of each major key indicated below.

63

Analyze the quality of the primary triads you constructed in the previous frames.

The quality of all primary triads in major keys is _____.

major

64

Identify the major key of the following example and circle the primary triads.

G major

Key _____

65

Are any of the nonprimary triads in Frame 64 major in quality? _____

No.

F major

D major

C major

Bb major

A major

Identify the *major key* of the following example and circle the primary triads.

Key _____

67

Continue as in Frame 66.

Key _____

68

Continue as in the preceding frame.

Key _____

69

Continue as in the preceding frame.

Key _____

70

Continue as in the preceding frame.

Key _____

DEVELOPING PERFORMANCE SKILLS

Exercises beginning on page 292 present initial performance skills on the autoharp.

	71 The primary triads of minor keys are also located on the first, fourth, and fifth scale degrees. In the key of D minor the roots of the primary triads are _____ , _____ , and _____ .
D, G, (and) A	
	72 In the key of F minor the roots of the primary triads are _____ , _____ , and _____ .
F, B-flat, (and) C	
	73 In minor keys the primary triads *most often* employ the notes of the *harmonic* minor scale. This is most important because of the effect upon triad *qualities.* As in major keys the primary triads in minor are constructed upon the first, fourth, and fifth scale degrees. All degrees of the harmonic minor scale are utilized (with some duplications). Notate the primary triads in the key of a minor. The a harmonic minor scale is already notated to assist you. Be sure to include any accidentals required in your answer.
	Answer:
	74 The primary triads in minor keys utilize the notes of the _____ form of the minor scale.
harmonic	

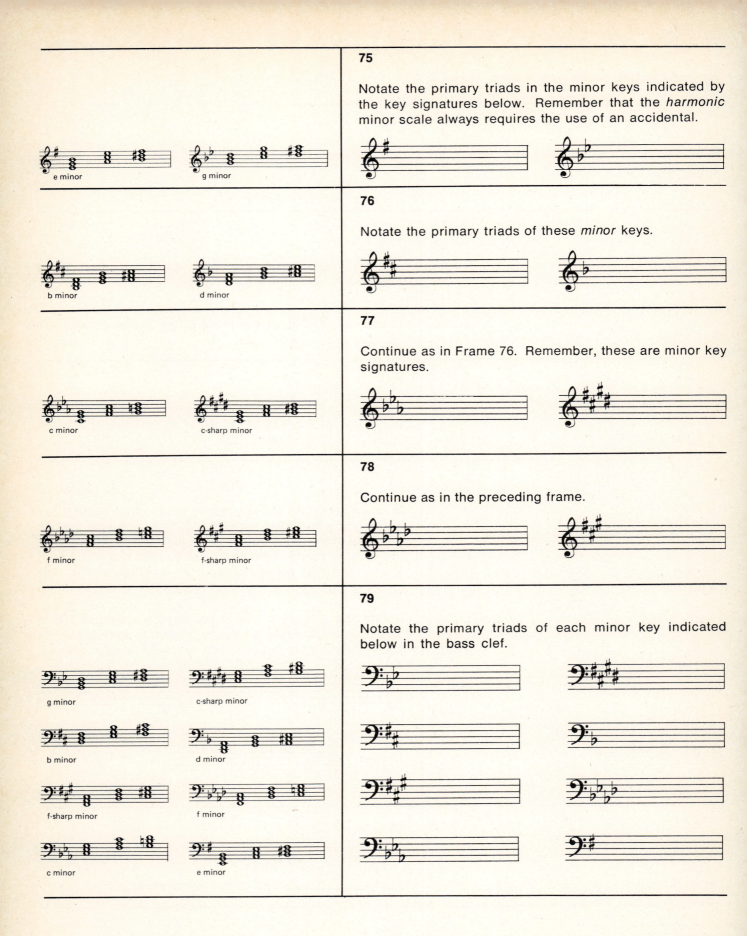

75

Notate the primary triads in the minor keys indicated by the key signatures below. Remember that the *harmonic* minor scale always requires the use of an accidental.

76

Notate the primary triads of these *minor* keys.

77

Continue as in Frame 76. Remember, these are minor key signatures.

78

Continue as in the preceding frame.

79

Notate the primary triads of each minor key indicated below in the bass clef.

	80
	Analyze the quality of the primary triads you have constructed in minor keys.
minor	The triad on the first scale degree is _____ in quality.
minor	The triad on the fourth scale degree is _____ in quality.
major	The triad on the fifth scale degree is _____ in quality.
	81
	The quality of all primary triads in minor keys is minor.
False.	(True/False) _____
	82
	Identify the minor key of the following example and circle the primary triads.
d minor	Key _____
	83
	Are any of the nonprimary triads in Frame 82 minor in quality? _____
No.	
	84
	The primary triad on the fifth scale degree in minor keys
major	is _____ in quality.

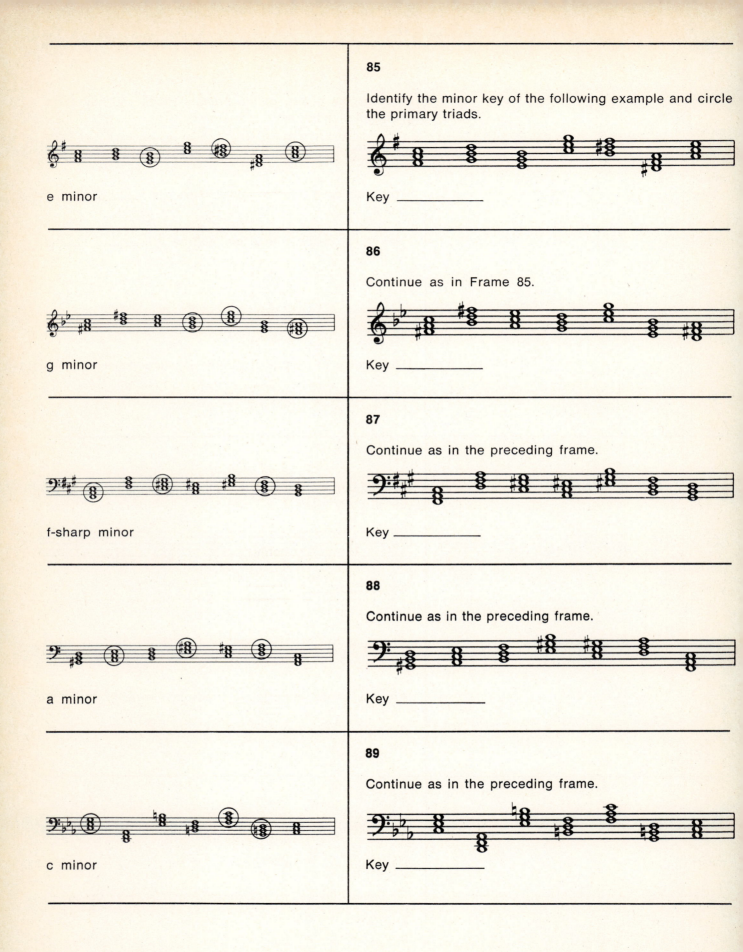

85

Identify the minor key of the following example and circle the primary triads.

Key _____

e minor

86

Continue as in Frame 85.

Key _____

g minor

87

Continue as in the preceding frame.

Key _____

f-sharp minor

88

Continue as in the preceding frame.

Key _____

a minor

89

Continue as in the preceding frame.

Key _____

c minor

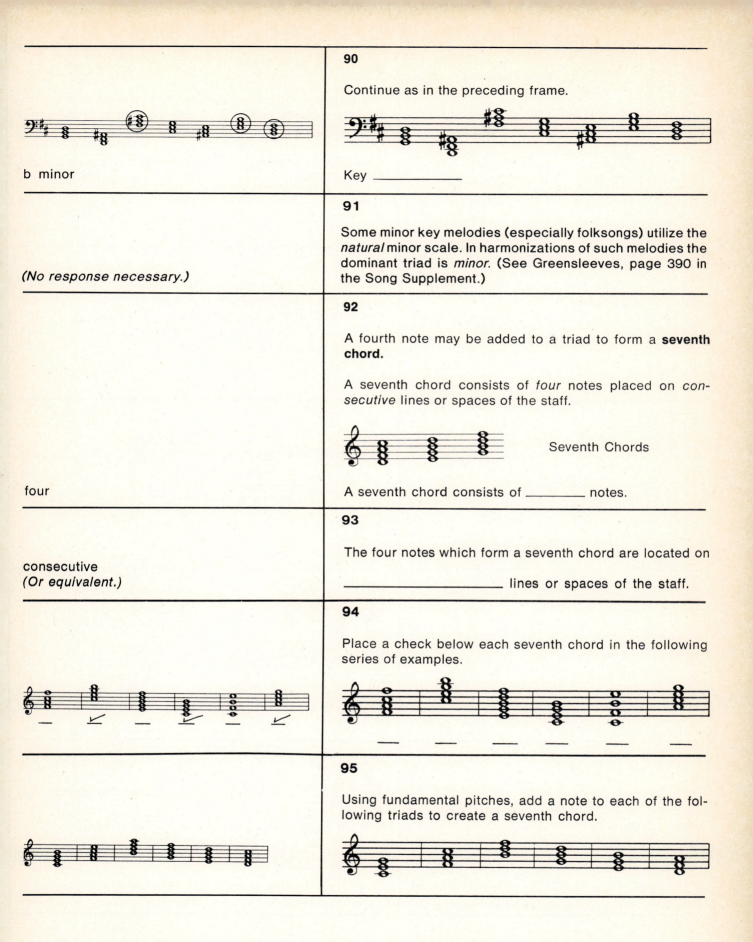

b minor

90

Continue as in the preceding frame.

Key _____

(No response necessary.)

91

Some minor key melodies (especially folksongs) utilize the *natural* minor scale. In harmonizations of such melodies the dominant triad is *minor*. (See Greensleeves, page 390 in the Song Supplement.)

92

A fourth note may be added to a triad to form a **seventh chord.**

A seventh chord consists of *four* notes placed on *consecutive* lines or spaces of the staff.

Seventh Chords

four

A seventh chord consists of _____ notes.

93

The four notes which form a seventh chord are located on

_____ lines or spaces of the staff.

consecutive
(Or equivalent.)

94

Place a check below each seventh chord in the following series of examples.

95

Using fundamental pitches, add a note to each of the following triads to create a seventh chord.

	96 The term seventh chord denotes both the numeric size of the interval between the root and fourth tone of the chord and the name of that fourth chord member. The uppermost note of a seventh chord is a _____ above the root.　　　　　*(interval)*
seventh	
	97 The names of the members of a seventh chord, from lowest to highest, are _____ , _____ , _____ , and _____ .
root, third, fifth, (and) seventh	
	98 The root of this seventh chord is _____ ; the seventh is _____ .
G　　F	
	99 G is the _____ of this chord; D is the _____ .
third　　　seventh	
	100 C is the _____ of this chord; E is the _____ .
fifth　　　seventh	

101

Triad qualities are identified by the quality of the intervals formed by the root and each of the upper tones. Since seventh chords consist of a triad plus a fourth note, their qualities are indicated by the quality of the *triad* they contain plus the interval quality from the root to the *seventh*.

The lower three tones of this seventh chord form a _____ triad. (Don't overlook the key signature.) The seventh is a _____ seventh
(quality)
above the root.

major

minor

102

A major triad and a minor seventh combine to form a **major-minor seventh chord.**

Place a check below each major-minor seventh chord in the following group.

103

Notate major-minor seventh chords on each of these roots. Be certain to include appropriate accidentals.

104

Although several additional triad and seventh chord qualities occur in tonal music the three you have studied thus far are the most prevalent and, therefore, considered the *basic* chord types.

The three basic chord types (as represented by this study) are _____ and _____ triads and _____ seventh chords.

major (and) minor (triads)

major-minor (seventh chords)

Fm   C⁷   D⁷   A♭   G⁷

105

You have learned to identify triads by their root and quality. Because the major-minor seventh chord is much more prevalent than other seventh chord types, it is most often named simply by its root plus the words "seventh chord." A major-minor seventh chord with E as its root is called an E seventh chord, abbreviated E⁷.

Place the proper abbreviation symbol below each of the following chords.

_____   _____   _____   _____   _____

A⁷   Am   C   E⁷   F⁷

106

Continue as in Frame 105.

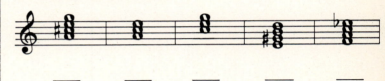

_____   _____   _____   _____   _____

E♭⁷   F♯m   A⁷   D⁷   B♭⁷

107

Notate the chords identified below.

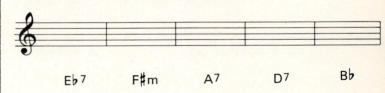

E♭⁷   F♯m   A⁷   D⁷   B♭

F⁷   C⁷   G⁷   A♭   E⁷

108

Continue as in the preceding frame.

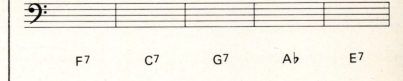

F⁷   C⁷   G⁷   A♭   E⁷

DEVELOPING PERFORMANCE SKILLS

Piano and singing exercises emphasizing the major-minor seventh chord begin on page 295. Listening exercises involving major and minor triads and major-minor seventh chords begin on page 295. Autoharp exercises introducing the major-minor seventh chord begin on page 295. An introduction to basic chord vocabulary on the guitar begins on page 297.

109

In musical study, triads are identified by Roman numerals corresponding to the scale degrees on which they are built. The primary triad on the first scale degree (tonic) is identified by a I (upper-case) if major or by a i (lower-case) if minor.

Place an I or i, as appropriate, below each of the following tonic triads. Be sure to identify quality properly.

110

The key of an example or composition is always identified prior to the first Roman numeral, upper-case for major, lower-case for minor, as in the following examples. Notice that this letter is followed by a colon.

(No response necessary.)

111

Identify the *tonic* triad with the appropriate Roman numeral in each of the following examples. Notice that the key has already been identified.

112

Continue as in Frame 111.

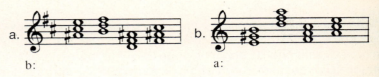

a.

b:

b.

a:

113

Continue as in the preceding frame.

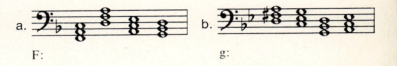

a.

F:

b.

g:

114

Continue as in the preceding frame.

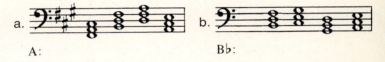

a.

A:

b.

B♭:

a.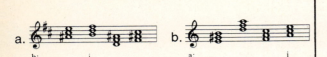

b: i

b.

a: i

a.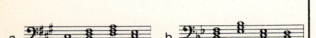

F: I

b.

g: i

a.

A: I

b.

B♭:   I

C: I   I   I   I   I

115

Identify the key of the following example and place the appropriate Roman numeral below each tonic triad.

Twinkle, Twinkle Little Star

France

a: i   i   i

i   i   i

116

Continue as in Frame 115.

Go Down Moses   Spiritual

117

Continue as in the preceding frame.

Old Dan Tucker   Dan Emmett

G: I

G   C   G   D   G

I   I   I   I

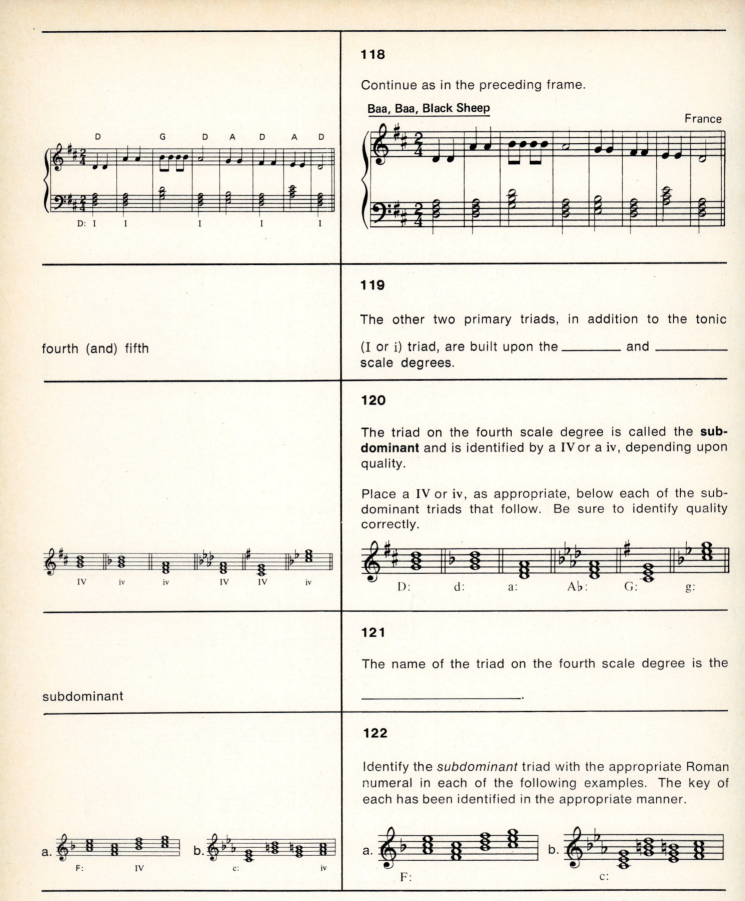

118

Continue as in the preceding frame.

Baa, Baa, Black Sheep

France

119

fourth (and) fifth

The other two primary triads, in addition to the tonic (I or i) triad, are built upon the _____ and _____ scale degrees.

120

The triad on the fourth scale degree is called the **sub-dominant** and is identified by a IV or a iv, depending upon quality.

Place a IV or iv, as appropriate, below each of the sub-dominant triads that follow. Be sure to identify quality correctly.

D: d: a: A♭:   G: g:

121

subdominant

The name of the triad on the fourth scale degree is the

_____.

122

Identify the *subdominant* triad with the appropriate Roman numeral in each of the following examples. The key of each has been identified in the appropriate manner.

a.   F: IV   b.   c: iv

a.   F: b.   c:

a.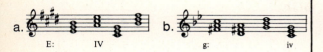

E: IV

b.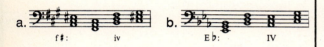

g: iv

123

Continue as in Frame 122.

a.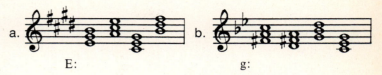

E:

b.

g:

a.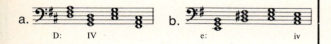

f♯:   iv

b.

E♭:   IV

124

Continue as in the preceding frame.

a.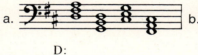

f♯:

b.

E♭:

a.

D: IV

b.

e: iv

125

Continue as in the preceding frame.

a.

D:

b.

e:

a.

C: I   IV   I   IV   I   I   IV   I

126

Identify the key of the following example and place the appropriate Roman numerals below all *tonic* and *subdominant* triads.

Jack and Jill

J. W. Elliott

127

Continue as in Frame 126.

On Top of Old Smoky   U. S.

128

Continue as in the preceding frame.

Loch Lomond   Scotland

129

Continue as in the preceding frame.

The Derby Ram   England

130

The term **dominant** refers to the triad on the fifth scale degree. Since the harmonic minor scale is employed in most minor-key situations, the dominant triad is almost invariably major in quality and is identified as V.

The triad on the fifth scale degree is termed the_____ _____ triad.

dominant

131

The dominant triad is almost invariably identified by the Roman numeral _____.

V

132

In each of the following examples place the appropriate Roman numeral below the *dominant* triad.

133

Continue as in Frame 132.

134

Continue as in the preceding frame.

g: V   G: V

135

Continue as in the preceding frame.

g: G:

136

Identify the key of the following example and place the appropriate Roman numerals below all *tonic*, *subdominant*, and *dominant* triads.

A: I   IV   I   I   V   I

Old MacDonald Had a Farm

U. S.

137

Continue as in Frame 136.

Dame Get Up

England

g: i   V   i   V

i   V   i   V   i

G: I   IV   V   I

138

Continue as in the preceding frame.

Old Dan Tucker

Dan Emmett

139

Continue as in the preceding frame.

Twinkle, Twinkle Little Star

France

C: I   I   IV   I   IV   I   V   I

140

Notate the primary triads indicated by the Roman numerals in each of the following exercises.

a.   g: i   b.   D: V   c.   F: IV

a.  b. c.

g: i   D: V   F: IV

141

Continue as in Frame 140.

a.  b. c.

B♭: IV   c: i   G: V

142

Continue as in the preceding frame.

a. C: V   b. F: V   c. E: IV

143

Continue as in the preceding frame.

a. a: V   b. e: i   c. A: V

144

Add primary triads as indicated by the Roman numerals to harmonize the following melody. Notate each chord in the proper note values according to the time signature.

A-Hunting We Will Go

England

F: I   I   V   V

I   IV   I   V   I

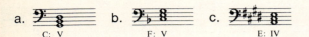

a. C: V   b. F: V   c. E: IV

a. a: V   b. e: i   c. A: V

F: I   I   V   V

I   IV   I   V   I

145

Continue as in Frame 144.

Sourwood Mountain

Appalachia

Eb: I   IV   I   I   V   I

I   IV   I   I   V   I

146

Continue as in the preceding frame.

Going to Boston

U. S.

C: I   IV   V   I   I   IV   V   I

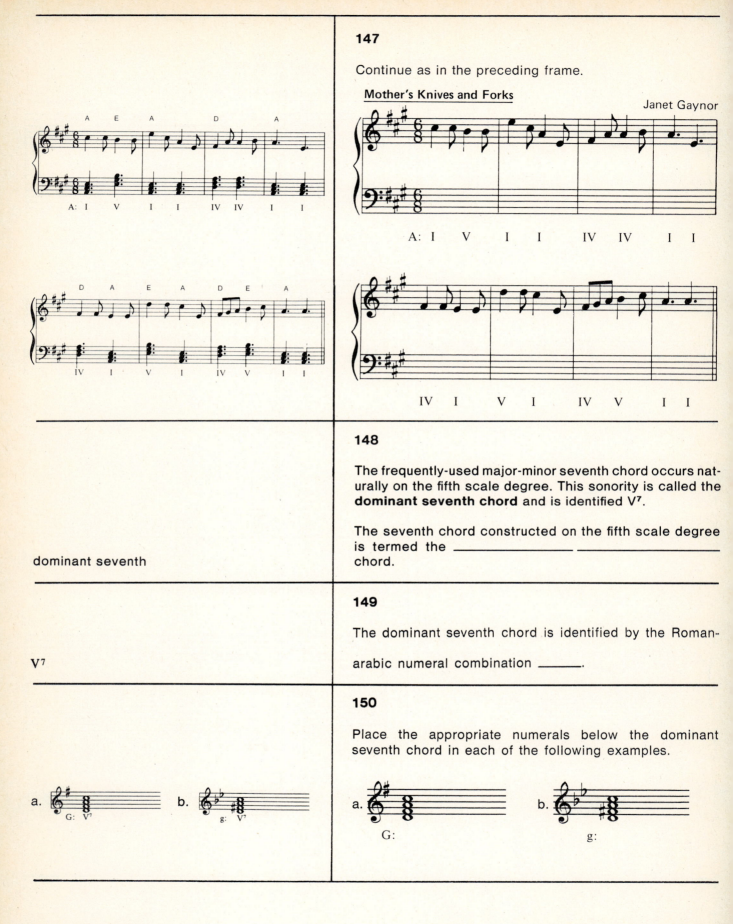

147

Continue as in the preceding frame.

Mother's Knives and Forks

Janet Gaynor

A: I   V   I   I   IV   IV   I   I

IV   I   V   I   IV   V   I   I

dominant seventh

148

The frequently-used major-minor seventh chord occurs naturally on the fifth scale degree. This sonority is called the **dominant seventh chord** and is identified V⁷.

The seventh chord constructed on the fifth scale degree is termed the _____ _____ chord.

V⁷

149

The dominant seventh chord is identified by the Roman-arabic numeral combination _____.

150

Place the appropriate numerals below the dominant seventh chord in each of the following examples.

a.   G: V⁷   b.   g: V⁷

a.   G: b.   g:

151

Identify the dominant seventh chord in each of the following examples by placing the appropriate numerals below it.

D: V⁷   F: V⁷

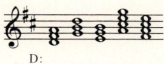

D:

F:

152

Continue as in Frame 151.

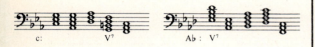

c: V⁷   Ab: V⁷

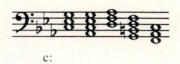

c:

Ab:

153

Continue as in the preceding frame.

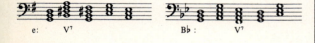

e: V⁷   Bb: V⁷

e:

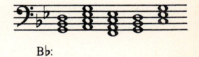

Bb:

154

Identify the key of the following example and place the appropriate numerals below each chord.

G: I   I   IV   I   I   V⁷   I

Bingo   Scotland

155

Continue as in Frame 154.

Early One Morning

England

156

Continue as in the preceding frame.

Erie Canal

U. S.

157

Continue as in the preceding frame.

Bow Belinda

U. S.

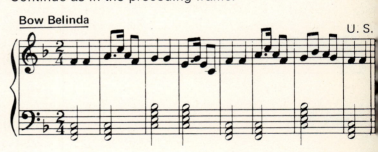

158

Notate the dominant seventh chords indicated in each of the following examples. Add the appropriate key signature.

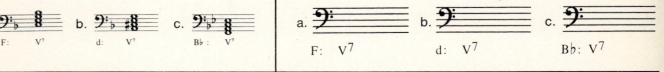

a. F: V⁷ b. d: V⁷ c. B♭: V⁷   a. F: V⁷   b. d: V⁷   c. B♭: V⁷

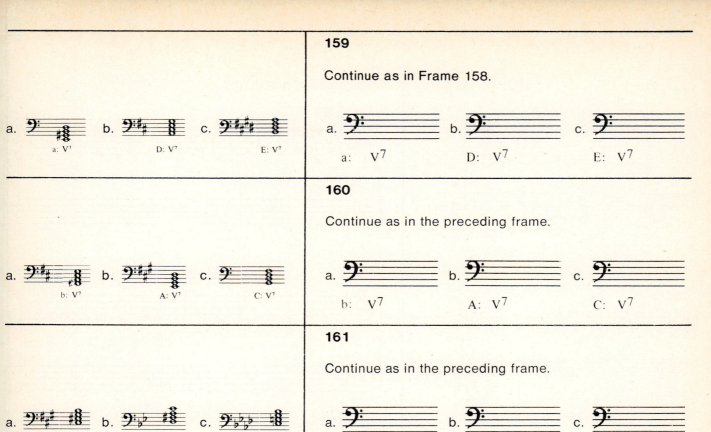

159

Continue as in Frame 158.

a.   a: V⁷   b.   D: V⁷   c.   E: V⁷

160

Continue as in the preceding frame.

a.   b: V⁷   b.   A: V⁷   c.   C: V⁷

161

Continue as in the preceding frame.

a.   f♯: V⁷   b.   g: V⁷   c.   f: V⁷

DEVELOPING PERFORMANCE SKILLS

Exercises in harmonizing melodies with basic chords at the piano begin on page 306. Exercises beginning on page 308 introduce additional accompanying techniques on the autoharp. Guitar exercises beginning on page 309 introduce new chord fingerings and strumming techniques for accompanying melodies.

162

Add triads and dominant seventh chords as indicated to harmonize the following melody. Notate each chord in the proper note values according to the time signature.

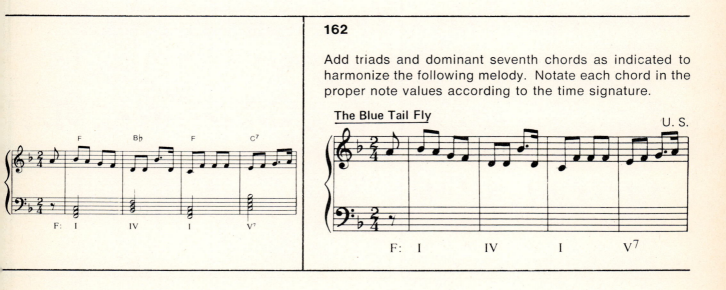

The Blue Tail Fly   U. S.

F: I   IV   I   V⁷

163

Continue as in Frame 162.

Aura Lee   U. S.

F: I   IV   V⁷   I

I   IV   V⁷   I

164

Continue as in the preceding frame.

Erie Canal   U.S.

d: i   i   V⁷   i   i   i   V⁷ i

i   i   iv   V⁷   i   i   i   V⁷ i

165

Continue as in the preceding frame.

Little Boy Blue

Mother Goose Rhyme

CHECK YOUR UNDERSTANDING

1. A triad consists of _____ notes placed on _____ lines or spaces of the staff.

2. The names of the three members of a triad, from lowest to highest, are

   _____, _____, and _____.

3. The tonic triad of a major key is always a _____ triad.
   (quality)

4. In the key of D major the primary triads are constructed upon the

   notes _____, _____, and _____.

5. In the key of F minor the roots of the primary triads are _____, _____,

   and _____.

6. The primary triads in minor keys utilize the notes of the _____ form of the minor scale.

7. Notate major triads above each of the following pitches.

8. Notate minor triads above each of the following pitches.

9. Notate the primary triads in each of the keys indicated below.

10. A fourth note is placed a third above the fifth of a triad to form a

    _____ chord.

11. The seventh chord constructed on the fifth scale degree is termed the

    _____ _____ chord.

12. Notate the dominant seventh chord in each of the following keys.

(Answers may be found on page 364.)

APPLY YOUR UNDERSTANDING

Identify the key of the following examples and place the appropriate numeral below each chord.

Mother's Knives and Forks

Janet Gaynor

Go Down Moses

Spiritual

(Answers may be found on page 365.)

Add triads and dominant seventh chords as indicated to harmonize the following melody. Notate each chord in the proper note values according to the time signature.

The Blue Tail Fly

U.S.

F: I   IV   I   V⁷   I

IV   V⁷   I   I   V⁷

V⁷   I   I   IV   V⁷   I

(Answers may be found on page 366)

DEVELOPING PERFORMANCE SKILLS

Performing triads on various instruments and vocally will help you become more familiar with their construction and sound and begin developing your skill in creating harmonic accompaniments on various instruments. These exercises are designed to develop varying levels of proficiency. You and your instructor may choose the extent to which mastery of these skills is required.

Piano, Singing (Frames 28–51)

Play each of these major triads on the piano and sing the structure as illustrated for exercise 1. Maintain a slow, steady tempo.

Exercise 1

Sing: 1 3 5 3 1   C E G E C   C major
(Sing the chord name on the pitch of the
root as you play the complete chord.)

Exercise 2

Continue as above. Play these major triads with your left hand.

Exercise 3

Play and sing these minor triads as in the preceding exercises.

Exercise 4

Continue as above. Play these minor triads with your left hand.

Listening (Frames 28–51)

Play random major and minor triads in both arpeggiated (broken) and harmonic (simultaneous) contexts for a partner. Your partner's task is to identify the quality of each triad. (Reinforcing the sound of each triad by singing it in the arpeggio 1–3–5–3–1 may help in identifying the quality.)

Autoharp (Frames 52–70)

The autoharp is versatile and easy to play. Since it is portable, it is often a practical substitute for the piano as an accompaniment instrument. It is played by pressing down a bar for each chord desired with the left hand and reaching across with the right hand to strum the strings with a pick or the thumb. The autoharp is usually placed on the player's lap or a desk or tabletop. Some performers prefer to hold it upright.

The two most commonly used autoharps have either 12 or 15 chord bars. A chord symbol appears on each bar as shown in these illustrations.

AUTOHARP CHART

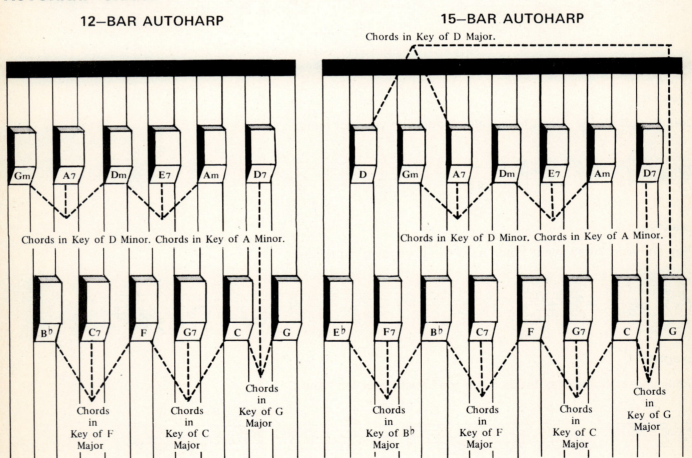

Locate the C chord bar. Press it down firmly with the left hand index finger. Cross your right hand over your left and strum across the strings from low to high (away from you). Using an autoharp pick or your thumb, try to strum quickly and evenly as demonstrated by your instructor.

Effective accompanying with the autoharp will require strumming in an appropriate rhythm. Play the following exercises using the C chord.

Strum each chord evenly at the same tempo, timing each motion of your right hand to coincide with the rhythm notated.

Exercise 1

You may emphasize the waltz flavor of $\frac{3}{4}$ meter by strumming louder on the first beat of each measure.

Exercise 2

Changing chords requires careful hand coordination. Try these exercises alternating the C and F chords. Strum the rhythm notated for each exercise in a steady tempo. Depress the appropriate chord bar a split second before the first strum of each chord change.

Exercise 3

Continue as in the above exercises using the C and G chords.

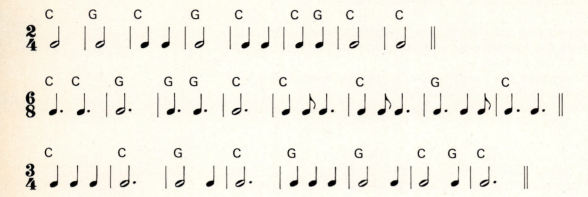

Exercise 4

Continue as above using the C, F, and G chords.

Exercise 5

Experiment further with these three chords by creating your own chord sequences and strumming rhythms.

Exercise 6

Try accompanying these familiar melodies by ear using the C, F, and G chords. Ask a partner to sing or play the melody if you wish. Start on the pitch indicated. Begin each accompaniment with the C chord.

Title	Melody begins on	Chords used
The Yellow Rose of Texas	G	I, V
Kookaburra	G	I, IV
Twinkle, Twinkle Little Star	C	I, IV, V
Bingo	G	I, IV, V
Battle Hymn of the Republic	G	I, IV, V

Piano, Singing (Frames 71–108)

Play each of these major-minor seventh chords on the piano and sing the structure as illustrated for exercise 1. Maintain a slow, steady tempo.

1. Play:

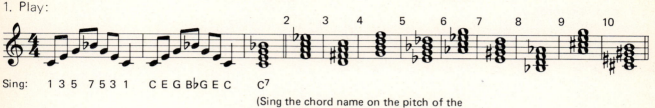

Sing: 1 3 5 7 5 3 1   C E G B♭ G E C   C⁷

(Sing the chord name on the pitch of the root as you play the complete chord.)

Continue as above. Play these major-minor seventh chords with your left hand.

Sound the root of each of the following chords on the piano in your own vocal range. Then sing each chord with note names in ascending order. Play each complete chord immediately on the piano to check your accuracy. Re-sing any missed chords correctly, with the piano if necessary. You may wish to do these exercises with a partner as an added check on your accuracy.

F Gm D⁷ G⁷ E A⁷ Dm C⁷ A♭⁷ D♭

E♭⁷ Bm F⁷ B♭⁷ E♭ Fm C⁷ E⁷ Am D⁷

Working alone or with a partner you may create additional drills of this type by selecting triad and seventh chord roots and qualities at random.

Listening (Frames 71–108)

Play random examples of the three basic chord types (major and minor triads, major-minor seventh chords) in both arpeggiated and harmonic contexts for a partner to identify by ear.

Autoharp (Frames 52–108)

Use of the major-minor seventh chord adds harmonic flavor to musical settings and facilitates the use of some instruments in playing accompaniments. These exercises illustrate that advantage on the autoharp.

Exercise 1

Place your index, middle, and ring fingers respectively on the C, G⁷, and F chord bars to play the following rhythmic patterns. (Notice that the left hand fingering is somewhat more simple than in previous autoharp exercises using the C, F, and G chords.)

Exercise 2

The use of seventh chords is absolutely necessary in playing minor key accompaniments on the autoharp. For instance an E chord would serve in place of E⁷ in two of these exercises but it is not available on the autoharp.

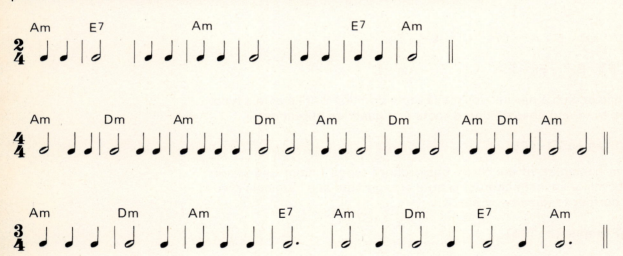

Exercise 3

The following rhythmic patterns provide an introduction to playing the three basic chord types in other major and minor keys. Find the chord bars required for each exercise first and try the required changes a few times before beginning each chord pattern.

Guitar (Frames 52–108)

The guitar is one of the most popular instruments in use today and is very appealing for the performance of harmonic components of music. (In the hands of a skilled player the guitar can perform melody as well as harmony.) Its gentle timbre is ideal in accompanying singing or the recorder and its design offers several advantages over the autoharp in choice of chord voicings and contrapuntal possibilities. These advantages, however, exact a price in terms of greater demand upon the player's physical technique. The exercises that follow explore some rudimentary possibilities in playing chords on the guitar. The development of broad technical fluency on the instrument will be a matter of individual inclination, practice time, and instructional guidance beyond the scope of this text.

The six strings of the guitar are named according to the pitch to which each is tuned as shown in the following view of the instrument as you face the fingerboard.

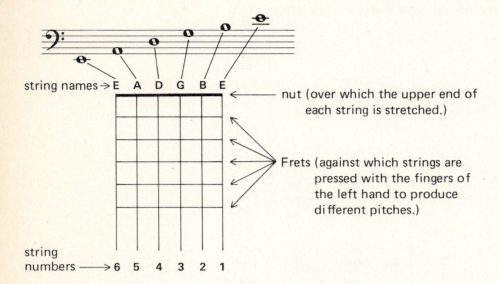

string names → E A D G B E

nut (over which the upper end of each string is stretched.)

Frets (against which strings are pressed with the fingers of the left hand to produce different pitches.)

string numbers ——→ 6 5 4 3 2 1

You may tune the guitar to a piano by plucking each string and turning the appropriate tuning peg *gently* until each corresponding pitch on the piano is matched. It is important to remember that the above diagram shows the *actual* pitch to which each string is tuned. Guitar music is traditionally notated in the *treble clef,* one octave higher than the actual sounding pitch. Guitar exercises in this text are presented only in terms of chord symbols so guitar notation on the staff will not be an issue.

Guitar pitch pipes available in most music stores can also be used for tuning. Each pitch will sound *one octave higher* than the corresponding string.

The guitar is most easily held resting on the right knee with the back of the instrument flat against your body as in illustration 1. The thumb of the left hand is placed *behind* the neck of the instrument and the fingers arch around the high E-string side of the fingerboard back toward your body. The right arm hangs comfortably over the lower body of the guitar at the elbow, with the hand in strumming position over the tone hole. Ask your teacher for guidance as needed.

An alternate tuning method may serve as your first attempt at using the left hand technique of the guitar. First tune the low E string with a piano or pitch pipe. Then, with your left hand in proper position (thumb behind guitar neck), press the E string firmly against the fingerboard with your left index finger between the fourth and fifth frets where Ⓐ appears in the following diagram. *Note that the finger is placed as close to the fifth fret as possible without touching it.* Pluck the E string with your right thumb or a pick held in your right hand. The pitch A will sound. Tune the A string to that pitch. Move your

Courtesy of Jerry Rouse, Chairman, Music Department, El Toro High School, Mission Viejo, California.

Folk style guitar playing position

index finger up the strings in this manner as shown in the diagram, tuning each in turn. *Note the altered finger location on the G string to produce the correct pitch for the B string.*

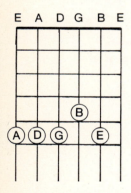

This action of the left hand fingers immediately behind the appropriate fret is referred to as "stopping" a string. This shortening of the vibrating length of each string raises its pitch one half-step at each fret. An "unstopped" string is referred to as "open." Guitar chords will be presented in reference to their root-name-and-quality symbol and left hand fingering diagrams similar to those used to explain tuning. The fingers of the left hand are numbered as follows:

index—1   middle—2   ring—3   little finger—4

Note that these numbers differ from piano fingerings. The left thumb always remains behind the neck of the guitar.

Numbers within circles in the fingering diagrams correspond to finger placement on the fingerboard. *Remember to press firmly.* An X above any string means it is *not* strummed by the right hand to produce a given chord. All other open strings *are* strummed.

These exercises involve playing individual triads in various rhythms.

Exercise 1

D major

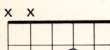

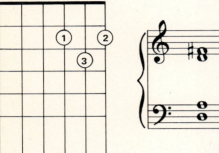

notes sounding

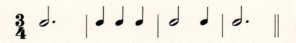

Strum the four upper strings in these rhythms at a moderate tempo.

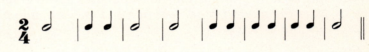

Exercise 2

A major

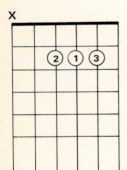

sound

Rhythms (5 upper strings)

(Placing the first finger *slightly* "behind" 2 and 3 ② ① ③ will facilitate this fingering.)

Exercise 3

G major

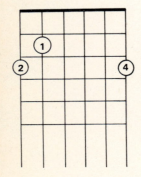

sound

Rhythms (all 6 strings)

Exercise 4

Shifting from one chord to another on the guitar is a more complex matter physically and mentally. Consider the shift from the D chord to the A chord by comparing the two fingerings.

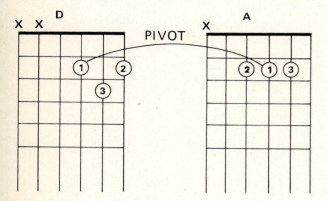

Even though the first (index) finger remains stationary, forming a pivot point, while the second and third fingers move, the shape of the left hand must change and the fingering of the A chord is "crowded" as you have already discovered in Exercise 2. The right hand must also switch from strumming four strings to five.

Here again the use of a seventh chord can simplify matters. Consider and try the shift from D to A⁷ as shown here.

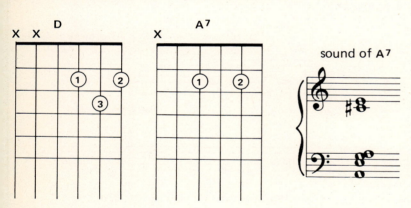

Although no pivot point exists and all fingers involved must move, the left hand retains essentially the same shape and one less stopped note is required. The right hand must still change its initial contact point from the fourth to the fifth string and back.

Try this shift a few times without regard for rhythm, then practice these rhythmic patterns.

Challenge

Exercise 5

Here is a familiar melody you can accompany using the D and A⁷ chords. Strum in even quarter notes throughout. Ask a partner to sing or play the recorder (using the recorder version) with you if you wish.

Down In the Valley (recorder version)

Kentucky

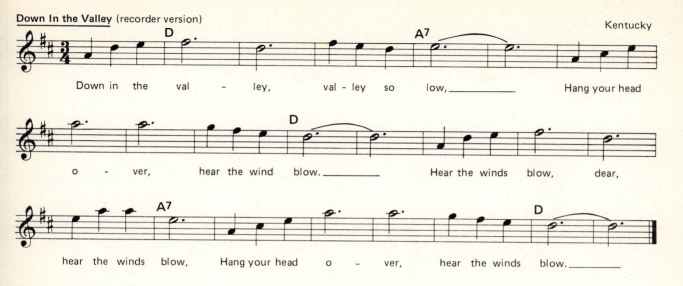

Down in the val - ley, val - ley so low,_____ Hang your head o - ver, hear the wind blow._____ Hear the winds blow, dear, hear the winds blow, Hang your head o - ver, hear the winds blow._____

This melody requires three chords for its accompaniment. Review the fingering for the G chord and practice that shift before attempting the complete accompaniment. Strum in quarter notes. Remember to strum all six strings on the G chord.

Camptown Races

Stephen C. Foster

The Camp-town la - dies sing this song, do - da, do - da! The Camp-town race track five miles long, Oh, do - da - day. Oh, see those hor - ses round the bend, do - da, do - da! Guess that race will nev - er end,

Chorus

Oh, do - da - day. Going to run all night, going to run all day, I'll bet my mon - ey on the bob - tail nag, Some-bod - y bet on the bay.

The same principles apply to playing basic chords in minor keys on the guitar. Locate these fingerings in the key of A minor and practice the rhythmic patterns for each chord.

Exercise 6

Exercise 7

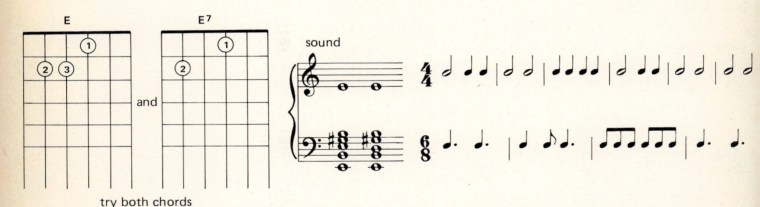

try both chords

Exercise 8

In this key the shifts are actually easier than in D major. The Am and E chords share the exact same hand position one string away from each other (making the use of E⁷ less essential but still harmonically interesting and slightly simpler). The Dm chord is more complex but essentially the same hand configuration. Using the alternate fourth finger on Dm may simplify matters physically, if not mentally. Each of these chords also involves strumming a different number of strings.

Exercise 9

Practice each shift without rhythm first, then practice these rhythmic patterns.

Challenge

Here are two melodies you can accompany in the key of A minor. For variety ask a partner to sing them while you accompany strumming in quarter notes.

Tum Balalaika   Russia

1. On the Don when once I was young, This, the song I once used to strum. Sing-ing of love and what it might bring. This was the song I once used to sing: "Tum ba-la, tum ba-la, tum ba-la lai-ka, Tum ba-la, tum ba-la, tum ba-la lai-ka, Tum ba-la-lai-ka, tum ba-la-lai-ka Tum ba-la-lai-ka, tum ba-la-lai."

2. Love is sky, but it can be bold,
   Love has moods which are thousand-fold.
   Love has so many beautiful shapes,
   You think you've caught it, then it escapes.
   Chorus

What a Court Hath Old England

England

What a court hath Old Eng - land of fol - ly and sin, spite of Chat - ham and Cam - den, Bar - re,

Burke, Wilkes and Glynn! Not con - tent with the game act they taxed fish and sea, and A -

mer - i - ca drench with hot wa - ter and tea. Der - ry down, down, _____ der - ry down. _____

Piano (Frames 109–161)

The piano is an excellent practical tool for working with the harmonic materials of music. It provides both aural and visual reinforcement of basic chord structures and quick access to relationships between melody and harmony.

Exercise 1

It will be helpful at the outset to develop some visual and physical familiarity with basic chord relationships at the piano. Cover the answer column of these exercises and play the chord sequences in the keys indicated with your *left hand*. **NOTE: These answers appear on the right so that you can cover them with your right hand.** Use the chord symbol equivalents in the answer column to check your accuracy. Consult a classmate or your instructor for additional assistance if necessary.

DRILL

1. C: I V I V IV V I

2. F: I IV I IV I V I

3. G: I V IV I IV V I

4. a: i iv i V i iv V

5. d: i V i iv i V i

6. e: i iv i V⁷ i iv V⁷

7. D: I IV I IV I V⁷ I

8. B♭: I V⁷ I IV V⁷ I V⁷

9. g: i iv i V⁷ i iv i

10. c: i V⁷ i iv V⁷ i V⁷

ANSWERS

	C	G	C	G	F	G	C
C:	I	V	I	V	IV	V	I

	F	B♭	F	B♭	F	C	F
F:	I	IV	I	IV	I	V	I

	G	D	C	G	C	D	G
G:	I	V	IV	I	IV	V	I

	a	d	a	E	a	d	E
a:	i	iv	i	V	i	iv	V

	d	A	d	g	d	A	d
d:	i	V	i	iv	i	V	i

	e	a	e	B	e	a	B
e:	i	iv	i	V⁷	i	iv	V⁷

	D	G	D	G	D	A	D
D:	I	IV	I	IV	I	V⁷	I

	B♭	F	B♭	E♭	F	B♭	F
B♭:	I	V⁷	I	IV	V⁷	I	V⁷

	g	c	g	D	g	c	g
g:	i	iv	i	V⁷	i	iv	i

	c	G	c	f	G	c	G
c:	i	V⁷	i	iv	V⁷	i	V⁷

Challenge

11. E♭: I IV I IV I V⁷ I

12. A: I V⁷ I V⁷ IV V⁷ I

13. f: i iv i V⁷ i V⁷ i

14. A♭: I IV I V⁷ I IV V⁷

15. b: i iv i iv V⁷ i V⁷

	E♭	A♭	E♭	A♭	E♭	B♭	E♭
E♭:	I	IV	I	IV	I	V⁷	I

	A	E	A	E	D	E	A
A:	I	V⁷	I	V⁷	IV	V⁷	I

	f	b♭	f	C	f	C	f
f:	i	iv	i	V⁷	i	V⁷	i

	A♭	D♭	A♭	E♭	A♭	D♭	E♭
A♭:	I	IV	I	V⁷	I	IV	V⁷

	b	e	b	e	F♯	b	F♯
b:	i	iv	i	iv	V⁷	i	V⁷

For further practice you may repeat these chord sequences in different keys.

Exercise 2

Playing a melody and its harmonic accompaniment simultaneously with both hands places greater demands on physical and mental coordination. The following exercises are based on the answer frames of drill exercises you have already completed. Refer to the page and frame numbers cited. Be aware of the Roman numeral analysis and equivalent chord symbols appearing in each frame. Repeat exercises as necessary to achieve a fluent performance at a tempo appropriate for each of these familiar melodies.

1. Pages 275-76, frames 126-129

2. Pages 278-79, frames 136-139

3. Pages 280-82, frames 144-147

4. Pages 283-84, frames 154-157

Autoharp (Frames 109–161)

Since the autoharp is oriented to chord-root-quality symbols rather than Roman numerals its use in playing harmonic accompaniments will provide additional experience in translating Roman numerals to specific chord equivalents in various keys.

Exercise 1

Cover the answers in the *right-hand* column of these exercises. Play the chord sequences indicated in Roman numerals in the left hand column. Reveal the appropriate answer to check your accuracy.

DRILL

1. C: I V⁷ I IV I V⁷ I
2. F: I V⁷ I V⁷ I IV I
3. B: I IV I IV V⁷ I V⁷
4. d: i V⁷ i iv V⁷ i V⁷
5. a: i iv V⁷ i iv V⁷ i
6. D: I V⁷ I V IV V⁷ I
7. G: I IV V⁷ I IV A V⁷

ANSWERS

1. C: C I   G V⁷   C I   F IV   C I   G V⁷   C I
2. F: F I   C V⁷   F I   C V⁷   F I   Bb IV   F I
3. B: Bb I   Eb IV   Bb I   Eb IV   F V⁷   B I   F V
4. d: d i   A V⁷   d i   g iv   A V⁷   d i   A V⁷
5. a: a i   d iv   E V⁷   a i   d iv   E V⁷   a i
6. D: D I   A V⁷   D I   A V⁷   G IV   A V⁷   D I
7. G: G I   C IV   D V⁷   G I   C IV   G I   D V⁷

Exercise 2

Play the accompaniment while singing the melody from the answer frames cited below. Be cognizant of the Roman numeral relationships as well as the chord symbols shown. Repeat exercises as necessary to achieve fluency at an appropriate tempo.

1. Page 275, frame 126   strum the accompaniment rhythm shown

2. Page 276, frame 127   strum the chord shown in each measure

3. Page 276, frame 128   strum the accompaniment rhythm shown

4. Page 276, frame 129   strum the appropriate chord on each ♩.

These exercises contain ideas for more interesting rhythmic patterns in the accompaniment.

5. Page 279, frame 138   Strum the lowest octave on the first beat of each measure and the remaining upper strings on the second beat of each measure. Substitute D⁷ for D.

6. Page 279, frame 139   Strum as in exercise 5. Use G⁷ for G if you wish.

7. Page 280, frame 144   Strum in ♩ ; alternate low/high registers as previously. Substitute C⁷ for C if you wish.

8. Page 281, frame 146   Strum in ♩ as previously. Use G⁷ if you wish.

9. Page 283, frame 154   Strum all strings in ♩ ; accent beat 1 of each measure.

10. Page 284, frame 156   Strum the rhythm shown placing each chord in the lowest octave of the autoharp. The slower tempo of this song suggests strumming each chord rather slowly. For contrast strum all strings on the fourth and last chords.

11. Page 284, frame 157   Strum in ♩. The alternating design of this melody suggests strumming the lower strings for measure 1, the upper strings for measure 2, etc. in measures 3–6. Then alternate low and high registers in measures 7 and 8.

12. Strumming the lowest octave on beat 1, the middle strings on beat 2 and the upper strings on beat 3 is a good accompaniment figure in $\frac{3}{4}$ meter. Try that pattern with this melody.

Flow Gently, Sweet Afton

Guitar (Frames 109–161)

Guitar fingerings are also oriented to chord symbols rather than Roman numerals. The guitar fingering chart beginning on page 417 of this text is organized around the I, IV, V, and V⁷ chords in several major and minor keys.

Exercise 1

You have already learned to play sequences applying these chords in the keys of D major and A minor. Review those chord structures by completing the following exercises.

Write the chord symbols for these harmonic relationships in the space provided. (Answers at bottom of page.)

D: $\overline{\text{I}}$ $\overline{\text{IV}}$ $\overline{\text{V}}$ $\overline{\text{V}^7}$ a: $\overline{\text{i}}$ $\overline{\text{iv}}$ $\overline{\text{V}}$ $\overline{\text{V}^7}$

Play these harmonic progressions in the rhythms indicated in a steady, moderate tempo.

1. $\frac{4}{4}$

D: I   V⁷   I   V⁷   I

2. $\frac{4}{4}$

D: I   IV   I   V⁷   I   IV   I V I

		D	G	A	A⁷		a	d	E	E⁷
Answers:	D:	I	IV	V	A⁷		a:	i	iv	V	V⁷

3. $\frac{3}{4}$

D: I   V⁷   IV   I   V⁷   I IV V⁷ I

4. $\frac{2}{4}$

a: i   V⁷   i   V⁷   i   V⁷   i V⁷   i

5. $\frac{3}{4}$

a: i   iv   i   V⁷ i   i   iv   i   iv   i   iv V⁷ i

6. $\frac{6}{8}$

a: i   V⁷   i   iv   i   iv i   V⁷   i   iv V⁷ i

Exercise 2

Expanding your guitar fluency to other keys involves learning some new chords. Practice the fingering changes required in each key first without regard to rhythm until they become familiar physically. Then play each rhythmic pattern several times to achieve a fluent performance at a moderate tempo.

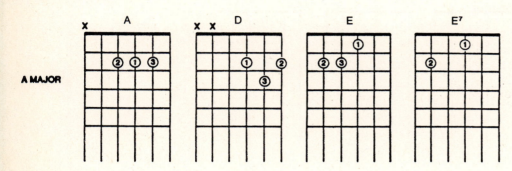

Notice that the "pivot" function of the first finger can be retained simply by sliding back and forth from the first to second fret in moving to and from the V or V⁷ chord. Use the V and V⁷ chords interchangeably as your left hand agility suggests.

Rhythmic figuration also adds interest to guitar accompaniments. In this exercise play the root of each chord on beats 1 and 3 and the remaining strings on beats 2 and 4.

An appropriate rhythmic accompaniment in $\frac{3}{4}$ meter sounds the chord root on beat 1 and the remaining strings on 2 and 3.

*Strum the entire chord on this beat.

Challenge

Create your own chord sequences and accompaniment rhythms in A major.

E minor

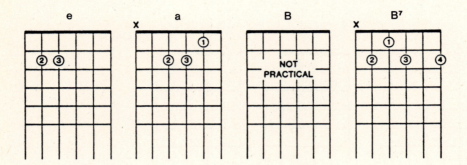

i to iv in this key is reasonably comfortable. The dominant harmonic function is another matter. The optional placement of the first finger shown for e minor may facilitate the shift to B⁷ (it will not alter the sound of i) but may impede the i to iv shift.

5. In $\frac{2}{4}$: i, iv, i, V7, i

6. In $\frac{6}{8}$: i, V7, i, iv, V7, i

Use the root-chord pattern of exercise 3 for this accompaniment figure in e minor.

7. In $\frac{4}{4}$: i, iv, i, V7, i, V7, i, iv, i, V7, i*

*root for beats 1 and 2; chord on 3 and 4

Use the root-chord-chord strum of exercise 4 for this $\frac{3}{4}$ accompaniment pattern.

8. In $\frac{3}{4}$: i, iv, V7, i, V7, i, V7, i*

*root on 1; chord on 2

Challenge

Invent additional chord sequences and rhythmic accompaniment patterns in e minor.

SUPPLEMENTARY ACTIVITIES

1. Practice playing I, IV, V, and V^7 chords in major and minor keys on the piano, autoharp and guitar.

2. Write out the harmonizations given in several songs in the Song Supplement.

3. Build chords with individual tone bells.

4. Try to sing the melody while playing the chords of the following pieces found in the Song Supplement. Try to create a short introduction for each of these pieces.
   Piano: Michael Finegan, page 377
         The Old Brass Wagon, page 380

   Autoharp: Bingo, page 377
         Skip to My Lou, page 382

   Guitar: Kum Ba Ya, page 394
         Michael, Row the Boat Ashore, page 379

Chord Inversion

10

1

The relationship among the notes of a chord produces its harmonic identity. Even when the notes of a chord are sounded with a member other than the root as the lowest pitch, this harmonic identity is retained.

harmonic identity

Sounding a chord with a tone other than its root as the

lowest pitch does not alter its _____ .

2

The G major triad may serve as an example of this phenomenon. Each of the following chords contains the notes g, b, and d.

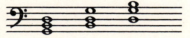

Yes.

Does each of the above examples possess the harmonic

identity of a G major triad? _____

3

Frame 2 demonstrates the principle of **triad inversion**. Moving the root of a root position triad up one octave inverts the triad. The following illustration applies this procedure to the F major triad.

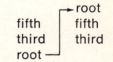

Apply this procedure to the following root position triads.

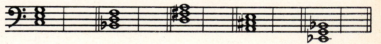

4

The procedure you applied in Frame 3 produced the **first inversion** of each triad. The lowest chord member of a

third

first inversion triad is the (root, third, fifth) _____.

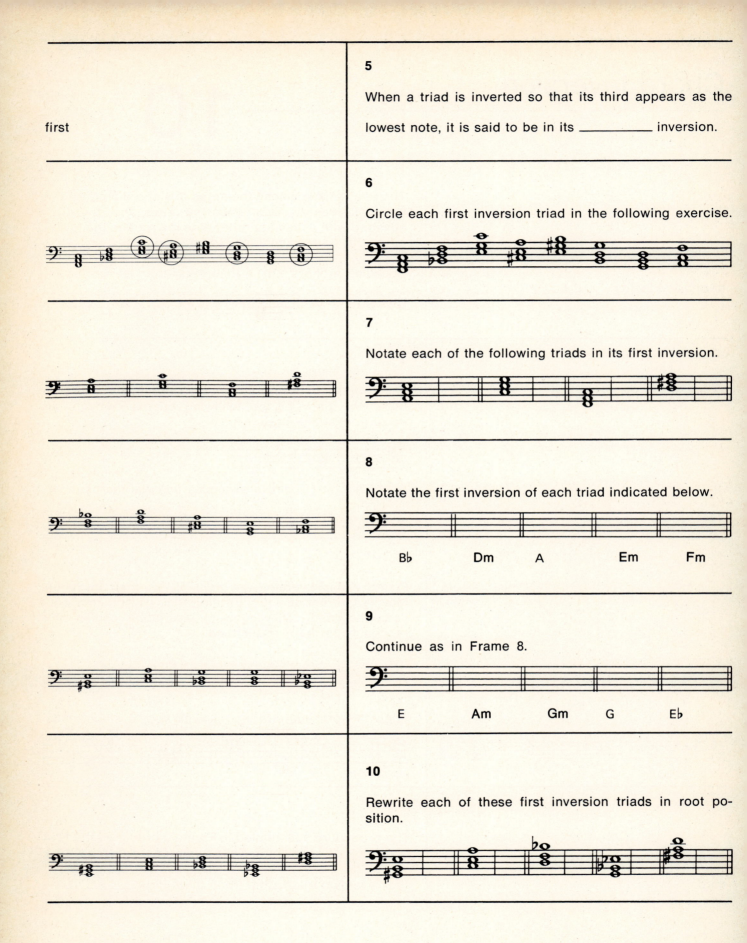

5

When a triad is inverted so that its third appears as the lowest note, it is said to be in its _____ inversion.

first

6

Circle each first inversion triad in the following exercise.

7

Notate each of the following triads in its first inversion.

8

Notate the first inversion of each triad indicated below.

Bb   Dm   A   Em   Fm

9

Continue as in Frame 8.

E   Am   Gm   G   Eb

10

Rewrite each of these first inversion triads in root position.

11

Identify the root and quality of each of the following triads by placing the proper chord symbols (i.e., C, Em, etc.) on the lines provided.

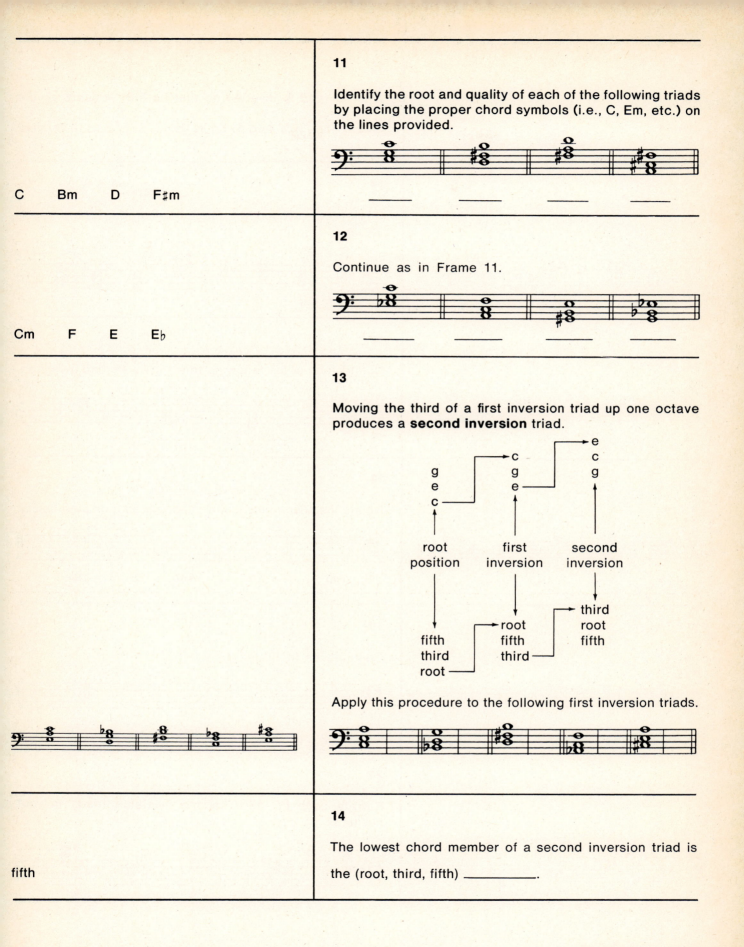

____   ____   ____   ____

C   Bm   D   F♯m

12

Continue as in Frame 11.

____   ____   ____   ____

Cm   F   E   E♭

13

Moving the third of a first inversion triad up one octave produces a **second inversion** triad.

```
                                        e
                    c                   c
        g           g                   g
        e           e
        c

      root        first            second
    position    inversion        inversion

                                      third
                    root              root
      fifth        fifth             fifth
      third        third
      root
```

Apply this procedure to the following first inversion triads.

fifth

14

The lowest chord member of a second inversion triad is the (root, third, fifth) _____.

Chord Inversion   **317**

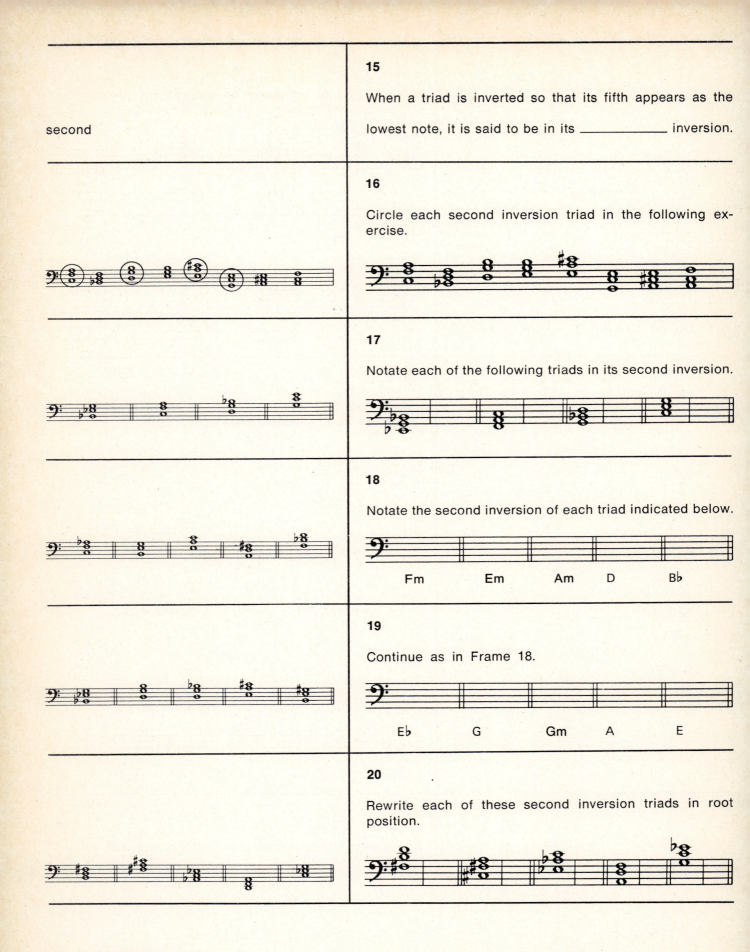

second

15

When a triad is inverted so that its fifth appears as the lowest note, it is said to be in its _____ inversion.

16

Circle each second inversion triad in the following exercise.

17

Notate each of the following triads in its second inversion.

18

Notate the second inversion of each triad indicated below.

Fm   Em   Am   D   Bb

19

Continue as in Frame 18.

Eb   G   Gm   A   E

20

Rewrite each of these second inversion triads in root position.

21

Identify each of the following triads by root name and quality using appropriate chord symbols.

E♭   Bm   Dm   C

_____   _____   _____   _____

DEVELOPING PERFORMANCE SKILLS

Turn to page 331 to reinforce your visual and aural familiarity with triad inversions by playing them on the piano.

22

The V⁷ chord may also be inverted without loss of harmonic identity. The only difference which applies to the V⁷ is that since it contains four notes, it may appear in three different inversions while a triad may be inverted only twice.

Complete the following table illustrating the vertical arrangement of chord members in each inversion of V⁷ in the key of B♭ major.

	root position	first inversion	second inversion	third inversion
root	third	fifth		
seventh	root	third		
fifth	seventh	root		
third	fifth	seventh		

	root position	first inversion	second inversion	third inversion
	seventh	_____	_____	_____
	fifth	_____	_____	_____
	third	_____	_____	_____
	root	_____	_____	_____

23

third

The lowest chord member of a first inversion dominant seventh chord is the _____.

24

second

When a dominant seventh chord is inverted so that its fifth appears as the lowest note, it is said to be in its _____ inversion.

seventh

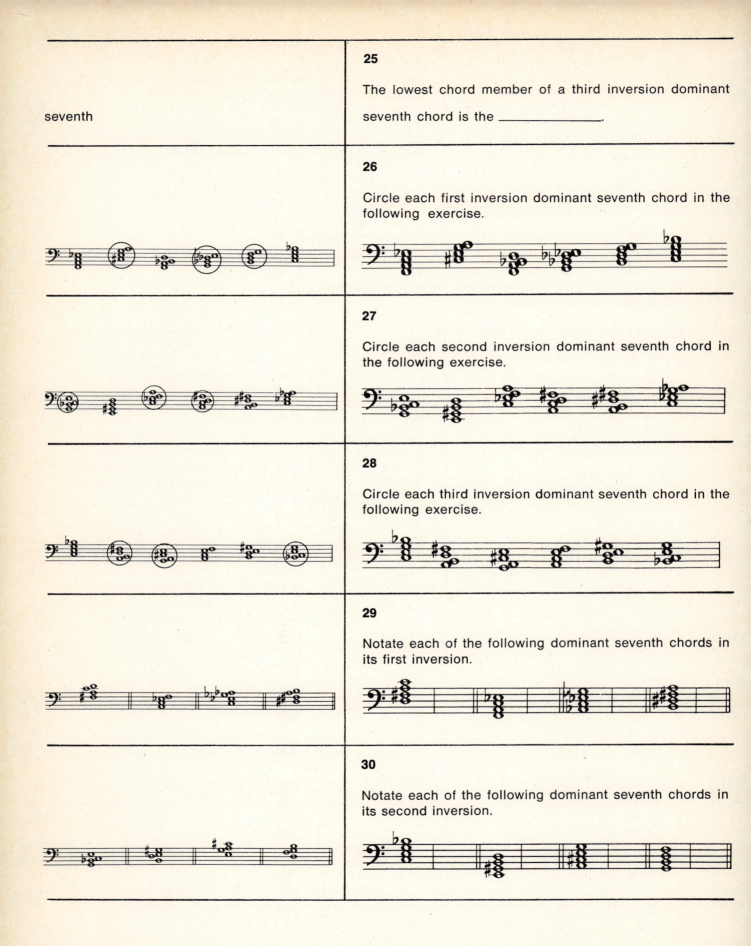

25

The lowest chord member of a third inversion dominant seventh chord is the _____.

26

Circle each first inversion dominant seventh chord in the following exercise.

27

Circle each second inversion dominant seventh chord in the following exercise.

28

Circle each third inversion dominant seventh chord in the following exercise.

29

Notate each of the following dominant seventh chords in its first inversion.

30

Notate each of the following dominant seventh chords in its second inversion.

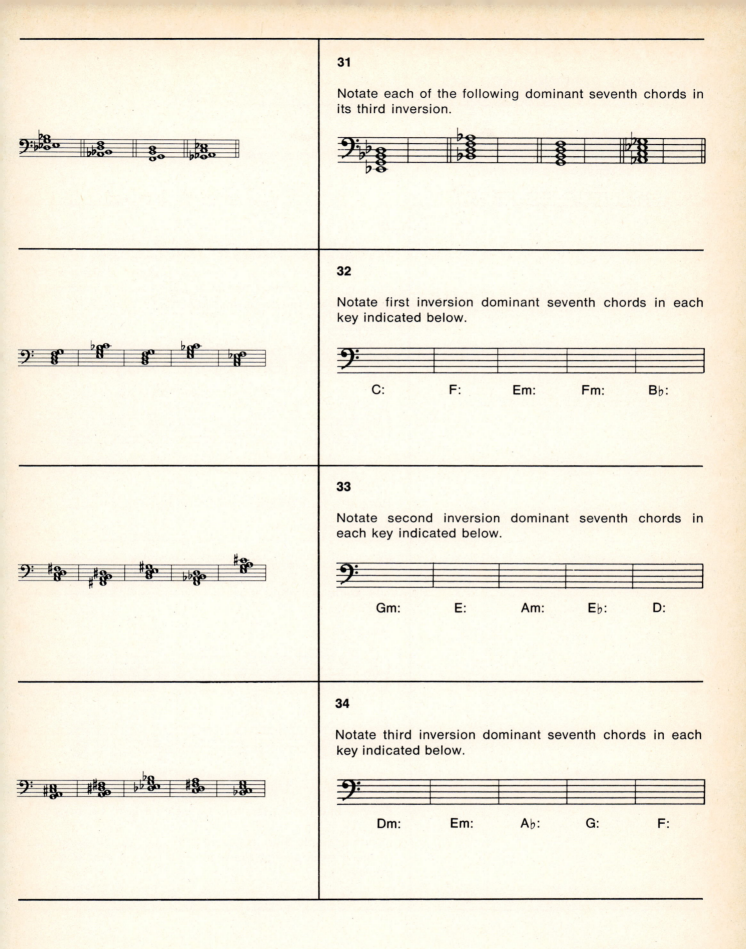

31

Notate each of the following dominant seventh chords in its third inversion.

32

Notate first inversion dominant seventh chords in each key indicated below.

C: F: Em: Fm: B♭:

33

Notate second inversion dominant seventh chords in each key indicated below.

Gm: E: Am: E♭:   D:

34

Notate third inversion dominant seventh chords in each key indicated below.

Dm: Em: A♭:   G: F:

DEVELOPING PERFORMANCE SKILLS

The piano exercises beginning on page 332 will reinforce your understanding
of dominant seventh chord inversion.

35

The use of chord inversion avoids large leaps from one chord to the next in a harmonization. Consider this harmonization from Chapter 9. Playing this example at the piano will illustrate this point.

Yes.

Does this harmonization contain large leaps? _____

36

The same harmonization is now presented using chord inversions.

Yes.

Do you find the horizontal flow of chords to be smoother in this example than in Frame 35? _____ (Playing both of these examples at the piano will help in reaching your decision.)

37

The harmonization from Frame 36 is repeated below. On the lines provided, indicate whether each chord is in root position, first inversion, or second inversion.

Aura Lee

U. S.

F: I _____   IV _____   V⁷ _____   I _____

root   second   first   root
position   inversion   inversion   position

38

The first inversion V chord or V⁷ chord and the second inversion IV chord are applicable to most keyboard harmonizations involving basic chords. The following symbols will provide a shorthand language for chord inversions adequate for the purposes of this text. Their more literal reference to first, second and third inversions is easier to recall than the more complex "figured bass" system of traditional music theory.

I or C indicates root position

I or C indicates 1st inversion
1   1

I or C indicates 2nd inversion
2   2

V⁷ or G⁷ indicates 3rd inversion
3   3

Notate the harmonization indicated (including inversions) for the following melody.

E :   I   IV   V   I   V⁷   I
              2   1   1

Sourwood Mountain

Appalachia

G: I   IV   I   I   V⁷   I
                    2   1

39

Harmonize the following melody using inverted chords as indicated.

Bingo   Scotland

G: I   IV   I   I   V⁷   I

40

Continue as in Frame 39.

Erie Canal   U. S.

d: i   i   iv   V⁷   i   i   i   V⁷   i

41

Continue as in the preceding frame.

Early One Morning   England

F: I   I   IV   V⁷   I
                         2   1

42

Continue as in the preceding frame.

Sourwood Mountain   Appalachia

G: I   IV   I   I   V⁷   I
                  2   1

G   C   G   D⁷   G

Dm   Gm   A⁷   Dm   A⁷   Dm

d: i   i   iv   V⁷   i   i   i   V⁷   i
                  2   1   1

F   B♭   C   F

F: I   I   IV   V⁷   I
                       2   1

G   C   G   D⁷   G

G: I   IV   I   I   V⁷   I
                 2   1

43

Other chord inversions are also useful in creating smoother voice leading and/or more interesting counterpoint between melody and accompaniment.

Using Roman numerals and inversion symbols as needed, identify each chord and inversion below this harmonization.

A-Hunting We Will Go   England

44

Continue as in Frame 43.

Mother's Knives and Forks   Janet Gaynor

A: I   V⁷₁   I

I   IV   V   I

45

Continue as in the preceding frame.

America   Henry Carey

A:

46

Continue as in the preceding frame.

Bow Belinda   U.S.

E:

E: I   I₁   V⁷₁   V⁷₁

I   I₂   V⁷₁   I

DEVELOPING PERFORMANCE SKILLS

Play the melody and harmony of each example in Frames 38–46 on the piano to practice using inverted chords in actual musical settings. You will find additional piano harmonization exercises involving chord inversions beginning on page 333.

Chord inversions can also add tonal and rhythmic interest to guitar accompaniments. Practice in those techniques begins on page 340.

CHECK YOUR UNDERSTANDING

1. Sounding the notes of a triad with either the third or the fifth as the

   lowest pitch demonstrates the principle of _____ _____.

2. The lowest chord member of a first inversion triad is the (root, third,

   fifth) _____.

3. Notate the first inversion of each triad indicated below.

   E   Em   D   F   Gm

4. When a triad is inverted so that its fifth appears as the lowest note,

   it is said to be in its _____ inversion.

5. Notate the second inversion of each triad indicated below.

   Fm   B   G   Am   A

6. The V^7 chord may appear in _____ different inversions.

7. The lowest chord member of a third inversion V^7 chord is the

   _____.

8. Notate the first inversion of each dominant seventh chord in each key
   indicated below.

   C   B♭   Bm   Dm   E♭

9. Notate the second inversion of each dominant seventh chord in each
   key indicated below.

   Cm   E   D   Am   F

10. Notate the third inversion of each dominant seventh chord in each key
    indicated below.

    G   Em   A   B♭   Gm

    (Answers may be found on page 366.)

APPLY YOUR UNDERSTANDING

Indicate whether each chord is in root position, first, second, or third inversion using symbols presented in Frame 38.

(Answers may be found on page 367.)

Harmonize the following melody using the chords indicated.

Ring, Ring the Banjo

Stephen C. Foster

(Answers may be found on page 368.)

DEVELOPING PERFORMANCE SKILLS

Piano (Frames 1–21)

As you play these drills at a slow but regular tempo listen to the sound of each triad inversion; watch the changing configuration of the three chord tones as you change inversions and try to cultivate the physical sensation as your left hand forms each inversion.

Group 1

Repeat the pattern illustrated for each triad given.

Group 2

You may find it easier to reach first inversions involving a black key by using your fourth finger. Try the same pattern with that alternative on these triads. (You may continue to use 5–3–1 if you find it more comfortable.)

Group 3

The following pattern employing the three primary triads will serve well as a basic harmonic background for many melodies. Practice it to develop your left hand coordination.

Group 4

Now try the same I $\begin{smallmatrix} \text{IV} & \text{V} \\ 2 & 1 \end{smallmatrix}$ I pattern spelling the triads and inversions your-self. Ask a classmate or your instructor to check your accuracy. Play in these keys: G: D: F: Bb: d: g: e: c:

Challenge

Repeat the same I $\begin{smallmatrix} \text{IV} & \text{V} \\ 2 & 1 \end{smallmatrix}$ I pattern in the keys of A: Eb: Ab: E: b:
f#:   c#:   f:

Piano (Frames 22–34)

Group 1

These drills emphasize the sound and configuration of dominant seventh chord inversions. Finger coordination is more complex with four notes. Listen to the characteristic sonority of the V⁷ as you play.

Group 2

Now try the first inversion V⁷ in place of V in the basic chord pattern you have learned. Play I $\begin{smallmatrix} \text{IV} & \text{V}^7 \\ 2 & 1 \end{smallmatrix}$ I in the following keys:

C: I   IV   V⁷   I   a: Bb: g:
            2   1

D: e:

Group 3

Practice the same pattern in the keys of G: D: F: d: a: c:

Challenge

Play the I $\begin{smallmatrix} & IV & V^7 \\ & 2 & 1 \end{smallmatrix}$ I pattern in the keys of E: b: A♭:   f♯:   E♭:   f:

Piano (Frames 35–46)

Practice the examples in frames 38–46 at the piano. Playing both melody and harmony will require maximum concentration. Ask a classmate or your instructor to check your accuracy.

These additional keyboard harmonizations will develop your piano skill further.

Minka

Battle Hymn of the Republic

Julia Ward Howe
William Steffe

U.S.

Germany

Streets of Laredo

Cowboy

Guitar (Frames 35–46)

Playing chord inversions on the guitar requires careful attention to the lowest string being strummed. Inverted chords have been added to the following progressions already presented in Chapter 9. Play them *slowly* in the rhythmic patterns notated. Numbers in parentheses below each rhythm indicate the lowest string to be strummed to produce each chord.

1. * Fingering chart indicates fifth string not normally strummed for this chord.

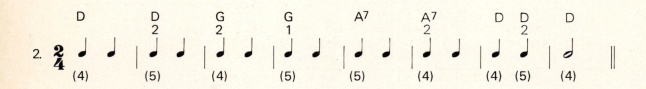

2.

3. * Fingering chart indicates sixth string not normally strummed for this chord.

4.

The previous exercises have used the inversion symbols presented in this text to associate a theoretical principle with the guitar. A more common method of indicating inversions in published music employs, for instance, D/A. This means "D chord with A bass", ie. finger D major and strum the fifth string as the lowest pitch. Play inverted chords as indicated by similar symbols in providing guitar accompaniments to these melodies. Arabic numerals in parentheses indicate the lowest string strummed in each chord. Notice how inversions add contrapuntal interest between bass line and melody.

5. **Mother's Knives and Forks**   Janet Gaynor

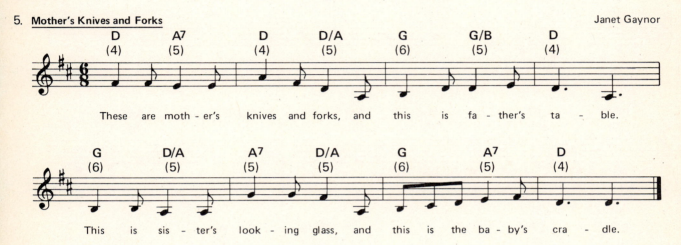

6. **Tum Balalaika**

1. On the Don when once I was young, This, the song I once used to strum. Singing of love and what it might bring. This was the song I once used to sing: "Tum ba - la, tum ba - la, tum ba - la - lai - ka, Tum ba - la, tum ba - la, tum ba - la - lai ka, Tum ba - la - lai - ka, tum ba - la - lai - ka Tum ba - la - lai - ka, tum ba - la - lai."

2. Love is sky, but it can be bold,
   Love has moods which are thousand-fold.
   Love has so many beautiful shapes,
   You think you've caught it, then it escapes.
   <u>Chorus</u>

Challenge

Adding inverted chords to guitar accompaniments quickly becomes too complex for many beginning guitarists. Students who do not find that to be so or are willing to devote the practice time required to develop more advanced performance skills may wish to explore some alternate strumming techniques. These also make more interesting use of the principle of chord inversion than the basic thumb or pick strum presented thus far and add rhythmic interest to accompaniments.

The **church lick** involves the thumb and index finger in three consecutive motions: (These three motions can also be executed with a pick, if desired.)

1. Thumb (T) strums bass note only, in normal fashion.

2. Back (nail) of index finger (I) strums the three upper strings in *downward* (toward the floor, lowest-to-highest string) direction.

3. Index finger (2) flicks back *up* (toward thumb) strumming only the top (E) string.

The starting and ending position for this strum places the right thumb and index finger roughly in the shape of a circle.

The most natural church lick rhythm is probably or equivalents.

The sound produced is

(Remember, ↓ means "toward the floor.")

The church lick can also be adapted to triple meter as follows: $\frac{3}{4}$ ♩ ♪ ♩

Practice the church lick on several familiar chord progressions.

The principle of chord inversion may be added to the church lick through the technique of alternating bass. This pattern will produce both tonal and rhythmic interest in an accompaniment. Try patterns like the following in various keys and meters.

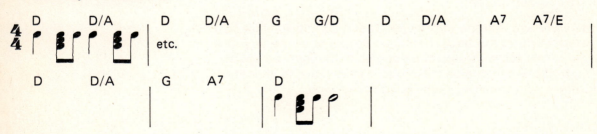

Plucking strings individually will produce an arpeggiated accompaniment. To experiment with this technique in its basic format:

1. Place your thumb just *above* (in relation to the floor) the desired bass note.

2. Place index, middle and ring fingers just *below* the three upper strings.

3. Strum *down* with the thumb and pluck *up* with 2, 3 and 4 in succession.

The most common rhythmic configuration in this style is  etc.

Adapting this figuration to triple meter is slightly more complex to coordinate.

Experiment with these and other rhythmic patterns of your own invention in familiar chord patterns. Alternating bass may also be added to this technique.

A more demanding application of the same basic hand position is **bass-chord** plucking.

1. Strum *downward* on the bass note with the thumb.

2. Pluck *upward* on the three upper strings simultaneously.

Common rhythms include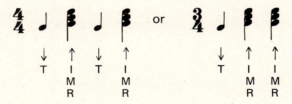

Alternating bass is also effective in this style.

Guitar (Frames 35–46 continued)

Combining chords you have learned in D major (A and D) and A minor (E⁷) will also allow you to perform the basic harmonic structure of the key of A major. Your first finger will serve as a pivot point among these three chords. Try accompanying these two melodies using chord inversions as indicated. Experiment with alternate strumming techniques if you wish.

Vesper Hymn   Russia

Hark! the ves - per hymn is steal - ing, o'er the wa - ters soft and clear;

Near - er yet and near - er peal - ing, soft it breaks up - on the ear.

Ju - bi - la - te! Ju - bi - la - ta! Ju - bi - la - te! A - men.

Far - ther now and far - ther steal - ing, soft it fades up - on the ear.

8. **Old Rosin, the Beau**   England

I live for the good of my na - tion And my sons are

all grow - ing low, But I hope that my next gen - er - a - tion Will re

sem - ble old Ros - in, the beau. _____ I've trav - el'd this coun - try all

o - ver, And _____ now to the next I will go, For I know that good

quar - ters a - wait me To wel - come old Ros - in, the beau. _____

If you have become relatively comfortable playing in D major, A minor and A major, you may wish to explore some additional tonalities. D or E minor will offer a more comfortable singing range for some students. These keys involve some chords you already know. One chord required in each is also rather awkward. Try both keys and concentrate on the one you find easier.

D minor begins with the chord you learned as the subdominant in A minor. The same A⁷ you learned in D major may be used although two alternate choices offer some advantages. The new chord Gm does not lie very close to i and V⁷ and involves a difficult stretch. Try these three chords in various combinations.

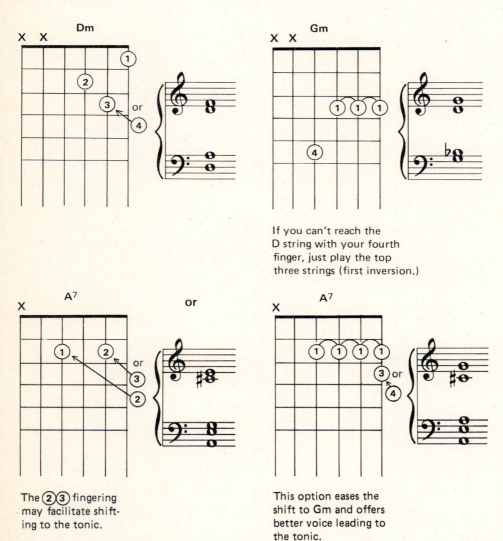

If you can't reach the D string with your fourth finger, just play the top three strings (first inversion.)

The ②③ fingering may facilitate shifting to the tonic.

This option eases the shift to Gm and offers better voice leading to the tonic.

Try accompanying these melodies in D minor. Apply inversions and alternate strumming techniques as you find appropriate.

9. Drill, Ye Tarriers, Drill!

Ear - ly morn - in' at sev - en o' - clock, There's twen - ty tar - riers drill - in' on the rock, And the boss comes a - long and says, "Keep still, and come down heav - y with the cast - iron drill," And drill, ye tar - riers, drill! Drill, ye tar - riers, drill. It's work all day for su - gar in your tay, Down be-hind the rail - way. Then drill, ye tar - riers, drill, and blast! and fire.

10. Wayfaring Stranger

I'm just a poor way - far - ing stran - ger, A' - trav - ling through this world of woe; But there's no sick - ness, toil, nor dan - ger in that bright world to which I go. I'm go - ing there to see my Fa - ther, I'm go - ing there no more to roam, I'm just a - go - ing o - ver Jor - dan, I'm just a' - go - ing o - ver home.

11. **High Barbaree**

There were two loft-y ships from old Eng-land came, blow high, blow low, and so ___ sailed we, one was the Prince of Lu-ther, and the oth-er, Prince of Wales, down a-long the coast of High Bar-ba-ree.

The subdominant chord in E minor is Am which you already know. Your second finger will provide a pivot between Em and the four-finger B⁷ which is difficult for many beginners. Experiment with these three primary chords.

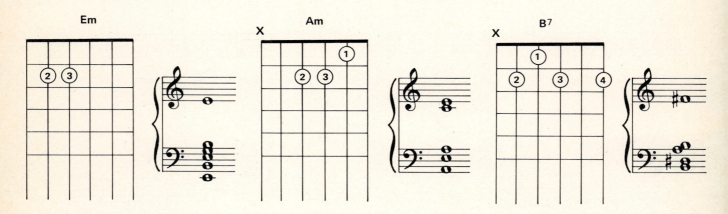

If you are relatively comfortable with these shifts try accompanying these same melodies in E minor. Add inversions and apply alternate strumming techniques as you deem practical.

Ear - ly morn - in' at sev - en o' - clock, There's twen - ty tar - riers

drill - in' on the rock, And the boss comes a - long and says, "Keep still, and

come down heav - y with the cast iron drill," And drill, ye tar - riers, drill!

Drill, ye tar - riers, drill. It's work all day for su - gar in your tay,

Down be-hind the rail - way. Then drill, ye tar - riers, drill, and blast! and fire.

10a. **Wayfaring Stranger** U.S.

I'm just a poor way - far - ing stran - ger, A' - trav - ling through this world of

woe; But there's no sick - ness, toil, nor dan - ger in that bright world to which I

go. I'm go - ing there to see my Fa - ther, I'm go - ing there no more to

roam, I'm just a - go - ing o - ver Jor - dan, I'm just a' - go - ing o - ver home.

11a. **High Barbaree**

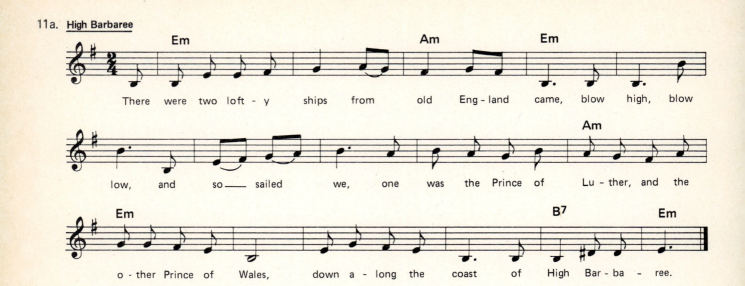

There were two loft-y ships from old Eng-land came, blow high, blow

low, and so — sailed we, one was the Prince of Lu-ther, and the

o-ther Prince of Wales, down a-long the coast of High Bar-ba-ree.

Adding two more chords to the G chord you learned as IV in D major will allow you to perform the same accompaniment pattern in G major. Practice the C and D^7 chords separately and in combination with G. The first finger will serve as a pivot in shifting from IV to V^7 in this key.

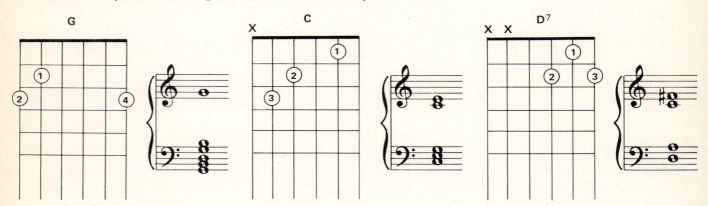

These three melodies offer additional practice in using chord inversions (and various strumming techniques if you wish) in the key of G major.

12. **Oats, Peas, Beans**

Oats, peas, beans and bar-ley grow; Oats, peas, beans and bar-ley grow; Do

you or I or an-y one know how oats, peas, beans and bar-ley grow?

13. Lovely Evening

Round

Oh, how love-ly is the eve-ning, is the eve-ning, When the bells are
sweet-ly ring-ing, sweet-ly ring-ing, Ding, Dong, Ding, Dong, Ding, Dong.

14. Walking Song

Switzerland

From Lu-cerne to Weg-gis fair, Hol-di-ri-di-a, Hol-di-ri-a,

Shoes and stock-ings we need not wear, Hol-di-ri-di-a, hol-di-a.

Hol-di-ri-di-a, hol-di-ri-di-a, hol-di-ri-a

Hol-di-ri-di-a, hol-di-ri-di-a, hol-di-a.

For additional practice in playing guitar accompaniments refer to the Song Supplement. Don't hesitate to transpose melodies to a key in which you are comfortable. Simply use Roman numeral analysis of the harmonization given to "translate" chord symbols to another key. Experiment with asking class-mates to play melodies on the recorder (or another instrument if they can) for variety.

SUPPLEMENTARY ACTIVITIES

Turn to the Song Supplement and, using the chords indicated, write out harmonizations to selected songs. Use chord inversions where appropriate for good voice leading and contrapuntal interest. Try to play these at the piano.

Answers to
Check Your Understanding
and Apply Your Understanding

The numbers in parentheses after each answer identify the frames in which
the information was originally presented.

CHAPTER 1   *(Answers to problems beginning on page 15.)*

CHECK YOUR UNDERSTANDING

1.   E-G-B-D-F   (9-12)

2.   F-A-C-E   (9-12)

3.   G-B-D-F-A   (21-23)

4.   A-C-E-G   (21-23)

5.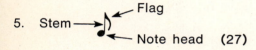

6.

7.   ledger lines   (34)

8.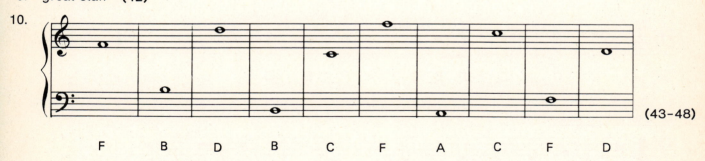

9.   great staff   (42)

10.

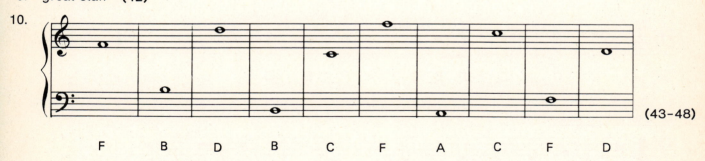

APPLY YOUR UNDERSTANDING

1. **This Old Man**　　England

G E G　G E G　A G F E　D E F　E F

G C C C　C D E F G　G D D F　E D C

2. **Little Piece**　　Robert Schumann

E F　G A D E　F　C D　E E D A

C B E F　G A D E　F　C D　E E D B　D C

3. **Lavender's Blue**　　England

C G G　G F E D C　C A A　A

C G G　G F E D C　F E D　C

4. **The Tailor and the Mouse**　　England

E　C A A A　G E G　E　E E E E

C A E　C A A A　G E G　E E E E C A

CHAPTER 1 (continued) *(Answers to problems beginning on page 24.)*

CHECK YOUR UNDERSTANDING

1. duration (49)
2. a. whole (51-55)
   b. quarter
   c. half

3. a.   b. (57-60)
4. rests (61)

5.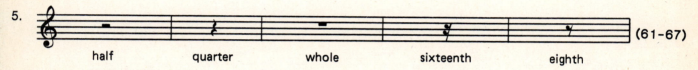

        half   quarter   whole   sixteenth   eighth

6. one-half (70)

7. a. ○ (70-75)

   b.

   c. +

   d.

8. a. (70-75)

   b.

   c.

   d.

APPLY YOUR UNDERSTANDING

1. a. sixteenth note
   b. dotted eighth note
   c. sixteenth rest
   d. dotted quarter note
   e. eighth rest

2. a. quarter note
   b. quarter rest
   c. eighth note

1. Rig-a-jig-jig

a. sixteenth   b. _____   c. _____   U.S.

B B B B B   C B G   B   B A F A   C B G   B

d. _____   e. _____

B B B B   C B G   E D   D D C D   E

2. Pony Song

Germany

a. _____   b. _____

G   B   D   D C B A   G   A A F D   D D B G

c. _____

A A F D   D D B G   G A B C   D   D C B A   G

CHAPTER 2   *(Answers to problems beginning on page 53.)*

CHECK YOUR UNDERSTANDING

1. rhythm   (1)

2. pulse or beat   (2-4)

3. measures   (12)

4. time signature or meter signature   (14)

5.   There are four quarter notes per measure. The upper number indicates the number of reference notes per measure. The lower number represents a reference note—in this case, a quarter note.   (15-17)

6. three   (15-23)

7. four   (15-23)

8. tie   (60-61)

APPLY YOUR UNDERSTANDING

1. time or meter signature

2. measure

3. bar line

4. tie

5. **The Old Brass Wagon** Midwestern U.S.

G G G G G G G G E D A A A A A A D D E G

B B B B B B A G E G A B E F G G

6. **Clementine** U.S.

G G G D B B B G G B D D C B A A B C C B A

B G G B A D F A G G G G D B B B G G B

D D C B A A B C C B A B G G B A D F A G

7. **The Tailor and the Mouse** England

E C A A G E G E E E E C A E C A A A

G E G E E E E C A C A E A C A E A

B D D D B D C A A A A G E E G E E E E C A

8. **Oats, Peas, Beans** England

B B B A G G C C C B A A A A

B C D C B B C D B A C B A G G G

9. 2/4

10. 3/4

11. 6/8

12. 4/4

CHECK YOUR UNDERSTANDING

1. b. and c.   (14-17)
2. four   (14-17)
3. two   (14-17)
4. two   (26-35)
5. four   (26-35)
6. one half beat   (26-35)
7. one half beat   (26-35)
8. b. and d.   **(59-60)**
9. true   **(61)**
10. two   **(61-62)**

APPLY YOUR UNDERSTANDING

Write the counting under the notes in the following songs.

1. **The Glendy Burk**   Stephen C. Foster

2. **The Riddle Song**   Kentucky

5. **Dancing Doll**

E. Poldini

1 2 & 3 &   1 2 3   1 2 3   1 (2 3)   1 2 3 &   1 & 2 (3)

1 2 3 &   1 & 2 (3)   1 2 & 3 &   1 2 3   1 2 3   1 (2 3)

1   2   3 &   1 & 2 & 3   (1) & 2 & 3 &   1   2   3

CHAPTER 4   *(Answers to problems beginning on page 117.)*

CHECK YOUR UNDERSTANDING

1. interval   (1)

2. half   (3)

3. whole   (3-4)

4. E *(and)* F, B *(and)* C   (6)

5. a. half   b. whole   c. whole   d. half   e. whole   (6-9)

6. Accidentals   (21)

7. raise   (26)

8. flat   (29)

9. natural   (33)

10. enharmonic   (49)

APPLY YOUR UNDERSTANDING

Circle and identify all accidentals.

CHAPTER 5 *(Answers to problems beginning on page 142.)*

CHECK YOUR UNDERSTANDING

1. scale   (1)

2. octave   (6)

3. 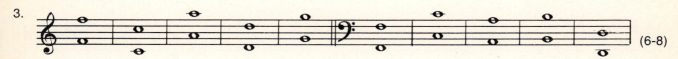   (6-8)

4. 3 and 4, 7 and 8   (12)

5. (12-14)

6. b.   (12)

APPLY YOUR UNDERSTANDING

1. B-flat major

2. A major

3. E-flat major

4. D major

CHAPTER 6   *(Answers to problems beginning on page 167.)*

CHECK YOUR UNDERSTANDING

1. tonality   (2)

2. key signature   (8)

3. beginning, clef   (8)

4. b.   (20)

5. F♯,   C♯,   G♯,   D♯   (20)

6. a.   (31)

7. B♭,   E♭,   A♭,   D♭   (31)

8. a.   b.   c.   d.

A major   F major   D major   B-flat major

APPLY YOUR UNDERSTANDING

a. A major   b. A♭ major   c. E♭ major   d. E major

1. G major

2. F major

3. D major

CHAPTER 7 *(Answers to problems beginning on page 195.)*

CHECK YOUR UNDERSTANDING

1. major   (1)

2. sixth   (2)

3. e minor   (4)

4.

G minor

E minor

5. 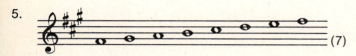 (7)

6. natural   (48)

7. seventh, half   (50)

8.

    a. C harmonic minor   b. B harmonic minor   c. A harmonic minor

APPLY YOUR UNDERSTANDING

a. C minor   b. C-sharp minor   c. E minor   d. D minor

1. C minor

2. E minor

CHAPTER 8   *(Answers to problems beginning on page 229.)*

CHECK YOUR UNDERSTANDING

1. numeric   (2)

2. a. third b. fifth c. fifth d. second e. sixth f. seventh g. octave   (3-9)

3. one, unison   (12)

4. major, minor, and perfect   (23)

5. perfect   (26)

6. major   (37)

7. minor   (50)

8. a. m3   b. P4   c. M6   d. m2   e. m7   f. M2   g. P5

APPLY YOUR UNDERSTANDING

a. P5   b. m3   c. P8   d. M6   e. m2   f. P4   g. M7

1. *m2*
2. *M2*
3. *P4*
4. *M3*
5. *m3*
6. *m6*
7. *P5*
8. *P8*

CHAPTER 9 *(Answers to problems beginning on page 288.)*

CHECK YOUR UNDERSTANDING

1. three, consecutive (5)
2. root, third, fifth (13-14)
3. major (28)
4. D, G, and A (53)
5. F, B♭, and C (53)
6. harmonic (73)

7.

8.

9.

A major   g minor   F major   e minor

10. seventh **(92)**
11. dominant seventh **(149)**

12.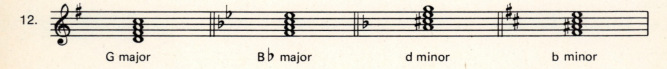

G major   B♭ major   d minor   b minor

APPLY YOUR UNDERSTANDING

Identify the key of the following examples and place the appropriate numeral below each chord.

Mother's Knives and Forks

Janet Gaynor

G: I   V⁷   I   I   IV   IV   I   I

IV   I   V⁷   I   IV   V⁷   I   I

Go Down Moses

Spiritual

a: i   V⁷   i   V⁷   V⁷   i   i   V⁷

i   V⁷   i   i   iv   i

i   i   i   V⁷   i

Add triads and dominant seventh chords as indicated to harmonize the following melody. Notate each chord in the proper note values according to the time signature.

CHAPTER 10 *(Answers to problems beginning on page 328.)*

CHECK YOUR UNDERSTANDING

1. chord inversion (2-3)

2. third (4)

3.

4. second (15)

5.

6. three (22)

7. seventh (25)

8. C major   Bb major   b minor   d minor   Eb major

9. C minor   E major   D major   a minor   F major

10. G major   e minor   A major   Bb major   g minor

APPLY YOUR UNDERSTANDING

Old Dan Tucker   Dan Emmett

I   I   IV   I   I   I   V⁷   V⁷   I   I

IV   I   I   I   V⁷   I   I   IV

V⁷   I   I   IV   V⁷   V⁷   I

Harmonize the following melody using the chords indicated.

Ring, Ring the Banjo

Stephen C. Foster

Song Supplement

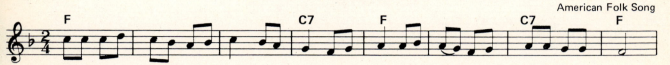

OVER IN THE MEADOW

American Folk Song

1. O-ver in the mead-ow, in the sand, in the sun, Lived an old Moth-er Toad and her lit-tle toad-ie one;

"Wink!" said the moth-er. "I wink," said the one; And he winked and he blinked in the sand, in the sun.

2. Over in the meadow, where the stream runs so blue,
   Lived an old Mother Fish and her little fishies two;
   "Swim," said the mother. "We swim," said the two;
   So they swam and they leaped where the stream runs so blue.

3. Over in the meadow, in a hole in a tree,
   Lived an old Mother Bird and her little birdies three;
   "Sing," said the mother. "We sing," said the three;
   So they sang and were glad in the hole in the tree.

DONA NOBIS PACEM

Traditional Round

Do - na no - bis pa - cem, pa - cem,

Do - na no - bis pa - cem.

Do - na no - bis pa - cem, Do - na no - bis

pa - cem. Do - na no - bis

pa - cem, Do - na no - bis pa - cem.

ONE MORE RIVER

Spiritual

1. Old No - ah built him - self an ark, There's one more riv - er to cross, And built it all of hick - o - ry bark, There's one more riv - er to cross.

Chorus

One more riv - er, ___ And that's the riv - er of Jor - dan; One more riv - er, ___ There's one more riv - er to cross. ___

2. The animals came two by two, there's one more river to cross,
   The elephant and kangaroo, there's one more river to cross.

3. The animals came three by three, there's one more river to cross,
   The baboon and the chimpanzee, there's one more river to cross.

4. The animals came four by four, there's one more river to cross,
   Old Noah got mad and hollered for more, there's one more river to cross.

5. The animals came five by five, there's one more river to cross,
   The bees came swarming from the hive, there's one more river to cross.

6. The animals came six by six, there's one more river to cross,
   The lion laughed at the monkey's tricks, there's one more river to cross.

7. When Noah found he had no sail, there's one more river to cross,
   He just ran up his old coat tail, there's one more river to cross.

8. Before the voyage did begin, there's one more river to cross,
   Old Noah pulled the gangplank in, there's one more river to cross.

9. They never knew where they were at, there's one more river to cross,
   'Til the old ark bumped on Ararat, there's one more river to cross.

CHRISTMAS IS COMING

England

1. Christ - mas is com - ing! The goose is get - ting fat! Please to put a pen - ny in an old man's ___ hat, Please to put a pen - ny in an old man's hat.

2. If you've no pen - ny, A ha' - pen - ny, will do, If you have no ha' - pen - ny, Then God bless ___ you, If you have no ha' - pen - ny, Then God bless you.

WALTZING MATILDA

Words - A. B. Patterson
Music - Marie Cowan

Australia

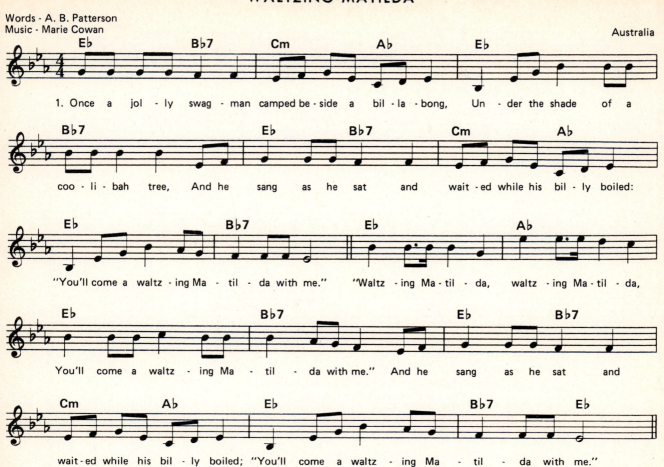

1. Once a jol - ly swag - man camped be - side a bil - la - bong, Un - der the shade of a
coo - li - bah tree, And he sang as he sat and wait - ed while his bil - ly boiled:
"You'll come a waltz - ing Ma - til - da with me." "Waltz - ing Ma - til - da, waltz - ing Ma - til - da,
You'll come a waltz - ing Ma - til - da with me." And he sang as he sat and
wait - ed while his bil - ly boiled; "You'll come a waltz - ing Ma - til - da with me."

2. Down came a jumbuck to drink beside the billabong,
Up jumped the swagman and seized him with glee,
And he sang as he stowed that jumbuck in his tuckerbag,
"You'll come a waltzing Matilda with me."
"Waltzing Matilda, waltzing Matilda,
You'll come a waltzing Matilda with me."
And he sang as he stowed that jumbuck in his tuckerbag,
"You'll come a waltzing Matilda with me."

3. Down came the squatter mounted on his thoroughbred,
Up came the troopers, one, two, three.
'Who's that jolly jumbuck you've got in your tuckerbag?
"You'll come a waltzing Matilda with me."
"Waltzing Matilda, waltzing Matilda,
You'll come a waltzing Matilda with me.
Who's that jolly jumbuck you've got in your tuckerbag?
You'll come a waltzing Matilda with me."

4. Up jumped the swagman and sprang into the billabong,
"You'll never take me alive," said he.
And his ghost may be heard as you pass by that billabong,
"You'll come a waltzing Matilda with me."
"Waltzing Matilda, waltzing Matilda,
You'll come a waltzing Matilda with me."
And his ghost may be heard as you pass by that billabong,
"You'll come a waltzing Matilda with me."

Swagman - a tramp

Coolibah tree - eucalyptus

Billabong - a water hole

Billy - a can to heat water for tea

Jumbuck - a sheep

Tuckerbag - a knapsack

Squatter - rancher

Trooper - sheriff

Waltzing Matilda - swagman's blanket roll

GOING TO BOSTON

1. Good - bye girls, we're going to Bos - ton Good - bye girls, we're going to Bos - ton,

Good - bye girls, we're going to Bos - ton, Ear - ly in the morn - ing.

Chorus

Won't we look pret - ty in the ball - room, Won't we look pret - ty in the ball - room,

Won't we look pret - ty in the ball - room, Ear - ly in the morn - ing.

2. Saddle up girls, and let's go with them, etc.
3. Out of the way, you'll get run over, etc.
4. Swing your partner, on to Boston, etc.
5. This is how we go to Boston, etc.

KOOKABURRA
(Round)

M. Sinclair

Australia

Kook-a - bur - ra sits on an old gum tree —— Mer - ry, mer-ry king of the bush is he. ——

Laugh, kook-a - bur - ra, laugh, kook-a - bur - ra, Gay your life must be.

Words and music from The Ditty Bag, Copyright 1946 by Janet E. Tobitt.
Used by permission.

ONCHIMBO

English words - Margaret Marks

Kenya

Leader

O take your fair share, ____ good fish - ing
                           good hunt - ing On - chim - bo bird.

Chorus

O take your fair share, ____ good fish - ing
                           good hunt - ing On - chim - bo bird.

Leader

Take fish from the stream, ____ good fish - ing On - chim - bo bird.
Take game from the plain, ____ good hunt - ing

Chorus

Take fish from the stream, ____ good fish - ing On - chim - bo bird.
Take game from the plain, ____ good hunt - ing

From Making Music Your Own - 4. Copyright 1966 by Silver Burdett Company.
Used by permission.

THIS OLD MAN

Steadily

England

F   Bb   C7

1. This old man, he played one, He played nick - nack on my thumb, With a

F   C7   F

nick - nack pad - dy whack give the dog a bone! This old man came roll - ing home.

2. This old man, he played two,
He played nick-nack on my shoe.

3. This old man, he played three,
He played nick-nack on my knee.

4. This old man, he played four,
He played nick-nack on my door.

5. This old man, he played five,
He played nick-nack on my hive.

6. This old man, he played six,
He played nick-nack on my sticks.

7. This old man, he played sev'n,
He played nick-nack up in heaven.

8. This old man, he played eight,
He played nick-nack on my gate.

9. This old man, he played nine,
He played nick-nack on my spine.

10. This old man, he played ten,
He played nick-nack over again.

THE ORCHESTRA SONG
(Round)

Austria

1. The vi - o - lin's ring - ing like love - ly ___ sing - ing. The

2. The clar - i - net, the clar - i - net makes doo - dle, doo - dle, doo - dle, doo - dle det, The

3. The trum - pet is sound - ing ta ta ta ta ta ta ta ta ta ta ta ta ta, The

4. The horn, the horn a - wakes me at morn, The

5. The drum's play - ing two tones and al - ways the same tones, Five

vi - o - lin's ring - ing like love - ly ___ song.

clar - i - net, the clar - i - net makes doo - dle, doo - dle, doo - dle det.

trum - pet is sound - ing ta ta ta ta ta ta ta ta ta ta.

horn, the horn a wakes me at morn.

one, one five, five, five, five, five one.

ERIE CANAL

1. I've got a mule, her name is Sal, Fif-teen miles on the E - rie Ca - nal. She's a good old work-er and a good old pal, Fif-teen miles on the E - rie Ca - nal. We've hauled some barg - es in our day, Filled with lum - ber, coal and hay, And we know ev - er-y inch of the way From Al - ba - ny —— to —— Buf - fa - lo. ——

Chorus

Low bridge, ev - er-y-bod - y down, Low bridge, 'cause we're com - ing to a town; And you'll al - ways know your neigh-bor, You'll al-ways know your pal, If you've ev - er nav - i - gat-ed on the E - rie Ca - nal.

2. We'd better get along, old pal, fifteen miles on the Erie Canal,
You can bet your life I'd never part from Sal, fifteen miles on the Erie Canal;
Get up there, mule, here comes a lock, we'll make Rome by six o'clock,
One more trip and back we'll go, back we'll go to Buffalo.

FUM, FUM, FUM

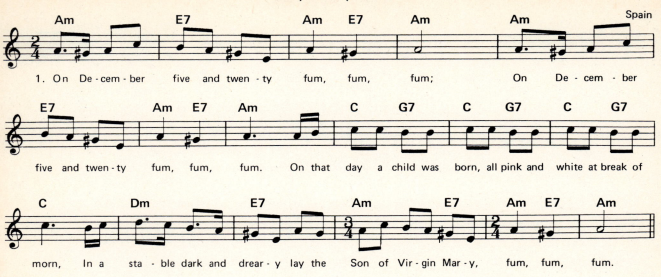

Spain

1. On De-cem-ber five and twen-ty fum, fum, fum; On De-cem-ber five and twen-ty fum, fum, fum. On that day a child was born, all pink and white at break of morn, In a sta-ble dark and drear-y lay the Son of Vir-gin Mar-y, fum, fum, fum.

2. Christmas is a day of feasting, fum, fum, fum;
Christmas is a day of feasting, fum, fum, fum.
In hot lands and in cold, for young and old, for young and old,
We tell the Christmas story,
Ever singing at its glory, fum, fum, fum.

WHEN JOHNNY COMES MARCHING HOME

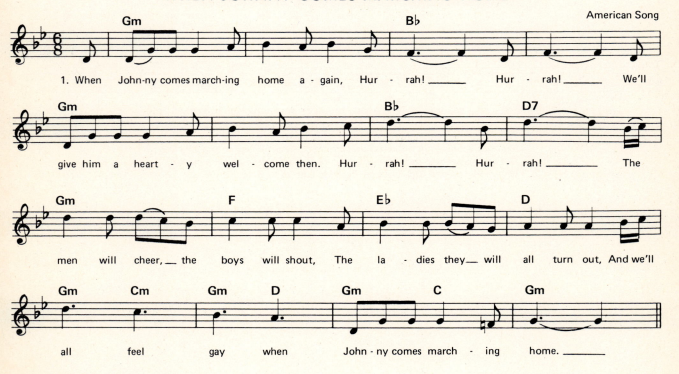

American Song

1. When John-ny comes march-ing home a-gain, Hur-rah! _____ Hur-rah! _____ We'll give him a heart-y wel-come then. Hur-rah! _____ Hur-rah! _____ The men will cheer, _ the boys will shout, The la-dies they_ will all turn out, And we'll all feel gay when John-ny comes march - ing home. _____

2. The old church bell will peal with joy, Hurrah! Hurrah!
To welcome home our darling boy, Hurrah! Hurrah!
The village lads and lassies say,
With roses they will strew the way,
And we'll all feel gay when Johnny comes marching home.

3. Get ready for the jubilee, Hurrah! Hurrah!
We'll give the hero three times three, Hurrah! Hurrah!
The laurel wreath is ready now,
To place upon his loyal brow,
And we'll all feel gay when Johnny comes marching home.

MICHAEL FINNEGAN

1. There was an old man named Mi-chael Fin-ne-gan.
He had whis-kers on his chin-ne-gan. He pulled them out but
they grew in a-gain. Poor old Mi-chael Fin-ne-gan. Be-gin a-gain.

2. There was an old man named Michael Finnegan,
   He went fishing with a pinnegan,
   He caught a fish but dropped it inagain,
   Poor old Michael Finnegan. Begin again.

3. There was an old man named Michael Finnegan,
   Climbed a tree and barked his shinnegan,
   He lost about a yard of skinnegan,
   Poor old Michael Finnegan. Begin again.

4. There was an old man named Michael Finnegan,
   He grew fat and then grew thinnegan,
   Then he died and that's the endegan,
   Poor old Michael Finnegan. Begin again.

BINGO

Scotland

There was a farm-er had a dog, And Bin-go was his name-O. B-I-N-G-O,
B-I-N-G-O, B-I-N-G-O, And Bin-go was his name-O.

The second time through, clap instead of saying the letter "B", the third time clap for both "B" and "I", etc. Continue until you are clapping the entire word Bingo.

OLD DAN TUCKER

Dan Emmett

1. I came to town the oth-er night, I heard the noise and saw the fight. The
watch-man, he was run-ning 'round, said "Old Dan Tuck-er's come to town."

Chorus

Get out the way, old Dan Tuck-er, Get out the way, old Dan Tuck-er,

Get out the way, old Dan Tuck-er, You're too late to come to sup-per.

2. Old Dan Tucker was a fine old man, he washed his face in the frying pan,
   He combed his hair with a wagon wheel, and died with a toothache in his heel.

3. Now, Old Dan Tucker and I fell out, and what do you think it was all about?
   He borrowed my old setting hen and didn't bring her back again.

4. Old Dan began in early life to play the banjo and win a wife,
   But every time a date he'd keep he'd play himself right fast asleep.

5. Now, Old Dan Tucker he came to town to swing the ladies all around,
   Swing them right and swing them left then to the one he liked the best.

6. And when Old Dan had passed away they missed the music he used to play,
   They took him on his final ride and buried his banjo by his side.

SIMPLE GIFTS

Shaker Song

'Tis the gift to be sim - ple, 'tis the gift to be free, 'Tis the gift to come down where we ought to be, And when we find our-selves in the place just right, 'Twill be in the val - ley of love and de-light. When true sim - pli - ci - ty is gain'd, To bow and to bend we shan't be a sham'd. To turn, turn will be our de-light till by turn - ing, turn - ing we come round right.

MICHAEL, ROW THE BOAT ASHORE

Black American Folk Song

1. Mich - ael, row the boat a - shore, Hal - le - lu - jah! Mich - ael, row the boat a - shore, Hal - le - lu - jah!

2. Sister, help to trim the sail, Hallelujah!
   Sister, help to trim the sail, Hallelujah!

3. River's deep and the river is wide, Hallelujah!
   Milk and honey on the other side, Hallelujah!

4. Jordan's river is chilly and cold, Hallelujah!
   Chills the body but not the soul, Hallelujah!

SOURWOOD MOUNTAIN

Appalachia

1. Chick-en crow-ing on Sour-wood Moun-tain, Hey de ing dang did-dle al-ly day.

So man-y pret-ty girls I can't count them, Hey de ing dang did-dle al-ly day.

My true love, she lives in Letch-er, Hey de ing dang did-dle al-ly day.

She won't come and I won't fetch her, Hey de ing dang did-dle al-ly day.

2. My true love's a blue-eyed daisy, Hey, etc.
If I don't get her I'll go crazy, Hey, etc.
Big dogs bark and little ones bite you, Hey, etc.
Big girls court and little ones slight you, Hey, etc.

3. My true love lives by the river, Hey, etc.
A few more jumps and I'll be with her, Hey, etc.
My true love lives up the hollow, Hey, etc.
She won't come and I won't follow, Hey, etc.

THE OLD BRASS WAGON

Midwestern U. S.

1. Cir-cle to the left, the old brass wag-on, Cir-cle to the left, the old brass wag-on,

Cir-cle to the left, the old brass wag-on, You're the one my dar-ling.

2. Circle to the right, the old brass wagon, etc.
3. Swing, oh swing, the old brass wagon, etc.
4. Promenade around, the old brass wagon, etc.
5. Swing your partner, the old brass wagon, etc.
6. Break and swing, the old brass wagon, etc.
7. Promenade in, the old brass wagon, etc.

WHO BUILT THE ARK?

American Folk Song

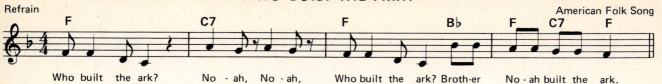

Who built the ark? No - ah, No - ah, Who built the ark? Broth-er No - ah built the ark.

1. Now didn't old No - ah build the ark?__ He built it out of a hick - o - ry bark.__ 2. He

2. He built it long, both wide and tall,
   Plenty of room for the large and small,

3. Now in come the animals two by two,
   Hippopotamus and kangaroo,

4. Now in come the animals three by three,
   Two big cats and a bumble bee,
   Refrain

5. Now in come the animals four by four,
   Two through the window and two through the door,

6. Now in come the animals five by five,
   Four little sparrows and the redbird's wife,

7. Now in come the animals six by six,
   Elephant laughed at the monkey's tricks,

8. Now in come the animals seven by seven,
   Four from home and the rest from heaven,
   Refrain

9. Now in come the animals eight by eight,
   Some were on time and the others were late,

10. Now in come the animals nine by nine,
    Some was a-shouting and some was a-crying,

11. Now in come the animals ten by ten,
    Five black roosters and five black hens,

12. Now Noah says, "Go shut that door,
    The rain's started dropping and we can't take more."
    Refrain

This song can be used to demonstrate the effect of syncopation. For example, the first measure can be sung without syncopation (♩ ♪ ♪ ♪ ‰) to illustrate the greater and more natural word rhythm created by the syncopation.

Who built the ark?

From Making Music Your Own - 2. Copyright 1966 by Silver Burdett Company.
Used by permission.

SKIP TO MY LOU

Brightly

Southern U. S.

1. Flies in the but-ter-milk, shoo fly shoo! Flies in the but-ter-milk, shoo fly shoo! Flies in the but-ter-milk,

shoo fly shoo! Skip to my Lou, my dar - ling. Lou, Lou, skip to my Lou.

Lou, Lou, skip to my Lou. Lou, Lou, skip to my Lou. Skip to my Lou, my dar - ling.

2. Lost my partner, what'll I do?
3. I'll get another one, prettier than you.
4. Can't get a red bird, a blue bird'll do.
5. Little red wagon, painted blue.
6. Skip a little faster, this'll never do.

TZENA, TZENA

English words - Phyllis Resnick

Israel

Tze - na, tze - na, tze - na, tze - na, come in - to the fields and we'll be
Hoe - ing, sew - ing, new things grow - ing, pi - o - neer - ing all to - geth - er,

gin _____ to work the land. hand.
come _____ and lend a

Tze - na, tze - na, build - ing a new na - tion, toil - ing bus - i - ly all day. _____

Soon we'll dance and have a cel - e - bra - tion, But first we'll work and then we'll play.

PAT-A-PAN

Tr. Janet Tobitt

French Carol

1. Wil-lie, take your lit-tle drum; Rob-in, bring your fife, and come; Play-ing on the fife and drum, Tu-re-lu-re-

lu, pat-a-pat-a- pan, We'll make mus-ic loud and gay, For our Christ-mas hol- i - day.

2. Shepherds glad, in ancient days, gave the King of Kings their praise;
   Playing on the fife and drum, Tu-re-lu-re-lu, pat-a-pat-a-pan,
   They make music loud and gay, on the Holy Child's birthday.

3. Christian men, rejoice as one, leave your work and join our fun;
   Playing on the fife and drum, Tu-re-lu-re-lu, pat-a-pat-a-pan,
   We'll make music loud and gay, for our Christmas holiday.

From The Ditty Bag, Copyright 1946 by Janet E. Tobitt. Used by permission.

ZUM GALI GALI

Israel

Zum ga-li, ga-li, ga-li, zum ga-li, ga-li.   1. He-cha-lutz le

'man a - vo - dah; _____ A - vo-dah le 'man he - cha - lutz.

2. Avodah le 'man hechalutz;   3. Hechalutz le 'man hab'tulah;   4. Hashalom le 'man ha'amim;
   Hechalutz le 'man avodah.   Hab'tulah le 'man hechalutz.   Ha'amim le 'man hashalom.

The chant may be sung twice as an introduction. Then it is repeated continuously as a background for the verses. The chant may also be sung between verses and after the last verse.

THE TAILOR AND THE MOUSE

England

1. There was a tai-lor had a mouse, Hi did-dle um-kum fee-dle. They lived to-geth-er

in one house, Hi did-dle um-kum fee-dle. Hi did-dle um-kum ta-tum, ta-tum,

Chorus

Through the town of Ram-say, Hi did-dle um-kum, o-ver the lea, Hi did-dle um-kum fee-dle.

2. The tailor thought the mouse was ill,
Hi diddle umkum feedle,
Because he took an awful chill,
Hi diddle umkum feedle.

3. The tailor thought his mouse would die,
Hi diddle umkum feedle,
And so he baked him in a pie,
Hi diddle umkum feedle.

4. He cut the pie, the mouse ran out,
Hi diddle umkum feedle,
The mouse was in a terrible pout,
Hi diddle umkum feedle.

5. The tailor gave him catnip tea,
Hi diddle umkum feedle,
Until a healthy mouse was he,
Hi diddle umkum feedle.

MAY DAY CAROL

English Folk Song

1. The moon shines bright, The stars give light, A lit-tle be-fore 'tis day. Our
3. A branch of May I bring to you As at ___ the door I stand. 'Tis

Heav-en-ly Fa-ther, He called to us And bid us to wake and pray.
but ___ a sprout well ___ bud-ded out, The work of ___ our Lord's hands.

2. A-wake, a-wake, O pret-ty, pret-ty maid, Out of your drow-sy dream. And
4. My song is done. I must ___ be ___ gone, No long-er can I stay. God

step in-to your dair-y be-low And fetch me a bowl of cream.
bless you all, both great and small, And send you a joy-ful May.

AURA LEE

Sentimentally

1. As the black-bird in the spring, 'Neath the wil-low tree, _____

Sat and piped, I heard him sing, Sing - ing Au - ra Lee.

Chorus

Au - ra Lee, Au - ra Lee, Maid of gold - en hair,

Sun - shine came a - long with thee, And swal - lows in the air.

2. In her blush the rose was born,
Music when she spoke,
In her eyes the glow of morn
Into splendor broke.

HE'S GOT THE WHOLE WORLD IN HIS HANDS

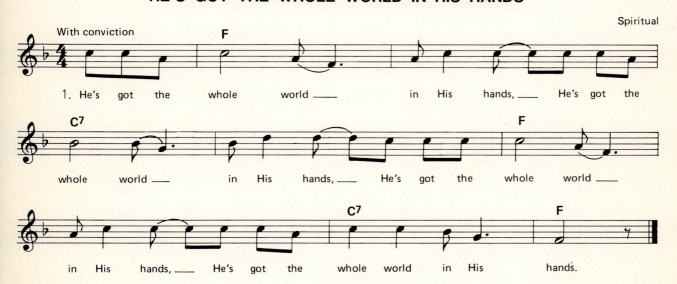

Spiritual

With conviction

1. He's got the whole world _____ in His hands, _____ He's got the

whole world _____ in His hands, _____ He's got the whole world _____

in His hands, _____ He's got the whole world in His hands.

2. He's got the wind and rain in His hands.
3. He's got that little baby in His hands.
4. He's got you and me in His hands.
5. He's got everybody in His hands.
6. He's got the whole world in His hands.

AMERICA

Samuel Francis Smith

Henry Carey

Expressively

1. My coun-try, 'tis of thee, Sweet land of lib-er-ty, Of thee I sing; Land where my fa-thers died, Land of the Pil-grims' pride, From ev-'ry —— moun-tain side Let —— free-dom ring.

2. My native country, thee, land of the noble free,
   Thy name I love.
   I love thy rocks and rills, thy woods and templed hills,
   My heart with rapture thrills
   Like that above.

3. Let music swell the breeze, and ring from all the trees
   Sweet freedom's song.
   Let mortal tongues awake, let all that breathe partake,
   Let rocks their silence break,
   The sound prolong.

4. Our fathers' God, to Thee, Author of liberty,
   To Thee we sing.
   Long may our land be bright with freedom's holy light,
   Protect us by Thy might,
   Great God, our King!

AMERICA THE BEAUTIFUL

Katharine Lee Bates
With dignity

Samuel A. Ward

1. O beau - ti - ful for spa - cious skies, For am - ber waves of grain, For pur - ple moun - tain maj - es - ties A - bove the fruit - ed plain! A - mer - i - ca! A - mer - i - ca! God shed His grace on thee, And crown thy good with broth - er - hood From sea to shin - ing sea!

2. O beautiful for Pilgrim feet,
   Whose stern impassioned stress
   A thoroughfare for freedom beat
   Across the wilderness.
   America! America! God mend thine every flaw,
   Confirm thy soul in self-control,
   Thy liberty in law.

3. O beautiful for heroes proved
   In liberating strife,
   Who more than self their country loved,
   And mercy more than life.
   America! America! May God thy gold refine
   Till all success be nobleness
   And every gain divine.

4. O beautiful for patriot dream
   That sees beyond the years,
   Thine alabaster cities gleam
   Undimmed by human tears.
   America! America! God shed His grace on thee,
   And crown thy good with brotherhood
   From sea to shining sea.

SHENANDOAH

Chantey

2. Oh, Shenandoah, I love your daughter,
Way, hey, you rolling river,
Oh, Shenandoah, I love your daughter,
Way, hey, we're bound away,
'Cross the wide Missouri.

3. Oh, Shenandoah, I love her truly,
Way, hey, you rolling river,
Oh, Shenandoah, I love her truly,
Way, hey, we're bound away,
'Cross the wide Missouri.

4. I long to see your fertile valley,
Way, hey, you rolling river
I long to see your fertile valley,
Way, hey, we're bound away,
'Cross the wide Missouri.

5. Oh, Shenandoah, I'm bound to leave you,
Way, hey, you rolling river,
Oh, Shenandoah, I'm bound to leave you,
Way, hey, we're bound away,
'Cross the wide Missouri.

THE TWELVE DAYS OF CHRISTMAS

England

Festively

1. On the first day of Christ-mas my true love sent to me, A par-tridge—in a pear tree.

2. On the sec-ond day of Christ-mas my true love sent to me,
3. On the third —— (etc.)
4. On the fourth —— (etc.)

2. 3. 4. two tur-tle doves, and a par-tridge —— in a pear tree.
3. 4. three French —— hens,
4. four call-ing birds,

(Sing in reverse order for verses indicated.)

5. On the fifth day of Christ-mas my true love sent to me,
6. On the sixth

(etc. through twelfth)

6. 7. 8. 9. 10. 11. 12. six geese a-lay-ing, five gold-en rings,
7. 8. 9. 10. 11. 12. seven swans a swim-ming,
8. 9. 10. 11. 12. eight maids a milk-ing,
9. 10. 11. 12. nine la dies danc-ing,
10. 11. 12. ten lords a leap-ing,
11. 12. eleven pip-ers pip-ing,
12. twelve drum-mers drum-ming,

(Sing in reverse order for verses indicated.)

four—call-ing birds, three French hens, two—tur-tle doves, and a par-tridge—in a pear tree.

GREENSLEEVES

1. A - las my love ___ you do me wrong, ___ To cast me off ___ dis - court-eous - ly; And

I have loved ___ you for so long, ___ De - light - ing in ___ your com - pan - y.

Chorus

Green - sleeves ___ was all my joy, ___ Green - sleeves ___ was my de - light,

Green - sleeves was my heart of gold, ___ And who but my lad - y Green - sleeves.

2. I long have waited at your hand
   To do your bidding as your slave,
   And waged, have I, both life and land
   Your love and affection for to have.

3. If you intend thus to disdain
   It does the more enrapture me,
   And even so, I will remain
   Your lover in captivity.

4. Alas, my love, that yours should be
   A heart of faithless vanity,
   So here I meditate alone
   Upon your insincerity.

5. Ah, Greensleeves, now farewell, adieu,
   To God I pray to prosper thee,
   For I remain thy lover true,
   Come once again and be with me.

BATTLE HYMN OF THE REPUBLIC

Julia Ward Howe

William Steffe

With fervor

1. Mine eyes have seen the glory of the coming of the Lord; He is tram - pling out the vin - tage where the grapes of wrath are stored; He hath loosed the fate - ful light - ning of His ter - ri - ble swift sword; His truth is march - ing on. Glo - ry, glo - ry hal - le - lu - jah! Glo - ry, glo - ry hal - le - lu - jah! Glo - ry, glo - ry hal - le - lu - jah! His truth is march - ing on.

2. I have seen Him in the watch-fires of a hundred circling camps,
They have builded Him an altar in the evening dews and damps,
I can read His righteous sentence by the dim and flaring lamps,
His day is marching on.
Chorus

3. In the beauty of the lilies Christ was born across the sea,
With a glory in His bosom that transfigures you and me;
As He died to make men holy, let us die to make men free,
While God is marching on.
Chorus

BARB'RA ALLEN

Scotland

1. In Scar - let town where I was born, There was a fair maid dwell - in', Made

ev -'ry youth cry, ___ "Well - a - day," Her name was Bar - b'ra Al - len.

2. All in the merry month of May,
   Where green buds they were swellin',
   Young Jimmy Grove on his deathbed lay,
   For love of Barb'ra Allen.

3. When he was dead and laid in grave,
   Her heart was filled with sorrow.
   "O mother, mother, make my bed
   For I shall die tomorrow."

4. And on her deathbed as she lay,
   She begged to be burried by him,
   And sore repented of the day
   That she did e'er deny him.

5. "Farewell," she said, "ye young girls all.
   And shun the fault I fell in.
   And take your warning by the fall
   Of cruel Barb'ra Allen."

MORNING HAS BROKEN

Gaelic Melody

Morn – ing has bro – ken like the first morn – ing Black-bird has spo – ken Like the first bird. Praise for the sing – ing! Praise for the morn – ing! Praise for them, spring – ing Fresh from the Word!

2. Sweet the rain's new fall,
   Sunlit from heaven,
   Like the first dewfall
   On the first grass.
   Praise for the sweetness
   Of the wet garden,
   Sprung in completeness
   Where his feet pass.

3. Mine is the sunlight!
   Mine is the morning
   Born of the one light
   Eden saw play!
   Praise with elation,
   Praise every morning,
   God's re-creation
   Of the new day!

KUM BA YA

African

Slowly, with dignity

Kum ba ya,* my Lord, kum ba ya. Kum ba ya, my Lord, kum ba ya, Kum ba ya, my Lord, kum ba ya. _____ Oh, Lord, ___ kum ba ya.

Verses (same tune as chorus):

1. Someone's crying, Lord, kum ba ya,
   Someone's crying, Lord, kum ba ya,
   Someone's crying, Lord, kum ba ya,
   Oh, Lord, kum ba ya.   *Chorus.*

Continue, as above:

2. Someone's praying, Lord, *etc.*
   Chorus.

3. Someone's singing Lord, *etc.*
   Chorus.

4. Someone's hoping, Lord, *etc.*
   Chorus.

I KNOW WHERE I'M GOING

Traditional

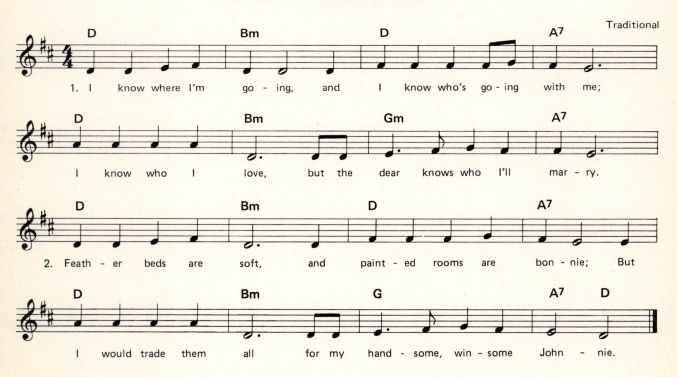

1. I know where I'm go - ing, and I know who's go - ing with me; I know who I love, but the dear knows who I'll mar - ry.

2. Feath - er beds are soft, and paint - ed rooms are bon - nie; But I would trade them all for my hand - some, win - some John - nie.

3. I have stockings of silk, and shoes of bright green leather;
   Combs to buckle my hair, and a ring for every finger.

4. Some say he's bad, but I say he's bonnie;
   Fairest of them all is my handsome, winsome Johnnie.

YOU'RE A GRAND OLD FLAG

Words and music by
George M. Cohan

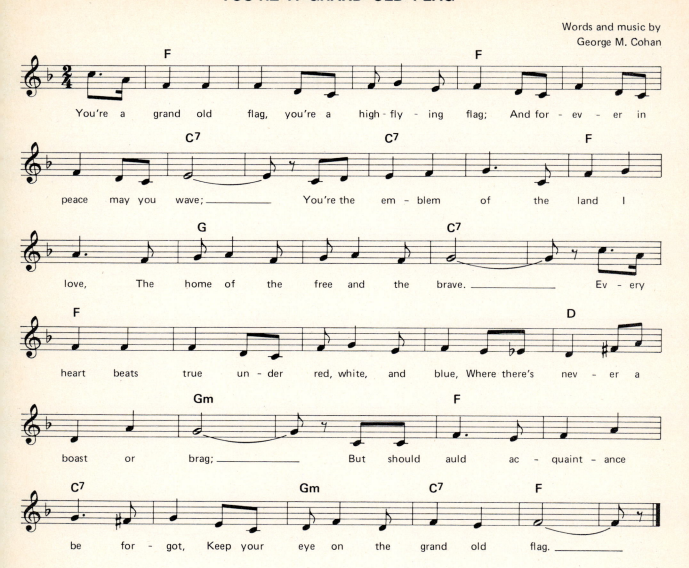

You're a grand old flag, you're a high - fly - ing flag; And for - ev - er in
peace may you wave; _____ You're the em - blem of the land I
love, The home of the free and the brave. _____ Ev - ery
heart beats true un - der red, white, and blue, Where there's nev - er a
boast or brag; _____ But should auld ac - quaint - ance
be for - got, Keep your eye on the grand old flag. _____

ROLL ON, COLUMBIA

Woody Guthrie

1. Green Doug - las fir where the wa - ters cut through, Down her wild
2. Oth - er big rivers add pow - er to you, Yak - i - ma,

moun - tains and can - yons she flew. Ca - na - di - an North - west to the
Snake, and the Klick - i - tat, too. Sand - y, Wil - lam - ette, and the

o - cean so blue, Roll on, Co - lum - bia, roll on. _____
Hood Riv - er, too. Roll on, Co - lum - bia, roll on. _____

Chorus

Roll on, _____ Co - lum - bia, roll on. Roll on, _____ Co -

lum - bia, roll on. Your pow - er is turn - ing our dark - ness to

dawn, Roll on, Co - lum - bia, roll on. _____

This song can be accompanied easily with the autoharp. Also chords can be spelled out on the tone bells having children stand in groups of three and each child holding one member of each chord. The three bells for each chord should be struck simultaneously where the chord symbols appear in the music.

Words by Woody Guthrie. Music based on ''Goodnight Irene'' by Huddie Ledbetter and John Lomax. TRO © Copyright 1957 (renewed 1985) and 1963 Ludlow Music, Inc., New York, N.Y. Used by permission.

WHAT WOULD THE WORLD BE LIKE WITHOUT MUSIC?

Words and Music by
Doug Nichol

Parts A) and B) can be sung simultaneously.

Words and music from <u>A Nichol's Worth</u>, copyright 1975 by Doug Nichol. Used by permission.

DO YOU BELIEVE IT?

Partner Song

Words and Music by
Doug Nichol

Once in a while I feel sort of cra-zy and I do things you might think dumb, like tick-lin' a worm on his un-der-neath and mak-in' him wig-gle his thumb. Then I find a cat and pull its trunk and sing a song with a dog, and kiss a cow and ride a snake, and eat my lunch with a hog!!

Words and music from <u>A Nichol's Worth</u>, copyright 1975 by Doug Nichol. Used by permission.

I DON'T BELIEVE IT!

Partner Song

Words and Music by
Doug Nichol

THREE LIMERICKS — PARTNER SONGS

Music: Doug Nichol
Words: anonymous

Words and music from A Nichol's Worth, copyright 1975 by Doug Nichol. Used by permission.

3

There was an old man of Black - heath who

sat on his set of false teeth. Said

he with a start, "Oh my, bless my heart, I've

bit - ten my - self un - der - neath!" _____

Words and music from A Nichol's Worth, copyright 1975 by Doug Nichol. Used by permission.

THE GLENDY BURK

Moderately Fast

Stephen C. Foster

1. The Glen - dy Burk is a might - y fast boat, With a might - y fast cap - tain,
I can't stay here for they work ___ too hard, I'm ___ bound ___ to leave this

too; He sits up there on the hur - ri - cane roof, And he
town; I'll take my duds and ___

keeps an eye on the crew. tote 'em on my back, When the Glen - dy Burk comes down.

Chorus

Ho! for Lou' - si - an - a! I'm bound to leave this town, I'll

take my duds and tote 'em on my back, When the Glen - dy Burk comes down.

2. The Glendy Burk has a funny old crew, and they sing the boatman's song,
They burn the pitch and the pine knot, too, just to shove the boat along;
The smoke goes up and the engine roars and the wheel goes round and round,
Then fare you well, for I'll take a little ride when the Glendy Burk comes down.

FUNNY SHAPE

Words and music by
Doug Nichol and Lisa Nichal

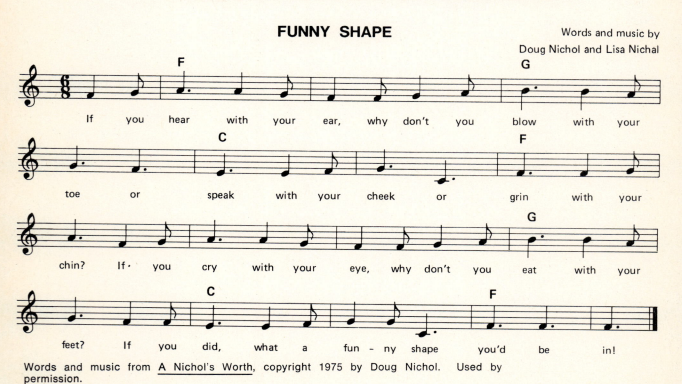

If you hear with your ear, why don't you blow with your

toe or speak with your cheek or grin with your

chin? If you cry with your eye, why don't you eat with your

feet? If you did, what a fun - ny shape you'd be in!

Words and music from A Nichol's Worth, copyright 1975 by Doug Nichol. Used by permission.

COUNTERMELODIES TO FUNNY SHAPE

1)

F   **G**   **C**   **F**

Fun - ny,   fun - ny,   you'd   look   fun - ny.

G   **C**   **F**

Fun - ny,   fun - ny,   you'd   look   fun - ny.

2)

F   **G**

You'd   look   fun - ny,   yes   you   would.

C   **F**

Would   you   look   like   this   if   you   could?

F   **G**

You'd   look   fun - ny,   yes   you   would.

C   **F**

Would   you   look   like   this   if   you   could?

CHESTER

Revolutionary War
William Billings

1. Let ty-rants shake their i-ron ___ rod, and slav-'ry clank ___ her ___ gall-ing ___ chains. We'll fear them not; we ___ trust ___ in ___ God: New ___ Eng-land's God ___ for ev-er reigns.

2. Howe and Burgoyne and Clinton too,
   With Prescott and Cornwallis join'd,
   Together plot our overthrow,
   In one infernal league combin'd.

3. When God inspired up for the fight,
   Their ranks were broke, their lines were forc'd.
   Their ships were sheltered in our sight,
   Or swiftly driven from our coast.

4. The foe comes on with haughty stride,
   Our troops advance with martial noise,
   Their vet'rans flee before our youth,
   And generals yield to beardless boys.

5. What grateful offering shall we bring,
   What shall we render to the Lord?
   Loud hallelujahs let us sing,
   And praise His name on every chord.

THIS IS MY COUNTRY

Don Raye

Al Jacobs

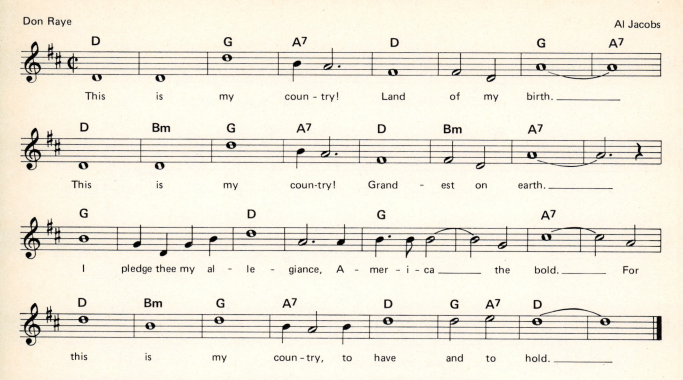

This is my coun-try! Land of my birth.

This is my coun-try! Grand - est on earth.

I pledge thee my al - le - giance, A - mer - i - ca the bold. For

this is my coun-try, to have and to hold.

THIS LAND IS YOUR LAND

Words and music by
Woody Guthrie

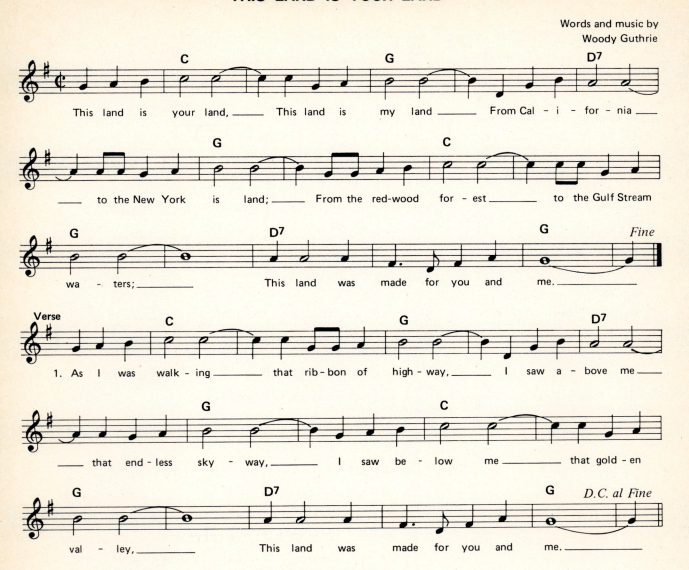

This land is your land, ____ This land is my land ____ From Cal – i – for – nia ____
____ to the New York is land; ____ From the red-wood for – est ____ to the Gulf Stream
wa – ters; ____ This land was made for you and me. ____

Fine

Verse

1. As I was walk – ing ____ that rib – bon of high – way, ____ I saw a – bove me ____
____ that end – less sky – way, ____ I saw be – low me ____ that gold – en
val – ley, ____ This land was made for you and me. ____

D.C. al Fine

2. I've roamed and rambled
and followed my footsteps
To the sparkling sands of
her diamond deserts,
And all around me
a voice came sounding,
This land was made for you and me.

3. When the sun comes shining,
and I was strolling
And the wheatfields waving
and the dust clouds rolling,
As the fog was lifting
a voice was chanting,
This land was made for you and me.

IF YOU'RE HAPPY

Gaily

1. If you're hap-py and you know it, clap your hands; *(clap)* *(clap)* If you're
hap-py and you know it, clap your hands; *(clap)* *(clap)* If you're
hap-py and you know it, Then your face will sure-ly show it; If you're
hap-py and you know it, clap your hands. *(clap)* *(clap)*

2. If you're happy and you know it, tap your foot.
3. If you're happy and you know it, nod your head.
4. If you're happy and you know it, do all three.

ALL NIGHT, ALL DAY

Negro Spiritual

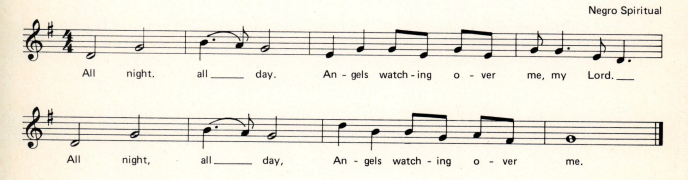

All night, all ___ day. An-gels watch-ing o-ver me, my Lord. ___

All night, all ___ day, An-gels watch-ing o-ver me.

CLEMENTINE

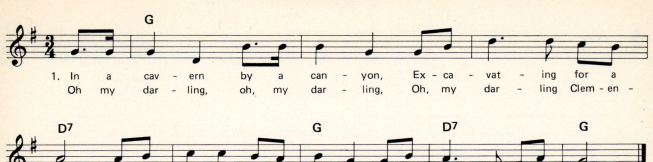

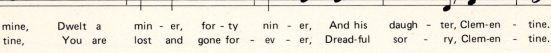

2. Light she was and like a feather,
   And her shoes were number nine;
   Herring boxes without topses,
   Sandals were for Clementine.

3. Drove she ducklings to the water
   Every morning just at nine;
   Struck her foot against a splinter,
   Fell into the foaming brine.

4. Rosy lips above the water
   Blowing bubbles mighty fine;
   But, alas! I was no swimmer,
   So I lost my Clementine.

TURN! TURN! TURN!

(TO EVERYTHING THERE IS A SEASON)

Music by Pete Seeger

Words from the Book of Ecclesiastes. Adaptation and music by Pete Seeger. TRO © Copyright 1962 Melody Trails, Inc., New York, N.Y. Used by permission.

* *D.S.* : Go back to the sign (𝄋) and repeat until the word *Fine*.

THE FOGGY, FOGGY DEW

When I was a bach - 'lor I lived by my - self, I worked at the weav - er's trade, ___ And the on - ly, on - ly thing I did that was wrong was to woo a fair young maid. I wooed her in the win - ter - time, And in the sum - mer too, And the on - ly, on - ly thing I did that was wrong was to keep her from the fog - gy, fog - gy dew.

One night she knelt close by my side
As I lay fast asleep.
She threw her arms around my neck,
And then began to weep.
She wept, she cried, she tore her hair,
Ah me, what could I do?
So all night long I held her in my arms
Just to keep her from the foggy, foggy dew.

Oh, I am a bachelor, I live with my son,
We work at the weaver's trade.
And every single time I look into his eyes
He reminds me of the fair young maid.
He reminds me of the winter time,
And of the summer too,
And the many, many times I held her in my
    arms
Just to keep her from the foggy, foggy dew.

PUTTING ON THE STYLE

Young man in a car-riage, driv-ing like he's mad,
With a pair of hors-es he's bor-rowed from his dad. He
cracks his whip so live-ly, Just to make the la-dies smile,
But they know he's on-ly put-ting on_____ the style.

Chorus: Putting on the agony,
Putting on the style,
That's what all the young folks
Are doing all the while.
And as I look around me
I'm very apt to smile,
To see so many people
Putting on the style.

Sweet sixteen and goes to church,
Just to see the boys,
Laughs and giggles
At every little noise.
She turns this way a little,
And turns that way a while,
But everybody knows she's only
Putting on the style.

Young man in a restaurant
Smokes a dirty pipe;
Looking like a pumpkin
That's only half-way ripe.
Smoking, drinking, chewing,
And thinking all the while
That there is nothing equal
To putting on the style.

Preacher in the pulpit
Shouts with all his might,
"Glory Hallelujah!"
Puts the people in a fright.
You might think that Satan's
Coming up the aisle;
But it's only the preacher
Putting on the style.

Young man just from college
Makes a big display
With a great big jawbreak,
Which he can hardly say.
It can't be found in Webster's,
And won't be for a while,
But everybody knows he's only
Putting on the style.

THE FOX

1. The fox went out on a chil-ly night, Prayed to the moon for to give him light, For he'd man-y a mile to go that night, Be-fore he reached the town, oh, town, oh town — oh, He'd man-y a mile to go that night be-fore he reached the town, oh.

2. He ran till he came to a great big pen,
   Where the ducks and the geese were kept therein,
   A couple of you will grease my chin
   Before I leave this town, oh-town, oh-town, oh
   A couple of you will grease my chin
   Before I leave this town, oh.

3. He grabbed the gray goose by the neck,
   Throwed a duck across his back.
   He didn't mind the quack, quack, quack,
   And the legs all dangling down, oh . . .

4. The old Mrs. Flipper-Flopper jumped out of bed,
   Out of the window she cocked her head,
   Saying, "John, John, the goose is gone,
   And the fox is on the town, oh . . ."

5. Then John he ran to top of the hill,
   Blowed his horn both loud and shrill,
   Fox, he said, "I better flee with my kill,
   For they'll soon be on my trail, oh . . ."

6. He ran till he came to his cozy den,
   There were the little ones: eight, nine, ten.
   They said, "Daddy, you'd better go back again,
   'Cause it must be a mighty fine town, oh . . ."

7. The fox and his wife, without any strife,
   Cut up the goose with a carving knife.
   They never had such a supper in their life,
   And the little ones chewed on the bones, oh . . .

IF I HAD A HAMMER

Words and Music by
Lee Hays and Pete Seeger

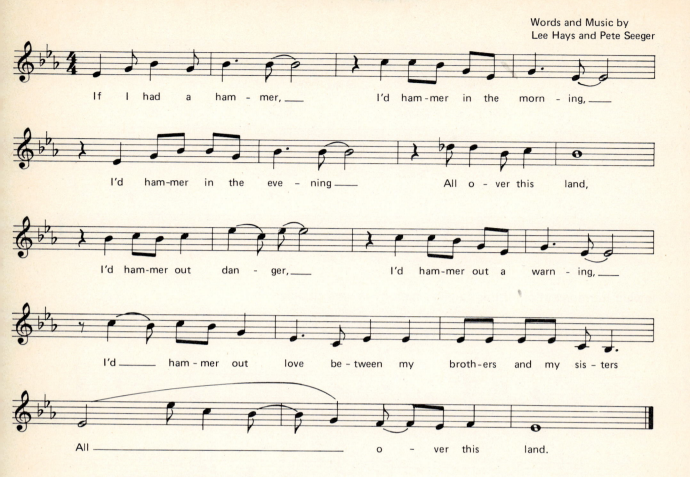

If I had a ham - mer, ___ I'd ham-mer in the morn - ing, ___

I'd ham-mer in the eve - ning ___ All o - ver this land,

I'd ham-mer out dan - ger, ___ I'd ham-mer out a warn - ing, ___

I'd ___ ham - mer out love be - tween my broth-ers and my sis - ters

All ___ o - ver this land.

2. If I had a bell I'd ring it in the morning,
   I'd ring it in the evening All over this land,
   I'd ring out danger, I'd ring out a warning,
   I'd ring out love between my brothers and my sisters All over this land.

3. If I had a song I'd sing it in the morning,
   I'd sing it in the evening All over this land,
   I'd sing out danger, I'd sing out a warning,
   I'd sing out love between my brothers and my sisters All over this land.

4. Well, I got a hammer and I got a bell,
   And I got a song to sing All over this land,
   It's the hammer of justice, It's the bell of freedom,
   It's the song about love between my brothers and my sisters All over this land.

TELL ME WHY

The following harmonization of this familiar melody is very popular.

TELL ME WHY

EENCY, WEENCY SPIDER

Playfully

Action Song

Een - cy, Ween - cy spi - der went up the wa - ter spout; Down came the

rain and washed the spi - der out; Out came the sun and

dried up all the rain, And the een - cy ween - cy spi - der went up the spout a - gain.

The familiar actions to this song can be done by touching the tip of the index finger on one hand to the tip of the thumb on the other. As you move up alternate thumb and index finger; hands come down with rain; hands over head for sun; finish with above spider movement.

ZUMBA, ZUMBA

English words - Margaret Marks
Collected by Beatrice Landeck

Spanish Folk Song

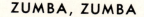

Zum - ba, zum - ba! Strike the cym - bal. Zum - ba, zum - ba! Strike the gong. Zum - ba,

zum - ba! Beat the tim - bal and the tam - bou - rine and drum!

Verse

1. Born on this night is a ba - by.   Ev - 'ry - one brings him a
2. What shall I take to the ba - by?   What shall I say when I

pres - ent,   Brings him a sa - vor - y meat - pie
take it?   I'll bring a gourd for a rat - tle,

Made out of par - tridge and pheas - ant.
I'll ask his moth - er to shake it.

This song can be accompanied with the autoharp using only the chords indicated, F and C7. The rhythm instruments mentioned in the words of the song, cymbal, gong and tambourine, can also be used.

SOPRANO RECORDER FINGERING CHART

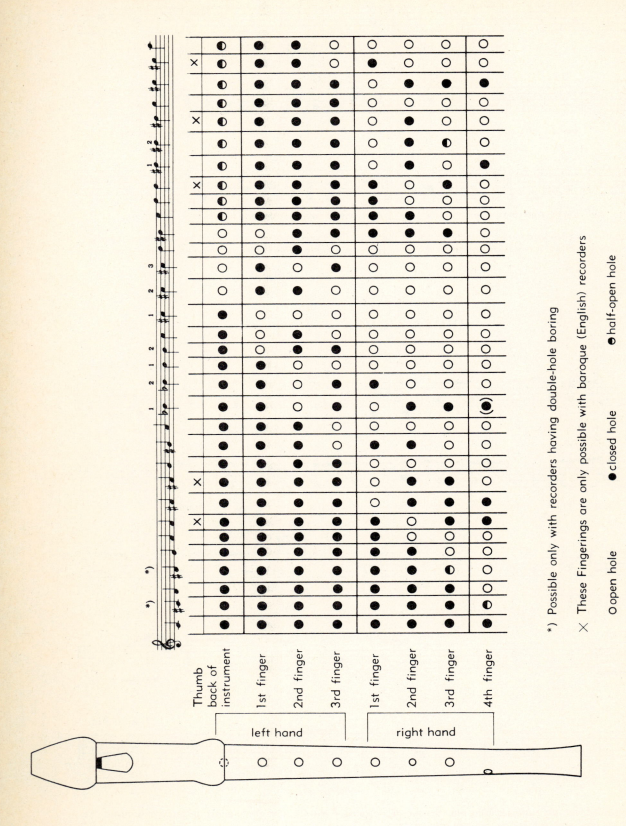

*) Possible only with recorders having double-hole boring

X These Fingerings are only possible with baroque (English) recorders

O open hole　　●closed hole　　◐half-open hole

Guitar Fingering Chart

Tune E A D G B E

The vertical lines in each fingering illustration indicate the strings as you face the fingerboard, beginning with the low E string on the left. The horizontal lines indicate the frets. The heavy top line represents the nut. The fingers of the left hand are numbered as follows:

index—1   middle—2   ring—3   little finger—4

The number within each circle indicates which finger is placed at that location on the fingerboard. Sometimes a single finger "stops" more than one string, indicated by ①①, etc. An X above a string means that string is *not* strummed to produce a given chord. All other strings may be strummed even if they are not stopped by a finger of the left hand.

The fingerings shown are root position chords except when otherwise noted. (Some root position chords are not practical.) Various strumming techniques may be applied to each fingering to produce chord inversions if desired.

When alternate fingerings are shown, choose the one offering the greatest continuity of fingering within a given chord progression. Rapid, facile shifting of the fingers from one chord to the next will produce the most fluent accompaniment.

Finally, and most importantly, a word about practicality! Because major and minor keys through four sharps and flats are used throughout this text, all of those keys are included in this fingering chart *for reference purposes.* As you will discover, however, only very accomplished players should attempt many of these keys. Beginners should concentrate on becoming fluent in a few of the most practical keys. D and A major are perhaps easiest (opinions vary). G and E major are usually considered next in difficulty. Among minor keys, A minor is probably easiest. Players seeking greater tonal variety may also wish to explore D or E minor. This selection should prove adequate for most accompanying needs. You may wish to sample other keys included in the chart to substantiate this advice.

MAJOR KEYS

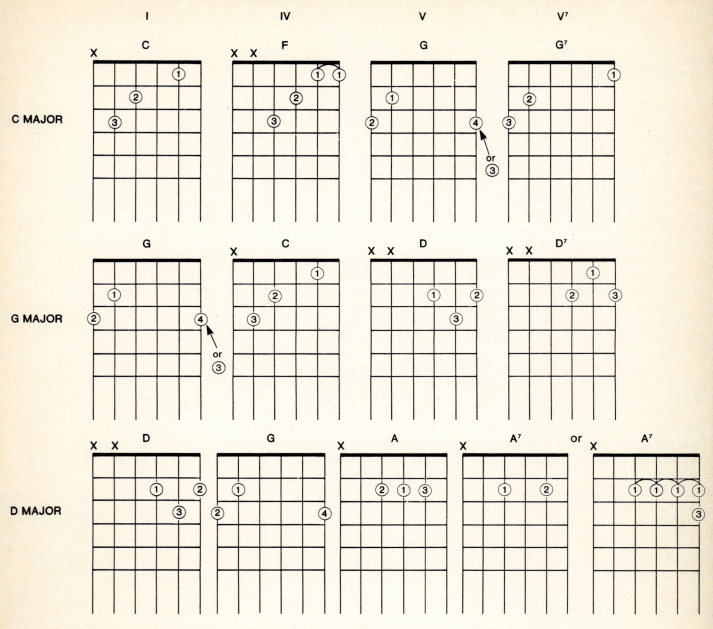

The second fingering for A⁷ will produce a preferable voicing of the chord in many musical contexts. The first may be easier to execute when moving from or to certain chords.

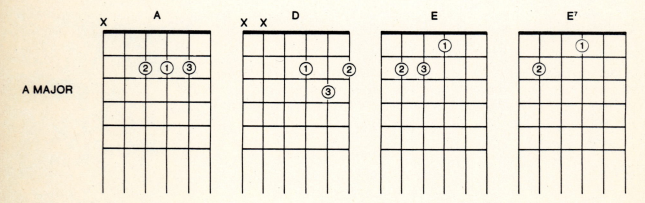

E MAJOR

E   X A   B   X B⁷

NOT PRACTICAL

In its standard tuning the guitar executes sharps more easily than flats. For this reason the following major keys require more awkward fingerings. Alternate tunings or the use of a *capo* are frequently employed to play in these keys.

F MAJOR

X X F   X X Bᵇ   X C   X C⁷

(1st inversion)

The first inversion Bᵇ chord is shown because the root position fingering is impractical.

Bᵇ MAJOR

X X Bᵇ   X X Eᵇ   Eᵇ   X X F   X X F⁷

(1st inversion)   (1st inversion)   (3rd inversion)

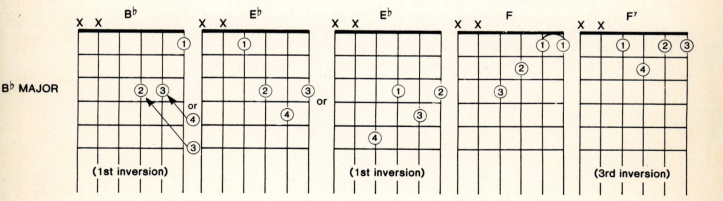

Both the root position and first inversion Eᵇ chords are awkward, especially for small hands. The third inversion F⁷ chord shown will serve most musical contexts best. First inversion may be played by adding the open A string. Root position is not practical.

The remaining two major keys involve even more strenuous fingerings.

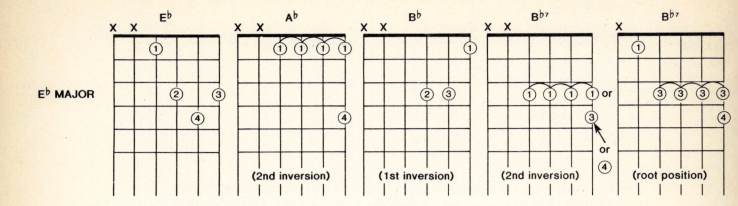

E♭ MAJOR

The second inversion A♭ chord offers helpful finger continuity and acceptable voice leading as the IV chord in E♭ major. The second inversion B♭⁷ has the same advantages as V⁷ in this key. The root position B♭⁷ is very awkward.

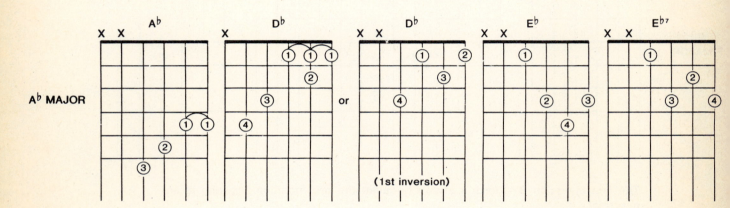

A♭ MAJOR

The second inversion A♭ chord used in E♭ major does not make a suitable tonic, thus the root position fingering is called for. The root position D♭ chord offers some continuity of hand formation with the root position A♭ and E♭ or E♭⁷ but is very awkward. You may find the first inversion D♭ more practical. (You may find transposing a piece up one half-step to A major an even more reasonable option!)

MINOR KEYS

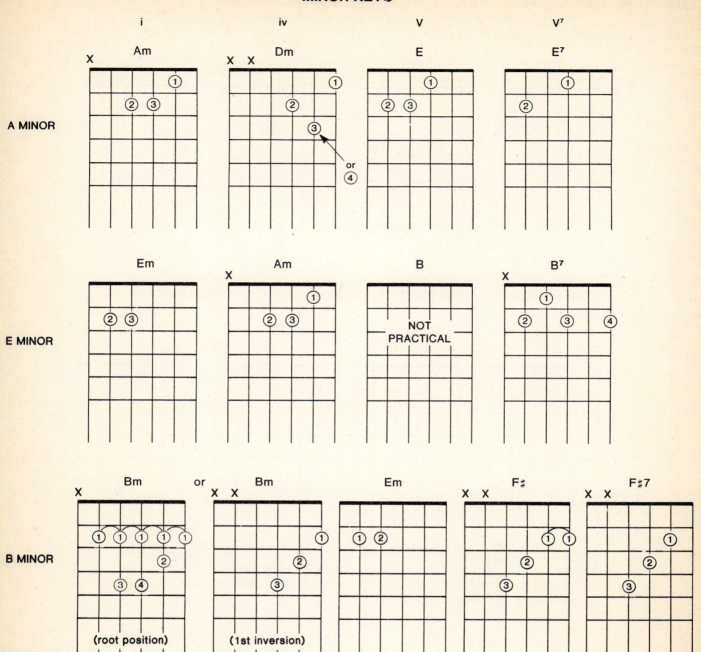

Players who prefer the more stable sound of a root position tonic chord may wish to attempt the very awkward root position b minor triad. The first inversion is much easier to play and offers greater finger continuity with other chords.

Even though these next two keys have sharps in their key signatures the jump in difficulty is severe. Notice the enharmonic equivalence of the dominant triad in each of these keys to chords required in the key of A♭ major.

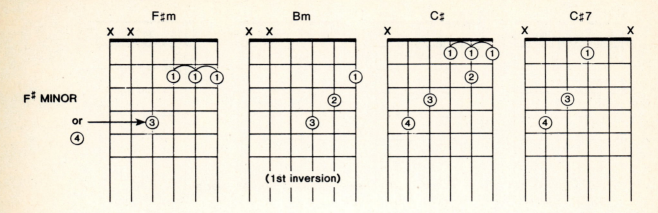

The first inversion b minor is definitely required here for continuity. Avoiding both outside strings in strumming the C♯7 chord requires a more careful right hand technique.

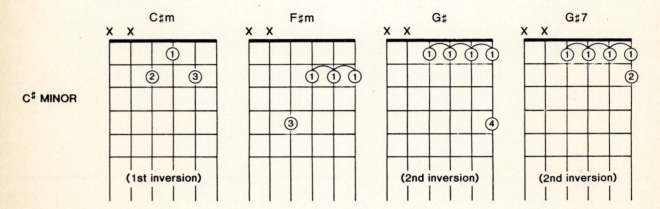

The first inversion tonic chord is the only reasonable choice here. The second inversion V and V⁷ are necessary for finger continuity, especially with the tonic. You may try the root position A♭ major triad (enharmonic equivalent) shown in the chart of that key for comparison.

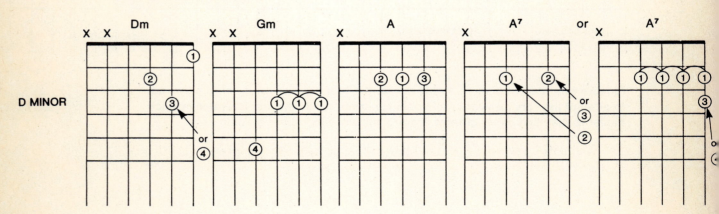

As in D major, the first A⁷ fingering is easier to execute, the second offers better voice leading to the tonic chord.

As in major keys, flats create more complex fingerings in the ensuing minor keys.

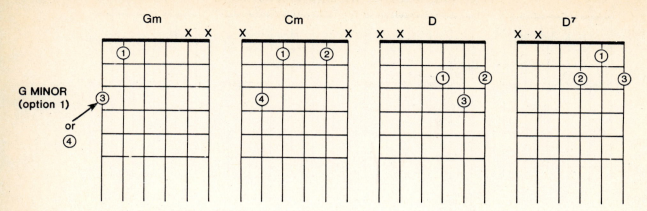

Notice in this first option for g minor the necessity of avoiding upper and outside strings in strumming the i and iv chords respectively.

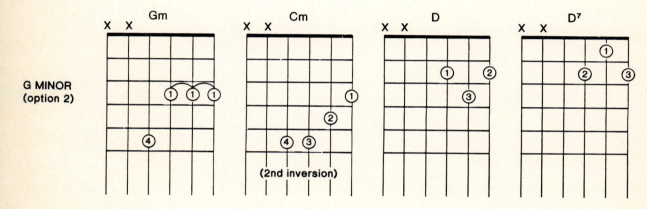

This option places all four chords in a similar pitch register and unifies the strumming technique but requires more strenuous left-hand positions. The second inversion iv chord is required for finger continuity with the tonic.

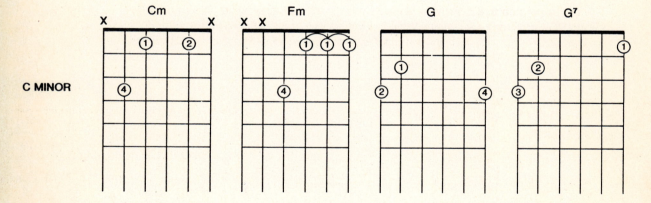

The root position c minor chord is preferable as the tonic. Finger continuity with iv is quite good. Shifting to V and V⁷ is more awkward.

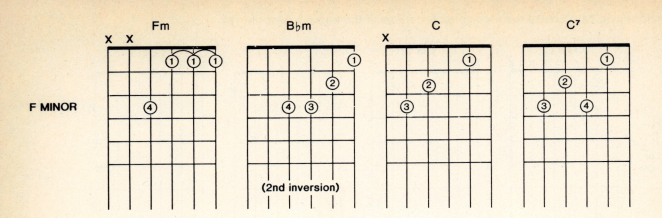

F MINOR

The second inversion offers the only practical fingering for the b♭ minor triad. Continuity with i is good but V and V⁷ require more awkward shifts.

Glossary

A tempo.   Return to normal tempo.

Accelerando, abbr. *acc.* A gradual increase in motion or speed.

Accidental.   A sharp, flat, or natural placed immediately before a note rather than in a key signature.

Adagio.   Slowly and with great expression. *See also tempo.*

Allegretto.   A moderately quick tempo of light and cheerful character. *See also tempo.*

Allegro.   A brisk lively tempo. *See also tempo.*

Andante.   At a walking pace. *See also tempo.*

Andantino.   Slightly faster than Andante. *See also tempo.*

Bar line.   Vertical lines through the staff that group patterns of strong and weak beats into measures of a fixed number of beats.

Bass clef. 𝄢   Also called the F clef because the two dots surround the fourth line of the staff designating it as the pitch F.

Cadence.   A point of rest in music.

Chord.   Usually three or more tones sounded simultaneously.

Circle of Fifths.   A graphic illustration showing that as sharps are added to a key signature (clockwise direction) the tonic notes ascend by perfect fifths and as flats are added to a key signature (counterclockwise) the tonic notes descend by perfect fifths.

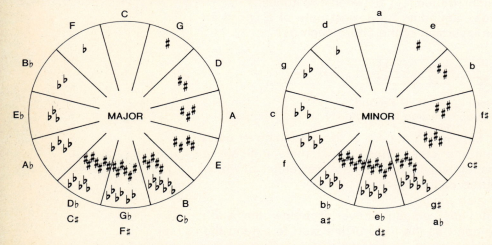

Clef.   A symbol placed on a staff which identifies the lines of that staff as representing specific pitches. *See also bass clef* and *treble clef.*

Compound meter.   A meter in which the upper number is a multiple of three, other than one. For example, $\frac{6}{8}, \frac{9}{8}, \frac{6}{4}, \frac{12}{8}$.

Crescendo, abbr. *cresc.* Gradually louder. Indicated by the symbol ◁.

Da capo, abbr. *D.C.*   Direction in a composition to return to the beginning and continue playing until further instructions such as *Fine.*

Dal segno, abbr. *D.S.*   Direction in a score to return to and repeat from the sign 𝄋 .

Decrescendo, abbr. *decresc.*   Gradually softer. Indicated by the symbol ▷ .

Diminuendo, abbr. *dim.*   Becoming gradually softer.

Dominant.   The fifth degree of the major or minor scale. Also a chord built upon that pitch.

Dotted notes.   A dot added to a note increases the value of that note by one-half.

Double bar.   Two vertical lines indicating the end of a composition or major section of a lengthy composition.

Dynamic level.   Degree of loudness and softness.

Enharmonic.   Pertaining to two names or identities for the same pitch such as C♯ and D♭ or E♯ and F.

Fermata ⌢ .   Pause or hold. Placed above a note to extend the duration of that note for an artistically appropriate length of time beyond the notated duration.

Fine.   The end, close.

First and second endings.   ⌐1.⌐ ⌐2.⌐ Play or sing through the first ending, then repeat, the second time skipping the first ending and playing or singing the second.

Flat, ♭.   A musical symbol appearing either in the key signature or to the left of the note head indicating the lowering of a pitch by one half step.

Forte, abbr. *f.* Loud.

Fortissimo, abbr. *ff.* Very loud.

Grave.   Slow, solemn. *See also tempo.*

Great staff.   The joining of the treble and bass staves by a brace forms the great staff. (Also referred to as the grand staff.)

Half step.   The smallest interval normally employed in our musical system.

Harmony.   The sounding of two or more tones simultaneously producing chords or implied chords. The vertical organization of musical sounds.

Interval.   The difference in pitch (frequency) between two tones.

Inversion.   Pertaining to chords. Sounding the lowest note of a chord an octave higher produces an inversion of the chord such as

Root   First   Second
Position   Inversion   Inversion

Key signature.   The sharps or flats which appear at the beginning of each staff immediately following the clef. These accidentals indicate a major scale and key and its relative minor scale and key either of which may provide the tonal source of the piece.

Largo.   Slow and stately. *See also tempo.*

Ledger line.   Short horizontal lines, placed above or below the staff, spaced the same distance apart as the lines of the staff to extend the staff in either direction.

Lento.   Slow, broadly.   *See also tempo.*

Measure.   One statement of the metric pattern or recurring group of beats on which the rhythm of a composition is based. Each repetition of this pattern is separated by a bar line.

Meter.   The grouping of beats into a regular and recurring pattern of strong and weak beats, indicated at the beginning of a composition by a meter signature such as $\frac{2}{4}$, $\frac{3}{4}$, and $\frac{6}{8}$.

Mezzo forte, abbr. *mf.* Moderately loud.

Mezzo piano, abbr. *mp.* Moderately soft.

Moderato.   At a moderate speed. *See also tempo.*

Natural, ♮.   A musical symbol indicating that a note is not to be sharped or flatted.

Notes. Graphic symbols placed on the staff to indicate pitch and relative duration.

𝅝 Whole note

𝅗𝅥 Half note   ♪ Eighth note

♩ Quarter note   ♬ Sixteenth note

Octave—The interval from any pitch to the next higher or lower pitch having the same letter name.

Pianissimo, abbr. *pp.* Very softly.

Piano, abbr. *p.* Softly.

Pitch. The highness or lowness of a tone determined by frequency of vibrations and represented musically by placing notes on a staff.

Presto. Quickly, rapidly, briskly. *See also tempo.*

Rallentando, abbr. *rall.* Gradually slower.

Repeat. ‖: :‖ Signs indicating to repeat music between the signs. If the first repeat sign does not appear repeat from the beginning of the song.

Rests. Notational symbols indicating durations of silence.

▬ Whole rest   𝄽 Quarter rest   𝄾 Sixteenth rest

▬ Half rest   𝄾 Eighth rest

Rhythm. Pertaining to the expression of time in music or the progression of relative durations within a given musical passage. Rhythm includes such additional factors as meter and tempo.

Ritardando, abbr. *rit., ritard.* Gradually slower.

Root. The tone upon which a chord is built.

Root position. A chord sounded with its root as the lowest pitch is said to be in root position.

Scale. The arrangement of pitches in alphabetical sequence usually through the interval of an octave. Not all scales employ all seven pitch letters.

Seventh chord. A chord of four notes placed on consecutive lines or spaces of the staff, so named because the interval from root to uppermost tone is a seventh.

Sharp, ♯. A musical symbol appearing in the key signature or to the left of the note head indicating the raising of a pitch by one half step.

Simple meter. A meter in which the upper number is not a multiple of three, such as $\frac{2}{4}, \frac{3}{4}, \frac{4}{4}, \frac{3}{8}, \frac{4}{8}$.

Staff. Five equally spaced horizontal lines and the four intervening spaces on which notes are written to signify pitch relationship.

Subdominant. The fourth tone of the major or minor scale. Also a chord built upon that pitch.

Syncopation. The occurrence of accents other than on strong beats.

Tempo. The pace or speed at which music moves. Some indications of tempo from slowest:

    Grave—slow, solemn.

    Lento—slowly, broadly

    Largo—slow and stately

    Adagio—slow, but with great expression

    Andante—at a walking pace, very moderate speed

    Andantino—slightly faster than Andante

    Moderato—at a moderate speed

    Allegretto—lightly, cheerfully

    Allegro—quick, lively, brisk movement

    Vivace—animated, vivacious, more movement than Allegro

    Presto—quickly, rapidly, briskly

Tie. A curved line joining two or more notes of the same pitch and indicating that one sounding of the pitch is to be sustained for a duration equal to the sum of the tied notes.

Tonality. An acoustic phenomenon in which the pitch organization of a composition aurally and aesthetically gravitates toward one central pitch or key center.

Tonic. The tonal center or key center. The first degree of a major or minor scale or a chord built on that pitch.

Transposition. The sounding of a composition in a different key than notated.

Treble clef. Also called the G clef because the circular lower portion surrounds the second line designating it as the pitch G.

Triad. The most predominant chord type heard in tonal music. A triad consists of three notes placed on consecutive lines or spaces of the staff.

Triple meter. A meter consisting of three beats per measure.

Triplet. The sounding of three notes in the time normally occupied by two, notated as in the following example.

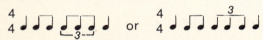

Vivace. Animated vivacious, more movement than Allegro. *See also tempo.*

Whole step. One of the two basic intervals in our musical system. Two half steps combine to form a whole step.

Whole-tone scale. A six-tone scale in which all intervals within an octave are whole steps.

Song Index

General Index